HISTORICAL ROMANCE FICTION

For Victor

Historical Romance Fiction
Heterosexuality and Performativity

LISA FLETCHER
University of Tasmania, Australia

ASHGATE

Published by
Ashgate Publishing Limited
Gower House
Croft Road
Aldershot
Hampshire GU11 3HR
England

Ashgate Publishing Company
Suite 420
101 Cherry Street
Burlington, VT 05401-4405
USA

Ashgate website: http://www.ashgate.com

British Library Cataloguing in Publication Data
Fletcher, Lisa
  Historical romance fiction : heterosexuality and
  performativity
  1. Fowles, John, 1926–2005. French lieutenant's woman
  2. Love stories, English – History and criticism
  3. Historical fiction, English – History and criticism
  4. English fiction – 20th century – History and criticism
  I. Title
  823'.085'09045

Library of Congress Cataloging-in-Publication Data
Fletcher, Lisa.
  Historical romance fiction : heterosexuality and perfomativity / Lisa Fletcher.
    p. cm.
  Includes bibliographical references (p.   ).
  ISBN 978-0-7546-6202-0 (alk. paper)
  1. Love stories, English–History and criticism. 2. Historical fiction, English–History and criticism. 3. Speech in literature. 4. Heterosexuality in literature. I. Title.

PR830.L69F56 2007
823'.08309–dc22

2007012681

ISBN: 978-0-7546-6202-0

Printed and bound in Great Britain by TJ International Ltd, Padstow, Cornwall.

Contents

Acknowledgments

This book would not have been possible without the guidance and support of Stephanie Trigg. Her unwavering enthusiasm for my approach to reading historical romance fiction fuelled my own determination to keep improving my work. I am deeply grateful for Stephanie's intelligent and thorough responses to drafts and for her generous support for all aspects of my academic life.

My colleagues in the School of English, Journalism and European Languages at the University of Tasmania offered guidance and advice when it was most needed; in particular, Ralph Crane, Lucy Frost, Anna Johnston, Elle Leane, Danielle Wood, and the members of the School's "book group." I am also grateful to Diana Barnes for compiling the index.

I owe an enormous debt to my parents for nurturing my childhood love of literature and learning, and for continuing to be my dearest friends and proudest advocates. My warmest appreciation is due Victor Stojcevski for his love, friendship and fierce intelligence and our daughters, Lily and Zhana, for enriching my life in immeasurable ways.

Different versions of some material in Chapters 3, 5 and 7 have been previously published. An earlier version of Chapter 3 was published as "'Mere Costumery'?: Georgette Heyer's Cross-Dressing Novels" in *Masquerades: Disguise in Literature from the Middle Ages to the Present*, eds. Jesús López-Paláez Casellas, David Malcolm and Pilar Sánchez Calle, Gdansk University Press, 2004, and is reprinted here with permission of the editors. Parts of Chapters 5 and 7 were originally published in my article "Historical Romance Fiction and Heterosexuality: John Fowles's *The French Lieutenant's Woman* and A.S. Byatt's *Possession*" in the Journal of Interdisciplinary Studies, 7.1 & 2, 2003, and are reprinted here with permission of the Journal of Interdisciplinary Studies, University of Newcastle. Quotations from two letters written by Georgette Heyer to Louisa Callender are reprinted by permission of Sir Richard Rougier. Quotations from three novels by Heyer are reprinted by permission of The Ampersand Agency acting on behalf of the Heyer Estate. *These Old Shades* Copyright © Georgette Heyer, 1926. *The Masqueraders* Copyright © Georgette Heyer, 1928. *The Corinthian* Copyright © Georgette Heyer, 1940. All three titles are published in the UK by Arrow Books. Quotations from *The French Lieutenant's Woman* by John Fowles, published by Jonathan Cape. Reprinted by permission of The Random House Group Ltd. Quotations from *The French Lieutenant's Woman* by John Fowles. Copyright © 1969 by John Fowles. By permission of Little, Brown and Co. Quotations from *Possession* by A.S. Byatt, copyright © 1991 by A.S. Byatt. Used by permission of Random House, Inc. Quotations from *Possession* by A.S. Byatt, published by Chatto & Windus. Reprinted by permission of The Random House Group Ltd.

Introduction

This book is a study of the historical romance genre in both its popular and literary manifestations. The following chapters examine the genre as a complex and ongoing discussion about gender and sexual norms and present a comprehensive theoretical model for analyzing this discussion. To begin, Part I, "Defining the Genre," offers a broad definition of romance: a fictional mode which depends on the force and familiarity of the speech act, "I love you." This utterance is the key to the genre's mutual dependence on and disavowal of its historicity. It therefore resonates in quite particular ways in *historical* romance novels. This book responds to debates in studies of literature and popular fiction (fields with more in common than recent scholarship suggests) and advocates the value of speech act and performativity theories for textual analysis. The crux of the book is the weaving together of these two strands of investigation (reading novels/reading theory) to make a contribution to the emerging area of critical heterosexuality studies.

"I love you" is the narrative and ontological turning-point of heterosexual romance fictions. This book deploys speech act theory (J.L. Austin, Shoshana Felman, Sandy Petrey) and theories of performativity (Judith Butler, Eve Kosofsky Sedgwick) to expose the assumptions and trace the various logics of the weightiest subgenre of heterosexual romance: historical romance fiction. My guiding assumption is that there is a definite relationship between speech acts and paradigmatic narratives in Western culture. The book explicates one of those relationships; however, rather than considering generic texts *as* enunciations or speech acts, it locates an idea of "speech" in the heart of the texts themselves and describes how historical romance novels both represent and *use* speech acts—and performatives in their broader sense—to produce and reproduce hegemonic ideas about romance, history and heterosexuality. I take my cue for this approach from Diane Elam's statement in *Romancing the Postmodern* that "Thinking romance is a questioning of how it is that one may say 'I love you'…" (27). My readings of historical romance novels seek to show the extent to which "I love you" is necessary to the telling of each and every romance. "I love you" is the *romantic speech act* because romance cannot proceed without the promise of its utterance. It is impossible to imagine a romance fiction which does not depend on the force of these three little words—as secret, promise, confession, declaration, or lie—for the progress of its plot and the development of its characters.

While writing this book I have been repeatedly struck by the extent to which romance fictions in general and historical romances in particular invite and provoke consideration of exactly the kinds of questions raised by theories of performativity. This is not just because much of the most important work in this field has focused on gender and sexuality, but also because historical romance fictions are themselves preoccupied with questions about the meaning and the *force* of language in its broadest sense (direct speech, symbols, gesture, costume). Indeed as my discussions of individual novels will demonstrate, the romance genre is obsessed with speech acts and, more generally, with performativity. It persistently represents the constitution of a heterosexual romantic subject in language. Further, historical romance fictions endlessly thematize and worry over the troubled line between the denotative and the performative capacities of language, and over the related distinctions between truth and lie, fact and fiction, reality and romance, which are so crucial to the genre's form and function. That these novels can neither resolve nor contain these oppositions in any meaningful or lasting way is the key paradox of historical romance fiction. This paradox is also the key to understanding the genre's need to incessantly reproduce and reclaim the terms by which it both makes sense to its readers and by which it seeks to guarantee the genre's lasting success as a cultural form.

The crucial insight of theories of speech acts and performativity can be represented by the figure of something turning back on itself both in the sense of a circuitous repetition or retracing *and* of an unravelling or undoing. The "logic of iterability" which the concept of performativity names and recognizes allows us to consider anew the ubiquity and apparent inexhaustibility of the romance genre as the result of an inherent failure ever to secure its terms with any finality. In Butler's formulation, bringing the key terms and themes of speech act and performativity theories together with those of heterosexual romance fictions allows us to "[work] the weakness in the norm" (*Bodies* 237) both with respect to the texts themselves and on a broader scale in relation to hegemonic concepts of sex, gender, and sexuality.

The idea that the ideological foundations of romance are unstable and uncertain is not without its precedents. There is a well-established scholarly tradition of highlighting the contradictoriness and indeterminacy of the romance genre in popular and literary contexts. While the terminology varies from study to study, this way of thinking about romance is exemplified most frequently by the claim that the romance genre is irresolvably both "conservative" and "progressive" in its form and function. Gillian Beer states quite simply that "Revolution is one function of the romance" (13). Beer begins her book by dismissing "sub-literary romances" from serious consideration. While she notes that it is works of "sub-literature," by which she means "magazines like *True Romances* or lightweight commercial fiction," that are now popularly called "romances," she is nevertheless reluctant to credit them with the title. For Beer, "Such 'romances' batten on the emotionally impoverished" (1); they do not merit discussion as a "literary" genre, as "romances," but rather as a popular and commercial phenomenon. To the contrary, in this book I insist that the very texts Beer excludes from her study must be read alongside those she includes if we are to recognize the extent to which these two categories are intertwined. Further, my choice of texts for this book shows that to consider commercially *and* critically "popular" novels such as *The French Lieutenant's Woman* and *Possession* without an awareness of their reliance on the storytelling devices and strategies of popular historical romance fiction is to miss one of the key aspects of their success. This position neither follows from a belief in the inherent quality or "literariness" of the popular romance novels I discuss, nor does it suggest that Byatt and Fowles do not deserve the critical accolades they receive. Instead, it was triggered by my ongoing frustration with the subdisciplinary distinction between literary scholarship and studies of popular fiction.

The almost synonymous relationship of popular romance fiction with "women's fiction" has prompted numerous feminist analyses of its history, content, production, and consumption—beginning in earnest with the publication of Janice Radway's seminal volume *Reading the Romance: Women, Patriarchy and Popular Literature* in 1984 (see for instance: Assiter; Cohn; Crane; Dubino; Ebert; Frenier; Krentz; Light, "'Returning to Manderley"; Mann; Modleski; Mussell; Radford; Taylor, Thurston, *Romance*; Woodruff). I will not be providing any detailed coverage or analysis of popular romance fiction studies as they have developed since 1984; however, I would like to make a number of general observations and comments in order to contextualize my own research. Most of the publications cited above focus on category romances (Mills and Boon, Harlequin). Apart from the work of Helen Hughes, Carol Thurston, and Kate McCafferty, comparatively few critics discuss popular *historical* romances as such. This is despite the fact that the "Smithton" women who form the basis for Radway's sociological study of romance reading had a marked preference for reading historical novels. The influence of Radway's text cannot be underestimated. Since its publication, "gender" has been taken as the immediate and principal critical focus in interrogations of romance. A number of critics have also endeavored to bring questions of class and race into the equation (Cohn; Cranny-Francis; Dubino; Ebert; McCafferty; Mann). A great deal of this work has been invaluable, but I am interested in questioning the apparent absence of examinations of the crucial relationship between compulsory heterosexuality, to use Adrienne Rich's term, and formations of romance. Such an absence betrays a certain blindness to the way in which popular romance is an almost paradigm case of "heterosexuality" as Butler describes it: "a compulsive and compulsory repetition that can only produce the *effect* of its own originality" ("Imitation" 21).

In order to ask pertinent questions about the relationship between Western formations of history, romance, and heterosexuality, I take historical romance fiction as a specific field of cultural production which encompasses both popular and literary texts. As explained below, Part II examines popular historical romance fiction and Part III looks at literary examples of the genre. Genre studies of romance tend to focus on its popular forms and to neglect the fundamental similarities between popular and literary fiction. This book argues that popular and literary romance are not distinct fields so much as subfields of a broader continuous category of literature. It takes issue, therefore, with the approach advocated in Ken Gelder's recent book, *Popular Fiction: The Logics and Practices of a Literary Field*, and insists that the work of genre undermines his argument that "popular fiction is best conceived as the opposite of Literature" (11). I just think this is taking an argument about the crucial differences between popular and literary texts too far. As the book's structure suggests, I don't think popular fiction and Literature (to adopt Gelder's capital "L," as I do throughout this book) are the same thing. There are of course important distinctions to be drawn between these two categories of historical romance fiction in terms of the broader context of their production and consumption, ranging from their cover art to the level of critical attention they receive from reviewers and academics alike. My feeling is that these kinds of considerations don't really matter as much as might first be imagined (which is not to say that they don't matter at all). The best way to begin to grasp the significance and impact of historical romance on ideas about heterosexuality is to address the similarities between its diverse texts.

Gelder identifies "genre" as a key word for popular fiction: "Popular fiction is, essentially, genre fiction" (1). In relation to romance my point is, quite simply, that genre's function exceeds popular fiction. Part I of this book, "Defining the Genre," defends this argument in broad terms and prepares the ground for the analyses of key historical romance novels in Part II and Part III. Most books about romance focus on popular fiction. It is relatively uncommon for critics to consider "literary" romances in a generic context. Novels such as *Possession*, or Susan Sontag's *The Volcano Lover* (both subtitled "A Romance") are more likely to be discussed in terms of their postmodernism or in the context of a longer author study. Similarly, it is unusual to find popular romance fiction discussed alongside literary romance fiction (Belsey, Elam, Strehle and Carden, and Wallace are notable exceptions). Parts II and III track the connections between popular "classics" by the "queen" of historical romance, Georgette Heyer, a selection of mass market historical romances published between 1980 and 2005, and John Fowles's and A.S. Byatt's acclaimed "Victorian romances," *The French Lieutenant's Woman* and *Possession*. To make a simple point, all of these novels can be accurately described as "bestsellers." Their common commercial, if not critical, success tests the limits of the classification "popular" to accurately name a particular type of fiction. There are also strong intertextual relationships between these romances. For instance, the work of Heyer, discussed in Chapter 3, impinges on Byatt's Booker prize-winning novel as strongly as it does on the "formula fiction" or "bodice rippers" I analyze in Chapter 4. This is not simply an instance of the later texts citing their historical precedents, nor can it be adequately explained by a general theory of postmodern citationality. Instead as Elam makes clear the permeability of the border between "high" and "low" culture is not simply displayed by, but characterizes romance. Further, reading these novels alongside each other reveals a closer relationship between them than might be expected—at the levels of both genre *and* ideology. As my analyses illustrate, the novels selected for this genre study share an allegiance to the tenets and motives of heterosexual hegemony. To make a broader and perhaps bolder claim: detailed textual analysis of these books also uncovers the instability of historical romance fiction's narratological and ideological foundations.

This book brings "literary" theory to bear on popular texts and uses some of the ideas which have emerged from studies of popular fiction to read literary texts. I am inspired in this approach by the following passage by Umberto Eco:

> The very dichotomy between order and disorder, between a work for popular consumption and a work for provocation, though it remains valid, should perhaps be reexamined from another point of view. In other words, I believe it will be possible to find elements of revolution and contestation in works that apparently lend themselves to facile consumption, and it will also be possible to realize, on the contrary, that certain works, which seem provocative and still enrage the public, do not really contest anything. (63–4)

As I remarked above, when I claim that there are "elements of revolution and contestation" to be found in the romance genre, I take my lead, at least in part, from the work of numerous other critics. The tradition of finding a dual impulse in the romance genre—an impulse to conform to hegemonic structures as it subverts them—manifests most often as an interest in the impact reading the romance genre has on its readers. In this regard, the distinction between conformity and subversion is frequently delineated along the lines of the opposition which Beer identified between escape and instruction. Radway writes that romance reading "is a profoundly conflicted activity centered upon a profoundly conflicted form" (14). She argues that popular romance fiction reaffirms the value and inevitability of patriarchal structures for women at the same time as the reading of romance affords women a means to protest against patriarchy's failure to fulfill the desires it engenders in women. For Jan Cohn the "surface plots" of popular romance novels are conventional in their emphasis on love and marriage but the "subtexts" are "subversive" in their drive to achieve wealth and power for the heroine. Rosalind Brunt draws similar conclusions in her study of Barbara Cartland whom she identifies as an "inadvertent feminist" (155). Brunt argues that the "moral" messages of Cartland's fiction are undercut by its representation of the material structures of patriarchy. Joseph Allen Boone frames his discussion of the romance in terms of an opposition between tradition and counter-tradition. Elam identifies romance as postmodern in order to explain its "uncertain" politics. Catherine Belsey uses the methodologies of poststructuralist and psychoanalytic theory to focus on the importance of a discourse of "desire" to understanding what is inherently contradictory in the form and function of love stories. Tania Modleski insists on the "importance of seeing both progressive *and* regressive elements in popular texts" ("Romance Writer" 67). Susan Strehle and Mary Paniccia Carden describe love stories as "cultural primers." They write, "Culture presses in on romance, dictating the forms love may take and its expression in language; romance exerts its own counterpressure, exceeding cultural prescriptions and erupting in unpredictable discursive moments" (xii). This is by no means an exhaustive list, but I hope it indicates that romance, before it is anything else, is a dynamic, difficult, and uncertain genre which warrants further study and consideration.

Elam begins *Romancing the Postmodern* by citing a promise offered on the covers of many Harlequin romance novels: "You can never have too much romance" (1). She explains: "Harlequin would like us to believe that romance is by definition a genre incapable of being exhausted. There will always be room for another romance, since a reader can never read, an author can never write, too many" (1). That is to say romance is constituted by its uncontainability; it is infinitely iterable. Romance's most notable characteristic, for Elam, is its excess. She argues that this excess extends beyond the genre's apparent inexhaustibility to infect "high literature" as a signature of postmodernism: "In postmodernism, as in romance, the division between high and low culture, the study and the boudoir, becomes blurred" (1). This claim both seeks to justify the scope of Elam's study of romance, in which she reads Walter Scott alongside Cartland and Eco and underpins her readings of individual texts. (I respond in more detail to Elam's argument about the inherent relationship between romance and postmodernism early in Part I.) For Elam "Romance, by virtue of its complex relationship to both history and novelistic realism, will have been the genre to address the problematic of postmodernity in narrative fiction" (1). Elam claims that postmodernism—which she defines as "the rethinking of history as an ironic coexistence of temporalities" (3)—*is* romance. While various critics have identified both *The French Lieutenant's Woman* and *Possession* as "postmodern" novels, I have kept my own use of Elam's preferred term, "postmodern romance," to a minimum in order to prevent this book becoming too cluttered with competing terminologies. I also want to keep open the possibility that those aspects of postmodernism and romance which Elam highlights are also present in popular historical romance. Further, too many scholars have left the term "romance" out of their discussions of Fowles and Byatt re-imaginings of the Victorian past.

Recent scholarship has noted significant changes in the structure and style of literary historical novels. The first chapter of Jago Morrison's *Contemporary Fiction*, "History and Post-Histories," argues that a broader "crisis in historical representation" (15) manifests in contemporary fiction in two ways. Firstly, it appears as scepticism of "grand narratives" of history and the "proliferation of local and regional historical narratives in their place." Secondly, contemporary writers recognize that the impact of globalization makes "the idea of self-contained, nationally and ethnically defined historical consciousness somehow outdated and inadequate" (14). Morrison argues that traditional conceptions of history which grant novelists the "imperious authority attributed to nineteenth-century novelists" are not "sustainable." Instead, he argues that "one of the characteristics of much contemporary writing is the way in which writers self-consciously acknowledge their *lack* of mastery of the historical, and of their own practices of narration" (14). Morrison uses the term "post-historical novel" to classify novels "about" history, novels "written against history's grain" (16). Over the last two decades, a number of critics have argued that a new classificatory term is necessary to signal the difference between traditional historical novels and recent manifestations of the genre.

In 1988, Linda Hutcheon famously coined the somewhat unwieldy "historiographical metafiction" in *A Poetics of Postmodernism* to group together novels which reflect on their treatment of history and the narrativization of history in general, at the same time as they sustain a belief in the validity and value of historical narratives. For Hutcheon, this paradox marks the postmodernism of the genre. More recently, Elam and Belsey have used the term "postmodern romance" to pose similar arguments to Hutcheon about the paradoxical nature of recent historical novels and the challenge they throw up to traditional ideas about the relationship between the past and the present. In addition, Del Ivan Janik and Martha Tuck Rozett both write about "new historical fiction." Certainly, the claims these critics make about developments in literary uses of history resonate with the literary novels I discuss in this book; however, my feeling is that this proliferation of terms hinders rather than helps new attempts to map the field of contemporary literary production. My preference is to use the more elastic and simpler term "historical romance fiction"; this classification already encapsulates the tensions and complexities the neologisms cited above have tried to name. It does not suggest that recent novels enact a radical break from the genre's traditions, but implies instead that the continuities in the genre are as significant as the changes, if not more so. More importantly though, using the term "historical *romance* fiction" intervenes in discussions about literary treatments of history by forcing the issue of the significance of "romance."

Elam offers a suggestive negative definition of "romance", under the subheading "What romance is not," beginning with the claim: "Romance is not just the kind of love story found next to the candy bars in supermarket checkout lanes: titles like *Always Love* or *Pagan Adversary* do not tell us all we need to know about romance" (5). However, her approach also makes clear that there *is* a relationship between this kind of love story and the kind more likely to be found on the shelves of "good" bookstores and university libraries. Any attempt to define romance, then, must be excessive since, in Elam's terms—by virtue of a generic leakage between high and pop culture—it refuses to be pinned down. It is no surprise then that Elam refuses to offer a straightforward definition of romance, arguing instead that "the generic function of romance is a complexity that belies singular definition" (4).

Romance, it might be said, plays the division between high and, to use Elam's term, "low" culture. As noted above, in this study I look at texts from both ends of this scale with a view to exposing their common ground. This study reveals that there are underlying similarities between all of the novels I discuss, most particularly in the way they *use* an idea of "history," which preclude any easy distinction between them in terms of their literary sophistication or erudition. To repeat, romance is a fictional mode which depends on the force and familiarity of the speech act "I love you." My definition of "historical romance fiction" aims to be as broadly inclusive. Simply put, this classificatory term applies to heterosexual love stories set in the past.

This book is principally motivated by feminist and antihomophobic politics in its efforts to interrogate the terms and discourses of heterosexual hegemony. In the introductory paragraph of *Epistemology of the Closet* Sedgwick proposes that many of the major tenets of "thought and knowledge" in twentieth-century Western culture are structured—and fractured—by a "chronic, now endemic crisis of homo/heterosexual definition" which she dates from the end of the nineteenth century. "Crisis" here refers to the infective vigor of the intractable incoherences and contradictions which Sedgwick argues permeate "each of the forms of discursive and institutional 'common sense'" about categories of sexuality in our present culture (1). The term "homosexual" entered common currency only in the late nineteenth century, earlier in fact than "heterosexual." As Sedgwick points out, it appears that "homosexual" practices, behaviors and even, she suggests, the "conscious identities" the term now denotes, had a long history preceding its coinage. Without precedence, however, was the way in which homo- and heterosexuality became identificatory *markers* by which every given person, just as he or she was necessarily assignable to a male or female gender, was now considered necessarily assignable as well to a homo- or hetero-sexuality, a binarized identity that was full of implications, however confusing, for even the ostensibly least sexual aspects of personal existence. It was this new development that left no space in the culture exempt from the potent incoherences of homo/heterosexual definition. (2)

Epistemology of the Closet takes as axiomatic Foucault's observation in *The History of Sexuality* that contemporary Western culture increasingly assumes a privileged and intimate relationship between "sexuality" and "our most prized constructs of individual identity, truth and knowledge." She adds, "it becomes truer and truer that the language of sexuality not only intersects with, but transforms the other languages and relations by which we know" (4).

For Sedgwick, the "crisis of homo/heterosexual definition" is as crucial to an understanding of Western cultural formations as the masculine/feminine gender binary. She argues persuasively that an exploration of "virtually any aspect of modern Western culture" is fundamentally flawed to the extent that it ignores the import of homo/heterosexual definition in its analyses. Despite Sedgwick's compelling definitional crisis the rampant *hetero*sexuality of popular and literary romance novels has not been subject to extended critique. Indeed, canvassing the principal, oft-cited texts in studies of the genre indicates that most, if not all, extended critiques of romance published to date have been flawed in this regard. In "Against Proper Objects," Butler repudiates the "mundane violence" of the institution of the disciplinary "proper object" of study. To this extent, she is interested in exposing the unfortunate and delimiting effects of the institutionally required distinction between the proper object for feminist studies and the proper object for gay and lesbian studies. Such a distinction, she argues, by reserving "sexuality" for gay and lesbian studies, threatens the prescriptive delimitation of feminism to an exclusive focus on "gender." Belsey raises the pertinent suspicion that as academic work in the field of gay and lesbian studies or "queer theory" becomes increasingly detailed and examines homosexual texts with correspondingly increasing sophistication, "there is a danger of leaving unproblematized our account of the erotic relation between men and women, and thus inadvertently reaffirming its naturalness by another route" (134). An awareness of this danger motivated me to write this book.

With these goals in mind, the two chapters in Part I build the theoretical scaffolding for the remainder of the book. My starting point is the extraordinary work of J.L. Austin, the British philosopher who coined the terms "speech act" and "performative" in 1955. The idea of "performativity" offers us another way to think through the question of "ideology," as it endeavours to describe that process whereby particular human practices become naturalized, taken for granted. Theories of performativity are seductive because of their capacity to describe the tenuousness of processes of naturalization or normalization. This aspect of theories of performativity fuels my optimism in this book. Not only does theory provide me with the tools to argue that it is possible to read some of our culture's most sexist and homophobic texts differently than might first seem possible; it also allows me to suggest that such readings are not only available to those of us who are in a position to bring a sophisticated and elaborate theoretical machinery to work on these texts. Instead the book seeks to demonstrate that the very forces which destabilize and subvert the principal messages of these texts are always already at work within them. This insight motivates the readings offered in the following chapters as they try to avoid presenting a constructivist account of gender and sexuality which leaves us no room within which to imagine a different and better future.

Part II does not offer a wide-ranging survey of popular historical romance fiction. A number of other scholars have already met the demand for such a study (Wallace, Strehle and Carden). Instead, the chapters in this section provide an introduction to an important and intriguing subgenre of popular historical romance which has been overlooked by earlier studies: cross-dressing novels. Chapter 3 examines the contribution to the form by Heyer and Chapter 4 presents a survey of cross-dressing novels published over the last twenty-five years by a range of contemporary popular novelists, including Kathleen Woodiwiss, Norah Roberts, Catherine Coulter, and Jude Deveraux. The discussion of popular romance applies and builds on the theoretical model developed in Part I. Cross-dressing novels are organized around a double scene of confession in which the pronouncement "I love you" is concomitant with the revelation of the cross-dressed heroine's sex. This section of the book includes an exploration of the logic of the "open secret" as it applies to heterosexual romance fictions, and a critique and reworking of Butler's claim that performativity theory involves "working the weakness in the norm."

Part III pursues two related questions: How have leading literary novelists treated the relationship between romance, history, and heterosexuality? What role does the romantic speech act play in the form and function of literary historical romance fiction? Whereas the chapters on popular romance focus on texts neglected by other studies, the chapters on literary romance focus on two novels which have attracted an extraordinary amount of critical attention: Fowles's *The French Lieutenant's Woman* and Byatt's *Possession*. The germ for this selection of texts was my frustration with the gaps and errors in scholarly discussion of these intimately related novels. Chapters 5 and 6 analyze *The French Lieutenant's Woman*. I decided to include two essays about this pivotal historical romance partly because of my strong sense that, throughout the volumes of essays I read during my research, the novel's core interest in heterosexuality had been largely overlooked by critics. While the secondary literature on this novel reveals a consensus that Fowles's approach to the historical novel broke new ground, little has been published about its representation of heterosexuality as such. Chapter 5 focuses on the representation of Sarah Woodruff as both an historical figure and one who exceeds history. (I take a similar approach to the analysis of Christabel LaMotte in *Possession*.) Chapter 6 approaches the novel along a slightly different path; it tests my claims about "I love you" by adding another speech act to the mix: "Shame on you." *The French Lieutenant's Woman* is organized and propelled by two related speech acts: "I love you" and "Shame on you." Sarah Woodruff's performances of shame and love raise the question of the place of agency in theories of performativity; they suggest also the interpellative role of speech acts. Chapter 7 is a feminist and antihomophobic critique of Byatt's *Possession*. It maps the links between Byatt's historical romance fiction and those discussed in earlier chapters. Like *The French Lieutenant's Woman*, *Possession* is self-conscious about the pivotal relationship between "I love you" and the heterosexual romance plot, between the romantic speech act and the formation of the heterosexual romantic subject. *Possession*, more particularly, demonstrates the mutual dependence between performatives and narratives in its representation of postmodern literary scholars who learn how to say "I love you" by reading an historical romance.

PART I
Defining the Genre

Chapter 1

Romance, History, Heterosexuality

Fredric Jameson begins his essay "Magical Narratives: Romance as Genre" by stating that genres are "essentially contracts between a writer and his readers" (sic). He adds that genres are literary "*institutions*, which like other institutions or contracts are based on tacit agreements or contracts" (135). He invokes the idea of "speech" to think about the form and function of literary genres and, more particularly, the romance genre:

> The thinking behind such a view of genres is based on the presupposition that all speech needs to be marked with certain indications and signals as to how it is to be properly used. In everyday life, of course, these signals are furnished by the context of the utterance and by the physical presence of the speaker, with his gesturality and intonations. When speech is lifted out of this concrete situation, such signals must be replaced by other types of directions, if the text in question is not to be abandoned to a drifting multiplicity of uses (or *meanings*, as the latter used to be termed). It is of course the generic convention which is called upon to perform this task, and to provide a built-in substitute for those older corrections and adjustments which are possible only in the immediacy of the face-to-face situation. Yet it is clear at the same time that the farther a given text is removed from a performing situation (that of village storyteller, or bard, or player), the more difficult it will be to enforce a given generic prescription on a reader; indeed, no small part of the art of writing is absorbed by this (impossible) attempt to devise a foolproof mechanism for the automatic exclusion of undesirable responses to a given literary utterance. (135–6)

Jameson describes generic texts as "speech acts" removed from the physicality and immediacy of conversation or live performance. He pictures the relationship between the writer and the reader of generic texts as a scene of utterance, in which the writer ("speaker") seeks to control or order the way their text is read ("heard"). He thus characterizes genres as authoritarian in their efforts to "enforce" certain attitudes or ideologies on readers. According to Jameson's model of genre, the writer seeks to alleviate or manage the threat of improper interpretation or usage of their text by the mobilization of appropriate "generic conventions." These conventions or stock devices take the place of the material context and physical gestures which accompany speech acts in their ordinary sense to determine the reception of generic texts. It is not the acceptance or enjoyment of the convention as such that matters. Instead, Jameson emphasizes the "generic prescription" which the devices and mechanisms of generic fiction work to communicate. Genres, that is, have ideological ends. What Jameson's model makes clear is that these ends are never easily or straightforwardly achieved. Rather, fictional genres are always haunted by the threat of disobedience to their terms, by their capacity to be read differently. Such an idea inheres in the authoritarian model of genre which he uses; to think of rules is also to imagine the possibility of their being broken.

As stated in the introduction, this book uses theories of speech acts to describe the ideological function of a particular genre and to make the argument that this function is never straightforward. To state my position baldly: historical romance fiction is constituted by an awareness of the instability of its narratological and ideological foundations. As the following chapters demonstrate, this self-awareness runs through the popular and literary subfields of the genre.

Jameson's representation of genres as "speech" occurs in the context of what Linda Hutcheon calls the "revenge of *parole*." In *A Poetics of Postmodernism* Hutcheon argues that theory has turned to an emphasis on the "enunciative situation" in its accounts of the subject's relationship to and use of language, and of the formation of subjectivity. She cites "speech act theory, pragmatics, [and] discourse analysis" as explicit examples of this phenomenon (*Poetics* 168). First published in 1988, Hutcheon's book predates the emergence of a body of theory which further exemplifies the trend she identifies. Most notably in the work of Judith Butler and Eve Kosofsky Sedgwick, theories of "performativity" bring speech act theory up to speed with accounts of the production of subjects in discourse offered by Louis Althusser, Michel Foucault, and Jacques Derrida among others. In Butler's words, theories of performativity describe and investigate "that aspect of discourse that has the capacity to produce what it names" ("Gender" 112). Hutcheon uses the term "enunciative situation" to name the entire complex of discursive relations within which a text is produced and received—"text, producer, receiver, historical, and social context" (115). While our terminology is somewhat different, I share her interest in the way fictional texts thematize and theorize precisely these aspects of textuality and discourse.

I am committed to locating what Sedgwick calls "the performative aspects of texts" (*Epistemology* 3). Taken performatively, texts are sites of definition, redefinition, and disruption—both in relation to readers and institutionally. That is to say, fictional texts are intimate participants in the production and reproduction of the logical (or illogical) systems and matrices through which we are defined and define ourselves. This approach to the analysis of an enduring popular and literary genre assumes that the importance and value of generic texts resides not just in their capacity to bear meaning, but also that the force of genres follows from their role in the ongoing construction of the various meanings by which we both make sense of and create ourselves and the "world." The three terms at the centre of this book's investigation of genre and its meanings are "romance," "history," and "heterosexuality."

Throughout this book, I employ speech act theory and theories of performativity to define and interrogate the parameters of the historical romance genre. In her concise history and study of romance, Gillian Beer argues that it "can be distinguished from other forms of fiction by the relationship it imposes between reader and romance-world" (8). Like Jameson, Beer draws an analogy between generic fiction and, to use his words, a "performing situation" when she compares the experience of reading a romance to that of a child listening to a storyteller. Whereas Jameson characterizes genres as authoritarian in a general sense, Beer suggests that the extent to which the romance seeks to determine reader responses sets it apart from other fictional genres. For Beer, in order to enjoy reading romance, in order to read it properly, we must "surrender" (8) to its demands by accepting first and foremost the fictional world it compels us to inhabit; reading romance is a question of being commanded rather than seduced. Nevertheless, what is implicit in her description of the romance genre is the idea that this genre may be constituted as much by the difficulty with which it achieves obedience to its terms as by any apparent success: "The absurdities of romance are felt when we refuse to inhabit the world offered us and disengage ourselves, bringing to bear our own opinions" (8). Beer's focus on the reading position assumed and produced by the romance leads to an emphasis on its "imaginative functions." She argues that this approach helps to overcome the difficulties of defining a term and of classifying a literary genre which has as broad a compass as "romance." Beer suggests that whereas the romance's "literary properties" have been too inconstant and too diverse over the centuries to provide the basis for meaningful classification, its principal "imaginative functions" persist. These are twofold: "escape" and "instruction." She explains that romance is instructive because in its construction of a fictional world for readers to escape into, it represents an "ideal" against which we can measure and assess our own experience and the world.

Beer's and Jameson's approaches to thinking about romance are valuable because of their emphasis on the way in which generic fictions might be said to function or *act*. However, both critics are preoccupied with talking about "writers" and "readers" rather than the wider enunciative context within which any given text circulates. Theories of performativity facilitate exactly this kind of broadening of focus. They also enable a greater emphasis on the extent to which romance fiction incessantly thematizes the very reading practices it engenders.

In all of the novels I discuss in this book, heterosexual love is precisely what exceeds history just as it enables a certain telling of history. Broadly speaking, the performative *force* of the romantic speech act (and of romance) depends on both a denial of its historicity, of the fact that it has always already been said before, at the same time as it relies on this fact for its familiarity and sense. In these terms "I love you" invokes a kind of continuous present. More particularly, there are two somewhat contradictory but mutually reinforcing aspects to this claim which are brought to the fore by my focus on heterosexual love stories set in the *past*: "I love you" is always said anew, but over and over again these texts insist that whenever and wherever it is said it means the same thing. The utterance "I love you" is not only the key to the plotting of historical romance novels, as it is to romances generally, but is also crucial to the link which they strive to draw between the present and the past. Bringing an idea of "history" to bear on performativity theory's insistence on the necessary iterability of language reveals how this fascinating speech act encapsulates heterosexuality's (impossible) claim to universality, timelessness and *truth*. Butler defines performativity as "the discursive mode by which ontological effects are installed" ("Gender" 112). Historical fictions of heterosexual love are performative to the extent that they participate in the establishment and maintenance of prevailing ideas about the links between sex, gender, and sexuality. This book charts one of the many ways in which romantic love is persistently and aggressively heterosexualized in Western culture and begins to consider the extent to which this campaign of normalization and exclusion is endlessly covered over.

Diane Elam writes that "the founding trope of historical romance is anachronism" (35). From the outset, a whole series of apparently oppositional discourses lock horns in historical romance, not least "history," in its promise to tell the truth about the past, and "romance" in its endeavors to offer a fantasy of an elsewhere. A whole series of complex binary oppositions lie, as on a palimpsest, beneath the term "historical romance": fact/fiction, truth/lies, real/false, past/present, here/there, linear/spatial, universal/contingent, mind/body, masculine/feminine, and so on. One of the pleasures and challenges of studying this genre is tracing the connections between these troublesome pairs. However, the binary which causes the most trouble and therefore demands the most urgent attention is homosexual/heterosexual. The link between historical romance's inherent anachronism and homo/heterosexual definition comes into clearer focus when we look carefully at the genre's organizing utterance, "I love you." The romantic speech act operates through an evacuation of "history," through an implicit denial of its historicity. This point has been indirectly made in theoretical accounts of the intersection of postmodernism with romance. However, while influential studies of postmodern historical novels have articulated the bond between two of the terms which entitle this chapter, "history" and "romance," they have largely overlooked the importance of the third term, "heterosexuality."

In *Reflections on* The Name of the Rose, Umberto Eco uses a variation of the romantic speech act to exemplify "the postmodern attitude." He writes:

> The postmodern reply to the modern consists of recognizing that the past, since it cannot really be destroyed, because its destruction leads to silence, must be revisited: but with irony, not innocently. I think of the postmodern attitude as that of a man who loves a very cultivated woman and knows he cannot say to her, "I love you madly," because he knows that she knows (and that she knows that he knows) that these words have already been written by Barbara Cartland. Still, there is a solution. He can say, "As Barbara Cartland would put it, I love you madly." At this point, having avoided false innocence, having said clearly that it is no longer possible to speak innocently, he will nevertheless have said what he wanted to say to the woman: that he loves her, but he loves her in an age of lost innocence. If the woman goes along with this, she will have received a declaration of love all the same. Neither of the two speakers will feel innocent, both will have accepted the challenge of the past, of the already said, which cannot be eliminated; both will consciously and with pleasure play the game of irony … But both will have succeeded once again, in speaking of love. (67–8)

This passage offers a beautiful illustration of the contradictory status of "I love you": its simultaneous circulation as both a confession and a cliché; its capacity both to hold the promise and betray the lie of the humanist subject; and its necessarily fraught link to history, to the "already said." Further, "I love you" encapsulates the key paradox of the referential concept of language or the "descriptive fallacy" (in the words of J.L. Austin): it is not enough to assess simply whether this statement is true or false. As Eco's hypothetical scene of utterance illustrates, a more critical criterion is the success or the "happiness" of a declaration of love.

The principal obstacle to the man's desire to confess his feelings is his (and his beloved's) knowledge that "I love you" is always a citation; it can never be owned by any individual speaker. The problem of proving his sincerity is compounded by this speech act's drive to conflate fiction and reality: "I love you" marks the imposition of romance on history. Eco draws attention to the performative force, not just of direct speech, but of the associated fictions and narratives which speech acts always carry with them. Reading this passage prompts consideration of the very questions which are my focus throughout this book. The joint problematics of referentiality and sincerity, citationality and history, fiction and reality which "I love you" registers for Eco—although he doesn't state this explicitly—are at the center of my analysis of its ubiquity and force in historical romance fiction.

For Eco, postmodernism demands "not the negation of the already said, but its ironic rethinking." It is for this reason, he explains, that modernism and postmodernism can "coexist, or alternate, or follow each other closely" in the same artistic work (68). In the short tale of postmodern love cited above, Eco equates the "already said" with the "past": "Neither of the two speakers will feel innocent, both will have accepted the challenge of the past, of the already said, which cannot be eliminated; both will consciously and with pleasure play the game of irony ... But both will have succeeded once again, in speaking of love." In these terms, saying "I love you" is a question of "history." Eco's conflation of citationality with history has two aspects. First, to say "I love you" is to recall the innumerable times it has been said before. It is also to cite an imagined (and impossible) past when saying "I love you" simply meant you were in love. Eco explains that the man's qualifying clause, "As Barbara Cartland would put it," allows him to say "I love you madly" without claiming the "innocence" of another "age." The man thus imagines a time when it was possible to say "I love you" with simple sincerity—a time before the excesses of twentieth-century popular culture had turned his speech into a cliché. Of course, he does not do this without irony, as is made clear by his reference to Cartland: a romance writer whose novels famously use an historical setting to picture an age when we believed in love, and when our dreams for a happy ending always came true (Brunt). That he manages to say what he wants despite (though with the help of) Cartland makes it clear that the romantic speech act has not been exhausted by its overuse; the language of heterosexual love persists and continues to be meaningful even when (or because) it is acknowledged as the stuff of formula fiction.

The man and the woman in Eco's story are distinguished from Cartland and the mass culture she represents by their "cultivation." At the same time, however, they desire precisely what fictions like Cartland's are most driven to represent: a happy ending for heterosexual love. That they "[succeed] once again, in speaking of love" is Eco's main point. That they manage to "revisit the past" with *both* irony and sincerity explains his use of this story as a parable for postmodernism as he understands it. Eco's short (and entertaining) love story describes not just the possibility that apparently opposed discourses (modernism and postmodernism, high culture and popular culture, history and romance, reality and fiction) can coexist without cancelling each other out, but it also demonstrates their primary interdependence. That he uses "I love you" to clarify and prove his point is germane to my study of this utterance as the ontological and narrative turning point for heterosexual romance. My analysis of "I love you" extrapolates on Eco's recognition of its duplicity to argue that this utterance indexes the ambivalence at the heart of fictions of heterosexual love (by writers shelved with Cartland at your local bookstore *and* those shelved with Eco). More broadly speaking, and as I argue in the next chapter, each and every reiteration of this utterance represents a moment of crisis for heterosexual hegemony and not just because it points to the foundational anachronism of heterosexual romance: "I love you" does not conceal its contradictions with ease. Instead its compulsive reiteration is symptomatic of its inability to do so in any lasting way: anxiety engenders reiteration.

The self-consciousness which characterizes Eco's man and woman in love is not the preserve of "cultivated" or educated lovers. Instead the very fictions to which they refer, but by implication do not read, themselves betray an awareness of the difficulties attendant on saying "I love you." At the least, Cartland's novels—their historical settings together with their spectacular popularity—signal a widespread if implicit acknowledgment that the language of heterosexual romance does not quite ring true in the present. The name "Barbara Cartland" is a synecdoche for popular romance. Eco's reference to her in a story of a distinctly "high culture" couple is suggestive of the entanglement of literary and popular versions of heterosexual romance I wrote of in the introduction, and further of the performative force of these fictions in culture generally—on the ways everyone speaks of love in their everyday lives.

Two of the most impressive and useful studies of the intersections of romance and history anchor their discussions in theories of postmodernism: Elam's *Romancing the Postmodern* and Catherine Belsey's *Desire: Love Stories in Western Culture*. Where I differ from both critics is in my insistence that postmodernism on its own cannot account for the ambivalence which inheres in the language and logic of our culture's principal hegemonies, not just of gender and sexuality, but also of class, race, ethnicity, and so on. This ambivalence is present, I demonstrate, in those cultural formations which are unlikely ever to merit the classification "postmodern." While I concede that postmodern literary theory is a useful device for analyzing the existence of contradictory positions in fictional texts and genres, it cannot go as far as the concept of performativity in foregrounding the capacity of historical romance fictions to reinforce ideological codes while they simultaneously interrogate them.

Performativity names processes of definition and subversion already at work in our language and texts and across a range of genres and cultural forms. Analysis of the role of the romantic speech act in historical romance novels highlights the inherent instability of the romantic imperative Western culture issues to its members. Further, it demonstrates the mutual implication of the historical romance genre and theories of performativity. Throughout this book, I argue that fictions of heterosexual romance and notions of performativity (both implicit and explicit) have a long-standing, if fraught, relationship. I come back to this point repeatedly in my discussions of individual novels and their characteristic (if not always enthusiastic) self-consciousness about the linguistic and discursive processes which produce and sustain the heterosexual romantic subject.

The narrator of Jeannette Winterson's *Written on the Body* (described as a "postmodern romance" by Belsey) neatly summarizes the problems of speaking of love in the present: the difficulty of reconciling emotion with cliché, passion with scepticism, romance with history:

> It's the clichés that cause the trouble. A precise emotion seeks a precise expression. If what I feel is not precise then should I call it love? It is so terrifying, love, that all I can do is shove it under a dump bin of pink cuddly toys and send myself a greeting card saying "Congratulations on your engagement." But I am not engaged I am deeply distracted. I am desperately looking the other way so that love won't see me. I want the diluted version,

the sloppy language, the insignificant gestures. The saggy armchair of clichés. It's alright millions of bottoms have sat here before me. The springs are well worn, the fabric smelly and familiar. I don't have to be frightened, look, my grandma and grandad did it, he in a stiff collar and club tie, she in white muslin straining a little at the life beneath. They did it, my parents did it, now I will do it won't I, arms outstretched, not to hold you, just to keep my balance, sleepwalking to that armchair. How happy we will be. How happy everyone will be. And they all lived happily ever after. (10)

The desire to say "I love you" is both banal and uniquely compelling. These three little words are inscribed across our culture in bold pink letters: on greeting cards, heart-shaped balloons and cuddly toys; in song lyrics ("I just called, to say …"), literature and poetry; on film and television; in postcards and letters; in conversations imagined and actual. They are both tacky and profound. Further, the passage quoted above traces the fine line between the desire to make our words match our experience and the fear that the opposite happens—that we are somehow compelled to make our experience match the available words. Winterson describes what we might call the inertia of the subject in love: "They did it, my parents did it, now I will do it won't I, arms outstretched, not to hold you, just to keep my balance, sleepwalking to that armchair."

Winterson's narrator shares this distrust of the language of love with the protagonists of A.S. Byatt's *Possession* (also considered a "postmodern romance" by Belsey). Byatt's novel tells the story of two late-twentieth-century English academics, Roland Michell and Maud Bailey, who stumble upon evidence of a secret romance between two well-known Victorian poets, Randolph Henry Ash and Christabel LaMotte. Roland and Maud fall in love as they pursue the story of the lovers from the past. Byatt's novel makes it explicit that the question of how to say "I love you" is one of imagining history. The contemporary characters are conscious of a distinction between the way they think about love and the way Ash and LaMotte conceived of it. Maud describes the difference: "We never say the word Love, do we—we know it's a suspect ideological construct—especially Romantic Love—so we have to make a real effort of imagination to know what it felt like to be them, here, believing in these things—Love—themselves—that what they did mattered" (267). To believe in love becomes a question of anachronism; it involves bringing an idea of the past into the present, or rather of imposing the present on a reimagined past.

Of course, what Winterson's, Byatt's and Eco's characters all have in common is their "cultivation," to use Eco's descriptor. My greater claim is that the ambivalence they articulate pervades discourses of heterosexual love; it is not exclusive to "postmodern romance" (to cultivated or high romance). The question of how to say "I love you" confronts all of its speakers. As the comparison of popular and literary romances in later chapters shows, awareness of this is merely a matter of degrees; it is not always "cultivated."

Belsey describes "love" in the present as "both silent and garrulous." Belsey draws out this contradiction by raising the question of how to say "I love you":

[Love] cannot speak, and yet it seems that it never ceases to speak in late twentieth-century Western culture. It is silent, first, in recognition of its banality. "Every other night on TV," Roland Barthes points out, "someone says: *I love you*." How can we, unique and autonomous as we long to be, capture the extraordinary experience of desire by echoing this worn-out commonplace, this blank performative, which lacks nuances and "suppresses explanations, adjustments, degrees, scruples" [Barthes *A Lover's Discourse* 148]? "I love you" obliterates the distinctiveness of the desire it sets out to capture, and affirms at the same time the difference it sets out to efface, the gap between "I" and "you," investing the performance in the process with a certain solitariness. (74–5)

Like Eco, Belsey suggests that the problem with saying "I love you" is one of achieving sincerity in the face of "scepticism" (72). For Belsey, this utterance encapsulates the ambivalence at the heart of postmodern conceptions of love. She clarifies this point by nominating "I love you" as a "performative." In these terms, the problem with saying "I love you" is the disjunction between its pronominal and semantic claim to uniqueness ("*I* love *you*") and its undeniable effect as citation. While Belsey's conception of postmodernism places less emphasis than Eco's on an ironic negotiation between the past and the present, her discussion implies a similar relationship between citationality and history to that which underpins his tale of postmodern love. How is it that we can say "I love you" anew (when we know that we can't)? She cites the protagonist of *Written on the Body*: "Why is it that the most unoriginal thing we can say to one another is still the thing we long to hear" (76). The key to Belsey's idea of "postmodern love" (like Eco's) is noticing that, despite our "recognition of its banality," we still want to find a way to say "I love you."

Belsey perceives postmodernism as an historical period more than any of the other critics I discuss in this chapter (see the discussion of Elam below for an example of a critic who actively dehistoricizes postmodernism). It is beyond the scope of this study to canvas debates over whether postmodernism is an historical period synchronous with late capitalism or a transhistorical cultural mode. For Belsey, postmodernism is inextricably tied to the "cultural logic of late capitalism." She argues that love holds a special place in the postmodern imagination to the degree that it lies beyond the reach of the "market." Love holds the promise of a fulfillment which is not tied to the forces of consumerism:

> Love thus becomes more precious than before because it is beyond price, and in consequence its metaphysical character is intensified. More than ever love has come to represent presence, transcendence, immortality, what Derrida calls proximity, living speech, certainty, everything in short that the market is unable to provide or fails to guarantee. (72)

At the same time, however, Belsey notes that postmodernism includes a distrust of precisely the kind of certainty the term "love" seeks to name:

> [T]he postmodern condition brings with it an incredulity towards true love. Where, we might ask, in the light of our experience, the statistics, our philosophy, or any documentary evidence outside popular romance, are *its* guarantees, its continuities, proof of its ability to fulfill its undertakings? (72)

In these terms, the idea of love attracts and repels us to the degree that it exceeds history. While Belsey does not make this last point explicit, as both of the extracts quoted above make clear, her distinction between our scepticism about love *now* and our implicit faith in it *before*, together with her insistence on its enduring relevance, reveals this double bind. She uses the term "postmodern love" to designate this new ambivalent position on love.

From Belsey's perspective the problem with saying "I love you" in postmodernity is one of referentiality: What does it *mean* to say "I love you"? If the postmodern condition is characterized by its resistance to precisely those things which this utterance seeks to represent (humanist principles of truth and a unified subject), then why does the idea of love remain so uniquely compelling? Perhaps the clue to making sense of this contradiction is to recognize that the conceptual and metaphysical tangle Belsey describes inheres in the romantic speech act; it is a linguistic *and* semantic inevitability.

Elam follows Eco both in her conception of postmodernism and in her use of romance as emblematic of its "attitude." As I've explained, her book was the first source for my nomination of "I love you" as a generic formula for romance. Shortly after I began research on this project I zeroed in on the following passage, with which she begins her chapter on Eco's *The Name of the Rose*:

> I love you.
> A statement that is pre-eminently pragmatic, "I love you" falls as prologue or epilogue to a story with which we are all familiar, as prefatory exhortation to, or concluding description of, intimacy. Yet we are not intimate, and we don't know where we are in the story. And "I love you" will have only appeared in quotation marks, marked as taking place in a world of textual apparatus. Thinking romance is a questioning of how it is that one may say "I love you," a statement undecidably descriptive or performative, whose whole drama is bound up in whether it belongs to a rhetoric of persuasion or a system of tropes. (26)

Elam discusses *The Name of the Rose* as an historical romance novel. She writes that it "becomes interesting because of the way it stages the textuality and intertextuality of the apparently vacuous 'I love you,' a phrase which comes to stand as characteristic of the entire problematic of postmodernity for Eco" (26). My efforts to make sense of the extract quoted above—particularly Elam's description of "I love you" as "undecidably descriptive or performative"—led me first to Butler and Sedgwick's versions of performativity theory and then to Austin's *How to Do Things with Words* and so on. What happened as I pursued the implications of using "I love you" to define romance was that this idea became unhinged from Elam's focus on postmodernism. I began to see that the implicit intertextuality of "I love you," together with the conceptual and political uncertainty which it phrases for Elam, Eco, and Belsey, was a condition of romance *per se*; the adjective "postmodern" became superfluous.

Elam does go some of the way towards suggesting my use (and abuse) of her conceptual framework when she argues that romance is *always* postmodern—a term which she says designates the very contradictions, ambivalences and uncertainties which characterize and constitute romance (12). My early reluctance to follow her lead in this regard stemmed from a recognition that the aspects of romance which Elam highlights (and which are the focus of my own readings of individual texts) need not be secured to an idea of postmodernism. Instead I sought to politicize my analysis of the romance genre from another direction: first by placing it in the context of hegemonic discourses of gender and heterosexuality; and second by tying the well-recognized indeterminacy of the romance genre to the ontological crises which, as feminist and gay and lesbian scholars have demonstrated, pervade normative notions of sex, gender, and sexuality. One of the reasons I focus on romance novels set in the past is that, as this chapter shows, tackling an idea of "history" is one of the first steps in recognizing and making sense of the performative force of the idea of heterosexual love.

Elam radically dehistoricizes the idea of postmodernism. (Her book includes chapters about the postmodernism of Scott, Joseph Conrad, George Eliot, and Eco. In fact she argues that Scott is more postmodern than Eco.) Her disengagement of postmodernism from a particular historical period is based on the claim that the romance genre "by virtue of its troubled relation to both history and novelistic realism, has in a sense been postmodern all along" (3). Elam draws an equivalence between romance and postmodernism—"postmodernism *is* romance" (12)—at the same time as she sustains a distinction between them. Her use of the term "postmodern romance" to describe novels by Eco and Kathy Acker, but not those by Cartland ("merely escapist" (49)) partitions the field of romance along the lines of a familiar high culture/low culture divide. However, she also suggests that even those romance narratives for sale at "airport bookstalls" (14) challenge the equation of history with realism. That she never resolves the question of which romance texts merit the classification "postmodern" and which don't further limits the usefulness of her preferred terminology.

In the context of Elam's complex theoretical framework, romance and postmodernism are mutually contaminating terms; they make sense only in relation to each other. For Elam, both romance and postmodernism confront "history as predicament" (53); they refuse to accept the past as past and insist instead on rethinking the past in the present. She argues that postmodernism confounds temporal boundaries to the extent that it refuses to be contained by them: it possesses the "paradoxical ability both to precede and to come after itself, to come both before and after modernism" (12). Elam draws an analogy between postmodernism's disrespect for linear history and the failure of traditional genre boundaries to contain romance: the romance genre persistently confounds the distinction between fictional and historical narratives. She writes that both postmodernism and romance are "flagrantly anachronistic, upsetting our ability to recognize the past as past, challenging the way we 'know' history" (12). Thus when postmodernism confronts the question of historical representation, it turns not to novelistic realism, but to romance. Romance is necessary to postmodernism: it makes possible postmodern fiction's radical questioning of the notion of the representable historical event. Romance provides postmodernism with the means to narrativize history even as it puts the status and the legitimacy of history in doubt.

Elam's book is a feminist project. When postmodernism invokes romance it raises, she says, the question of the "figure of woman." This follows in part from romance's reputation as a "women's genre" and from the heterosexist paradigm which circumscribes romance. In short, Elam argues that the "figure of woman" both enables and problematizes postmodern romance's negotiation with the past. The representation of the figure of woman marks the persistence of a modernist discourse of gender to the extent that she operates as the principal metaphor for the unrepresentability of history. Elam cites Eco's postmodern parable of a man who struggles to tell a very cultivated woman that he loves her. The woman, Elam argues, functions as "the silent other who silences men" (47); the only voice women have in this story is that of popular romance ("as Barbara Cartland would say"). In these terms, she concludes, the "postmodern attitude" is that of a heterosexual man, and postmodernism becomes "one more seductive technique, a way for men to talk to, or at, women" (47). As described by Eco, "the postmodern is a romance encoded as heterosexist and classist" (17). However, for Elam, the key to understanding the role of the "figure of woman" in postmodern romance is that the question of her uncertain status is never resolved. The incommensurability of her capacity to enable historical representation at the same time as she stands beyond its reach is characteristic of what Elam calls the "politics of uncertainty."

Elam argues that "feminism is the most obvious political question posed by romance" (19). This follows in part from the degree to which romance (in all of its guises) must continually struggle with the question of gender. It is also linked to her claim that both postmodernism and romance display a "constant difficulty in calculating their politics" (19). Feminism, she notes, persistently redefines the political and therefore shares common ground with the romances of postmodernity:

> To rethink the political as uncertain may be something more than merely relinquishing the possibility of action. It may just be a way of inventing new modes of political calculation that can resist the growing certainties of nuclear annihilation, multinationalist capital expansion, and the rule of heterosexist patriarchy and other cultural orthodoxies. (19)

While Elam notes the prevailing heterosexism of romance, her principal focus is on the relationship between gender and genre. My study of romance practices a similar politics to Elam in its emphasis on the capacity of historical romance novels both to comply with and critique cultural hegemonies. But I want to bring a consideration of the relationship between sexuality and genre into the picture; to examine the extent to which the role of the "figure of woman" in romance is inextricably linked to the romance genre's heterosexualization of history.

Hutcheon describes her book *A Poetics of Postmodernism* as "an attempt to see what happens when culture is challenged from within: challenged or questioned, but not imploded" (xiii). This book has a similar objective. Like Elam though, Hutcheon limits her focus to "postmodern" novels—all "cultivated," all literary. Hutcheon's key point is that postmodernism installs humanist principles only to undermine them; it "always works *within* conventions in order to subvert them" (5). She is careful to point out that her emphasis on the contradictions and paradoxes of postmodernism does not seek to name a dialectic process, "just unresolved contradictions" (106). There are clear parallels between Hutcheon's insistence on postmodernism's drive to question and unsettle cultural hegemonies and Elam's advocacy of a politics of uncertainty. Hutcheon's work on the politics of postmodernism (see also *Narcissistic Narrative: The Metafictional Paradox* and *The Politics of Postmodernism*) predates Elam's. It is therefore surprising that Elam makes little mention of Hutcheon in *Romancing the Postmodern*. The key difference between these studies is their choice of texts. Whereas Elam seeks to revalue romance as *the* postmodern genre, Hutcheon famously coined the term "historiographical metafiction" to classify a body of novels which she argues "characterize postmodernism in fiction" (ix). The elasticity of the term "postmodernism" has both guaranteed its popularity among literary critics and at the same time generated the confusion which dogs its fans and critics alike (see Butler "Contingent Foundations"). Like Elam, Hutcheon claims that postmodernism is defined by its uncertainty and uncontainability. One aspect of this is a problematizing return to history. For Hutcheon, the term "historiographical metafiction" designates narratives which reflect on their treatment of history and the narrativization of history in general, yet paradoxically sustain a belief in the validity and value of historical narratives. She discusses, for example, John Fowles's *The French Lieutenant's Woman*, Salman Rushdie's *Midnight's Children*, E.L. Doctorow's *Ragtime*, and John Berger's *G*.

Importantly, like the literary novels I discuss in Part III of this book, all of Hutcheon's primary texts are remarkable for their critical and commercial success—for their popularity. Hutcheon sees in these texts "a curious mixture of the complicitous and the critical" (201). She speculates further that their use of conventional narrative structures and their related mobilization of humanist ideologies might explain why these novels are frequently bestsellers: "Their complicity guarantees accessibility." Hutcheon insists that this last statement is not meant to be cynical and suggests instead the idea that the "most potent mode of subversion" might be that which speaks to a "conventional" reader (202). This kind of thinking encourages my interest in seeking out the errors of romance—in underlining, to use a phrase from performativity theory, "the weakness in the norm" (Butler *Bodies* 237). While my theoretical framework is different from both Elam's and Hutcheon's, there are strong similarities between our approaches to the reading of historical novels which make both critics an important influence on my work. What distinguishes my study is that, whereas they use the discourse of postmodernism to discuss texts which are remarkable for their capacity to problematize our key cultural hegemonies, I use the idea of performativity to contend that the processes they name are at work in texts which are typically treated as unremarkable in this regard.

This chapter brings together Eco, Belsey, and Elam's brief references to "I love you" with Hutcheon's "poetics of postmodernism" because when read together they raise and clarify issues key to historical romance fiction. Beginning this way places my insistence on the political uncertainty of the historical romance genre in the context of a well-established if not fully articulated critical debate. I have also taken this approach because it alleviates some of the anxiety which has accompanied focusing on a phrase whose usage is so widespread and obvious that it has received remarkably little academic attention. "I love you" is so trivial, so taken for granted in the Western idiom that—as a kind of weird proof of its obviousness—it is not listed as a specific usage of the verb "love" in the recently revised edition of the Oxford English Dictionary. I now go on to offer a detailed account of the meaning and usage of this phrase which goes some of the way toward filling this gap.

Chapter 2

"I Love You": The Romantic Speech Act

Performativity—as any reader of Austin will recognize—lives in the examples. (Parker and Sedgwick 5)

Roland Barthes designates "I-love-you" as one of the "figures" which make up and circulate in a "lover's discourse." Of the term "figure," he says a "figure is established if at least someone can say: '*That's so true! I recognise that scene of language*'" (4). Of the figure "I-love-you" he explains: "The figure refers not to the declaration of love, to the avowal, but to the repeated utterance of the love cry" (147). He elaborates:

> *I-love-you* is without nuance. It suppresses explanations, adjustments, degrees, scruples. In a way—exorbitant paradox of language—to say *I-love-you* is to proceed as if there were no theater of speech, and this word is always *true* (has no referent other than its utterance: it is a performative). (148)

Barthes's conception of "I love you" as an utterance which both lacks any identifiable referent besides itself and yet always tells the truth, rests on his nomination of it as a "performative." While it is clear that his use of this term seeks to name the paradoxical operations of "I love you," Barthes does not elaborate on his choice of words. What does the term "performative" encapsulate which makes it a useful descriptor for the phrase "I love you"? Why isn't it enough to assess this utterance as a descriptive statement of its speaker's feelings? What, more precisely, does it mean to say that "I love you" (which claims at each instance to speak of "love") behaves as if it has no referent? If it assumes no referent, then where does its meaning reside and what guarantees its continual usage? From where, that is, does "I love you" draw its reiterative force? With no referent other than its utterance, can "I love you" do nothing but refer to itself—over and over again? How can an utterance which "proceeds as if there were no *theater* of speech" be said to perform, to *act*? This chapter addresses these questions in order to develop a theoretical vocabulary for reading heterosexual romance fictions; it analyzes "I love you" as a speech act and anchors this analysis in an argument about the thematic significance of secrecy and confession in romance.

An Analysis of "I Love You" as a Speech Act

The notion of a "performative" utterance or "speech act" was first introduced by British philosopher J.L. Austin in his Harvard lectures of 1955, published in 1962 as *How to Do Things with Words*. The cluster of sentences which are his central examples in these lectures—"I do...," "I bet...," "I dare you..." and so on—does not include "I love you." Of these examples, he writes: "it seems clear that to utter the sentence ... is not to *describe* my doing of what I should be said in so uttering to be doing or to state that I am doing it: it is to do it" (6). That is to say, a performative utterance contains its own referent; the act does not precede the utterance. To utter "I love you" is, in both the Austinian sense and in common understanding, to do something; love is not declared/confessed/promised until these "three little words" are spoken. It is not enough for the amorous individual to behave lovingly towards his or her beloved; he or she must say "I love you."

Austin begins *How to Do Things with Words* by distinguishing between utterances which *do* something (performative utterances) and those which purely *say* something (constative utterances). Sandy Petrey succinctly summarizes this distinction: "Constative utterances describe the world, performative utterances become part of the world" (4). Petrey's paraphrase anticipates the flaw in Austin's initial formulation which eventually led him to refute his own performative/constative distinction in favor of a general theory of performativity: such a distinction mistakenly assumes that utterances might exist which are *not* part of the world. As Max Black noted a few years after its publication, *How to Do Things with Words* might as well be subtitled "In Pursuit of a Vanishing Distinction" (401). Petrey uses the "banal everyday phrase," "I'm sorry," as an example to explain the classificatory confusion which undermined Austin's theory even as he developed it. As Petrey puts it, "I'm sorry" can be seen as both a constative description of feelings and a disguised performative, a paraphrase of the explicit first-person speech-act "I apologize." He asks: "How can constative and performative be separate kinds of language when the same words belong on both sides of the dividing line without really fitting in either place?" (26). Petrey might just have successfully used the banal everyday phrase "I love you" to make his point. Does "I love you" simply describe the speaker's feelings, or is it a performative ("I declare/promise/confess my love") masquerading as a constative?

In his initial formulation of the performative, Austin refers to performatives as "masqueraders": utterances which are quite commonly disguised as "statement[s] of fact, descriptive or constative" but are actually something quite different (4; see also Butler *Excitable* 51). Austin's initial error might be that he begins his exposition attempting to see "through" this disguise, rather than by looking *at* the disguised figure.[1] To look at the masquerader is to recognize that the uncertainty it represents may well be irresolvable; simple classification becomes impossible. Marjorie Garber makes this important distinction between looking *through* and looking *at* a disguised figure (human, linguistic or otherwise) in her book *Vested Interests: Cross-Dressing and Cultural Anxiety.* She writes: "the tendency on the part of many critics has been to look *through* rather than *at* the cross-dresser, to turn away from a close encounter with the transvestite, and to want instead to subsume that figure within one of two traditional genders" (9). Garber argues that the function of transvestism (masquerade, disguise, cross-dressing) is to indicate the place of "category crisis"

---

1   "Grammarians have not, I believe, seen *through* this 'disguise,' and philosophers at best only incidentally. It will be convenient, therefore, to study it first in this misleading form, in order to bring out its 4 characteristics by contrasting them with those of the statement of fact which it apes." Austin 4.

(16). I make this seemingly odd comparison between two very different types of "disguise"—linguistic and gender—for two reasons. First, because it allows me to classify the performative as a critical figure for "category crisis." Second, in order to anticipate the arguments I pose in Part II when I consider the relationship between the performative operations of the phrase "I love you" and the characterization of the cross-dressed heroine in popular historical romance. For Garber, cross-dressing serves as an "index, precisely, of many different kinds of 'category crisis'—for the notion of 'category crisis,' ... is not the exception, but rather the ground of culture itself." She explains that "category crisis" describes "a failure of definitional distinction, a borderline that becomes permeable, that permits of border crossings from one (apparently distinct) category to another" (16): male/female, heterosexual/homosexual, ... constative/performative.

My fascination with measuring the performative dimensions of the utterance "I love you" began with Diane Elam's description of it as "a statement *undecidedly descriptive or performative*, whose whole drama is bound up in whether it belongs to a rhetoric of persuasion or a system of tropes" (26, my emphasis). Austin writes: "There seem to be clear cases where the very same formula seems sometimes to be an explicit performative and sometimes to be a descriptive, *and may even trade on this ambivalence*: for example, 'I approve' and 'I agree.' Thus 'I approve' may have the performative force of giving approval or it may have a descriptive meaning: 'I favour this'" (78, my emphasis). How might a "formula" profit from playing on such a categorial confusion? Recognizing the inherent contradiction in the *simultaneous* "descriptive" and "performative" status of "I love you" is crucial to an understanding of its ubiquitous and apparently veracious circulation.

Despite Austin's incremental assertion throughout *How to Do Things with Words* that *all* utterances act, his initial formulation of the *explicit* performative persists even as it is superseded: "The thing seems hopeless from the start ... nevertheless the type of performative upon which we drew for our first examples, which has a verb in the first person singular present indicative active, seems to deserve our favour: at least, if issuing the utterance is doing something, the 'I' and the 'active' and the 'present' seem appropriate" (67). Eve Kosofsky Sedgwick remarks that the "self-evidence" of Austin's principal examples as indisputable "performatives" subtly belies his gradual repudiation of his theory as the lectures progressed ("Queer Performativity" 2–3). All language acts, has effects, but utterances like "I do," "I bet," and "I dare you" have retained a kind of purity in speech-act parlance.

"I love you" is a performative in the terms of Austin's initial definition of the category. It is also performative because, according to his later formulation of a general theory of illocution, every utterance performs. In his article "The Unhappy Performative," Timothy Gould persists with the constative/performative distinction despite remarking that such a distinction "can also seem quite simple and even simple-minded" (20). Despite such risks, developments in performativity theory over the last twenty-five years have shown the validity and usefulness of keeping both Austin's definitions of the term "performative" in play. Even in its earliest formulation, in Austin's *How to Do Things with Words*, the idea of the performative utterance has rich critical and interpretive potential for researchers interested in examining the role and significance of language in literary texts. The key aspects of

Austin's theory provide a framework for the order in which I present my ideas about the romantic speech act: the constative/performative distinction; the possibility of an impure performative; the idea of an utterance's felicity; and his rejection of the notion of an explicit performative in favor of a general theory of illocutionary force.

Had Austin acknowledged the performative dimension of "I love you," he might have nominated it an "impure performative." He distinguishes between pure and impure (or "half-descriptive") performatives: for example "I apologize" is pure and "I am sorry" is impure; "I thank" is pure and "I am grateful" is impure. Austin's attempt to find criteria with which to assess whether any given instance of an impure performative is operating descriptively or performatively flounders on the untenability of the constative/performative distinction. Significantly, Austin introduces the idea of impure performatives when he considers performative phrases which express (or claim to express) "emotion":

> There are numerous cases in human life where the feeling of a certain "emotion" (save the word!) or "wish" or the adoption of an attitude is conventionally considered an appropriate or fitting response or reaction to a certain state of affairs, including the performance by someone of a certain act, cases where such a response is natural (or we should like to think so!). In such cases it is, of course, possible and usual actually to feel the emotion or wish in question; and since our emotions or wishes are not readily detectable by others, it is our common wish to inform others that we have them. Understandably, though for slightly different and perhaps less estimable reasons in different cases, it becomes *de rigueur* to "express" these feelings if we have them, and further even to express them when they are felt fitting, regardless of whether we really feel anything at all which we are reporting. (78–9)

Significantly, convention—the extent to which an utterance has become "*de rigueur*"— infects "emotive" speech acts with performativity. With his typically evasive wit, Austin questions the possibility of an emotive or affective utterance which is uttered independent of an established convention.

Austin formulated his theory of speech acts in order to dispute what he called the "Descriptive Fallacy": the prevalent philosophical idea that "statements" are either true or false and can only be assessed on the basis of this distinction. He argued instead that utterances can also be assessed according to whether they are "happy" or "unhappy," "felicitous" or "infelicitous." His "Doctrine of the Infelicities" lists six "rules" which must be followed for a speech act to be happy:

(A. 1)   There must exist an accepted conventional procedure having a certain conventional effect, that procedure to include the uttering of certain words by certain persons in certain circumstances, and further,

(A. 2)   the particular persons and circumstances in a given case must be appropriate for the invocation of the particular procedure invoked.

(B. 1)   The procedure must be executed by all participants both correctly and

(B. 2)   completely.

(Γ. 1)   Where, as often, the procedure is designed for use by persons having certain thoughts or feelings, or for the inauguration of certain consequential conduct on the part of any participant, then a person participating in and so invoking the procedure must in fact have these thoughts and feelings, and the participants must so intend to conduct themselves, and further

(Γ. 2)   must actually so conduct themselves subsequently. (14–15)

When I say "I love you," when I declare/confess/give my love to you, I *also* say "I (promise to) love you (forever)." However, if you are not present, or you are a figment of my imagination or a small furry animal, then you are an "inappropriate" lover and the speech act does not come off, it fails. However, if you are a living human and, as the dictates of a heterosexist culture demand, male, we "pass" and may proceed happily (A. 2). If you fail to return my love, to say "I love you (too)," then my "I love you" has "misfired." The procedure has not been executed by all participants correctly and completely (B.1–2). The script has not been read all the way through and my "I love you" is hollow, void. Alternatively, we might argue that you don't need to say "I love you (too)" in order for my words to have the force of a declaration; in which case, my act succeeds. If you do say "I love you (too)," but feel no affection for me whatsoever, the speech act succeeds despite your insincerity; it has been "abused" (Γ. 1). Similarly, the act is abused if we are both "sincere," but I fail to conduct myself like one in love: I ignore your letters, don't return phone calls, ban you from my home (Γ. 2). There is clearly an important distinction in Austin's account between rules A. 1-B. 2 and rules Γ. 1-Γ. 2 and one which has particular resonance for the performative utterance "I love you."

Once Austin realized the limited theoretical scope of the performative/constative distinction, he introduced instead a general theory of "illocutionary force," according to which every utterance performs. The general theory redefines the explicit performative as a "special" class of performative. To this end, he distinguished between three processes which belong to every speech act: "locution," "illocution," and "perlocution." Briefly: locution describes the act *of* saying something (saying the words "I love you"); illocution describes the act *in* saying something ("I love you" may have the "force" of a declaration, a confession, or a promise); and perlocution describes the act *by* saying something ("I love you" might have the short-term perlocutionary effect of delighting, surprising or confusing the addressee, or, in the long term, it may usher in a whole series of other performatives—"I do...," "It's a girl!").

(Of course, the felicitous perlocutionary consequences of any actual "I love you" may not be forthcoming, whereas in heterosexual romance fictions, "I love you" is assumed to operate proleptically; we know that the hero and heroine will live happily ever after. To this extent, the romance genre institutes the mechanism of what I call "perlocutionary guarantee" by shifting any suspense or delay which might inhere in the declaration of love to precede the utterance of "I love you," that is to precede locution. Careful theorization of the romantic speech act prepares the ground for tracing the broader ideological implications of this genre and its promises.)

The most remarkable attribute of the cluster of sentences which exemplified Austin's initial conception of the performative is their immediate and indisputable familiarity, so too with "I love you" and "Shame on you." Jacques Derrida complicated Austin's theory by illustrating that the power behind a performative is not volitional, but *always* derivative. He drew attention to "a general citationality—

or rather a general iterability—without which there would not even be a successful performative" (17). "I" never own "I love you"; I say it only because it has been said before, *only because it is conventional.* Romance can only quote. "I love you" is always and only a reiteration; yet to maintain its descriptive status, it must assert its originality or uniqueness at each utterance; the romantic speech act relies on its impurity to *work.* "I love you" is not simply constative or performative, it is always, and necessarily, undecidably either, and hence, incoherently both. That is, it both claims a peculiarly intimate moment for its speaker, ("I (like no other) love you (like no other)") and, retaining its ubiquitous history and corresponding reiterative force, continues to circulate as an infinitely and endlessly appropriable utterance. To this extent it conforms to the interpretation of myth offered by Barthes in *Mythologies.* As a mythic utterance, "I love you" carries the baggage of innumerable citations. At each utterance, however, "I love you" is emptied out, its history hidden, in order to facilitate the supposed and essential uniqueness of the particular relation it intends to communicate. This discussion is not intended to evacuate "I love you" of the material (historical, cultural, and political) factors which elaborately structure and determine its peculiar operations, but rather to begin to describe the way in which "I love you" depends upon its material evacuation for its circulation and operation. "I love you" is both a confession and a cliché; it is simultaneously meaning and form—an apparently empty utterance to be refilled by each lover, but which silently retains its history.

Andrew Parker and Sedgwick, in their introduction to *Performativity and Performance*, argue that adequate analysis of the performative force of an utterance requires a "disimpaction" of the scene: "To begin with, while [the explicit performative] ostensibly involves only a singular first and a singular second person, it effectually depends as well on the tacit requisition of a third person plural, a 'they' of witnesses—whether or not literally present" (8). The Austinian performative is an utterance ruled by social convention; it presumes a consensus between speaker, witnesses and addressee. But, as Sedgwick and Parker argue, it only presumes; it cannot guarantee.

Parker and Sedgwick invoke the scene of consensus and convention demanded by the classic performative through an analysis of one of Austin's core examples, "I dare you," which he includes in his "baggy category" (Parker and Sedgwick 8) of the behabitives: "a kind of performative concerned roughly with reactions to behaviour and with behaviour towards others and designed to exhibit attitudes and feelings" (Austin 83). "I love you" might also be a behabitive, or it might belong to that other "baggy category," the commissive: "an assuming of an obligation or the declaring of an intention" (163). Both of these categories are peculiar, for Austin, because of their "special scope for insincerity";[2] their vulnerability to rules Γ. 1-Γ. 2. Sedgwick and Parker note that the presumption of consensus is contained in the "positive" performative ("I dare you") and in the lack of a "formulaic negative response to being dared or being interpellated as a witness to a dare" (9). Despite the relative difficulty

---

2   Austin makes this remark specifically about behabitives (159). However, both commissives ("There is a slide towards descriptives." (157)) and behabitives are potentially "impure"; citing "emotion" as their motivation and blurring the distinction between insincerity and falsehood.

of finding an utterance with which to "disinterpellate"—for instance, the closest we might have to a formulaic refusal of the romantic speech act is silence—Sedgwick and Parker argue that it is possible and thus each "I dare you" "constitute[s] a crisis as much as it constitutes a discrete act" (9). Their argument illustrates the "risk" inherent in every performance of a positive speech act. As my readings of historical romance novels show, the desire to deny or to dispel such a risk, or crisis, compels the incessant repetition of "successful" and "happy" romantic speech acts in this genre. To state my argument bluntly, popular and literary historical romance novels are hyperbolic denials of the infelicitous performative.

It would be an error to locate this anxiety, this secret lack of confidence, in the positive performative utterance—in either the unverifiability of "sincerity" or in the possibility of a negative response, both of which imply the primacy of "intention." Instead performativity is structurally imbued with risk or danger. Discussing his favorite explicit performative, "I do (take this woman to be my lawful wedded wife)," Austin locates the "danger" of his theory in the suggestion that the logical extension of his argument might be to say "to marry is … simply to say a few words" (8). He attempts to dispel this fear by calling attention to the necessity for appropriate circumstances and legitimate actors to perform a marriage. However, as Shoshana Felman demonstrates in her extraordinary book *The Scandal of the Speaking Body: Don Juan with J.L. Austin, or Seduction in Two Languages*, the "conceptual economy of the performative" is "scandalous" because it threatens to divulge that the speaking body "subsists only insofar as it speaks" (79); that the romantic, in our case, might always be linguistic. She writes:

> Now for Austin, the capacity for failure is situated not outside, but *inside* the performative, both as speech act and as theoretical instrument. Infelicity, or failure, is not for Austin an *accident* of the performative, it is inherent in it, essential to it. In other words, … Austin conceives of failure not as external but as internal to the promise, as what actually constitutes it. (45–6)

The performative is normative, conventional, absolutely prescriptive *in the first instance*. However, the misfires and abuses that Austin's "Doctrine of Infelicities" legislates against, must be outlawed not only because they are always already possible, but because they constitute the performative, bring it into being.

Felman's book is an extended analysis of "I promise…," a popular exemplar amongst speech act theorists (Petrey 6). She asks: "In what way does a promise constitute a paradox, a problem? In what way is the very logic of promising a sign of a fundamental contradiction which is precisely the contradiction of the human?" (3–4). She confronts this question by bringing together *How to Do Things with Words* and Molière's play *Don Juan*, a text which she says "raises the problem of the performative in a spectacular way" (4). In the terms of Felman's argument, Austin becomes Donjuanian and Don Juan Austinian.

The particular promise at the center of this textual and figural congruence is the promise of love (and of marriage). Felman exposes, "the scandal of the promise of love insofar as this promise is *par excellence* the promise that cannot be kept; the scandal of the promising animal insofar as what he promises is precisely the *untenable*"

(5). Further, she concludes *The Scandal of the Speaking Body* by remarking that the performative scandal is always, in some sense, the scandal of the promise of love: "the scandal of the *untenable* ... the scandal—Donjuanian in the extreme—of the promising animal, incapable of keeping his promise, incapable of not making it, powerless both to fulfill the commitment and to avoid *committing* himself" (111). The scandal is embodied in the subject who is compelled to promise (love) but who knows that there is no necessary relation between making the promise and "truth"; no "thing" precedes the promise, rather the promise is an "event." The performative is "self-referential"; it does not describe "some action, inner or outer, prior or posterior, occurring elsewhere than in the utterance itself" (Gould 20). In short, for Felman's scandalous figure (Don Juan, Austin) "*truth is only an act*" (111). Briefly, Don Juan makes and breaks a series of promises of love and marriage to a series of women. The scandal of the performative, in Felman's account, is exemplified by the diegetic scandal of Don Juan's broken promises.

Petrey criticizes Felman for defining the performative in terms of self-referentiality. He argues that this makes the performative "anti-social" when Austin formulated it as precisely "social": For Austin "truth that is an act is by definition enacted as true. Language's freedom from facts brute and objective comes from its tight connection to facts institutional and social" (108). I would respond that Don Juan manipulates the performative as a mechanism which both covers over and relies on the social (on history). A performative such as "I (promise to) love you" needs the pretence that it exists independently of sociality in order to work. It must appear to be an utterance sprung from the "heart," predicated on the "I," in order to be believed. At the same time, however, it would have no impact, no force without its history, a kind of invisible scaffolding for each instance of any given performative. Don Juan hangs from this invisible scaffolding, so to speak. The performative is self-referential to the extent that it contains its own action, but it would fail to act if it did not cite and thus invoke an established convention.

Felman identifies two opposed forces in *Don Juan*: Don Juan himself, for whom language is performative; and his pursuers, for whom language is "transparent" (constative). For his pursuers, "language is an instrument for transmitting *truth*, that is, an instrument of knowledge, a means of *knowing* reality" (13). They assess utterances according to their truth or falsehood, assuming and demanding a perfect congruence between referent and utterance. For the promise of love, believers in this order of language insist on an absolute correspondence between words and "feeling." They are therefore willing victims for Don Juan's "trap of seduction [which] consists in producing a *referential illusion* through an utterance that is by its very nature *self-referential*: the illusion of a real or extralinguistic act of commitment created by an utterance that refers only to itself" (17). For Don Juan, language is not about knowing, but about doing. Because he "knows" this, he is able to play with language without being implicated in its purported meanings. His pursuers, then, are subjects who have been successfully interpellated into the romance or marriage plot which "I love you" invokes, whereas Don Juan abuses the romantic speech act by ignoring the sincerity rule and failing to conduct himself appropriately by following his promises.

Don Juan fails to be bound by his word, because his word is constituted by the possibility of failing: "Don Juan himself is thus only the symptom of a perversity inherent in the promise" (32). This failure, generated in part by the noncoincidence of what is promised with the act of promising, drives the Donjuanian repetition of the promise: "the entire drama is made of a signifying chain of promises which engender each other reciprocally, and whose connecting principle is their own failure to be kept" (33). The ceaseless reiteration of "I love you" in heterosexual romance is engendered by this same noncoincidence; however, as I will show in Parts II and III, this generic reiteration is precisely non-Donjuanian. For instance, the compulsory "happy ending" of popular romance fiction insists upon the transparency of language. Here, the scandal of the performative is embodied in the reiteration itself, a positive harping on the promise of love which works to deflect attention from the anxiety which begets it.

For Felman, the Don Juan myth *is* the myth of performativity to the extent that the performative, when "pushed to its extreme logical consequences en*acts* its own subversion" (34). As Austin himself recognized, the performative, as both theoretical tool and speech act, has potentially dangerous implications for cultural norms, conventions, and obligations. Sandy Petrey writes:

> The mark's penchant for self-destruction in fact makes even more impressive the capacity of language communities to produce and preserve illocutionary force. Focus on social conventions, speech-act theory's great imperative, is more rather than less rewarding because the reality performed by language not only manifests collective identity but triumphs over the mark's inherent slipperiness in order to do so. (144)

Certainly, one must be "impressed" by our culture's capacity to reconstitute its norms in the face of massive internal contradictions and incoherences. However, as Judith Butler's stunning reformulation of performativity makes clear, the performative's triumph over its "penchant for self-destruction" can only ever be provisional.

In her book *Excitable Speech: A Politics of the Performative* Butler writes:

> If a performative provisionally succeeds (and I will suggest that 'success' is always and only provisional), then it is not because an intention successfully governs the action of speech, but only because that action echoes prior actions, and *accumulates the force of authority through the repetition or citation of a prior and authoritative set of practices*. It is not simply that the speech act takes place *within* a practice, but that the act is itself a ritualized practice. What this means, then, is that a performative "works" to the extent that *it draws on and covers over* the constitutive conventions by which it is mobilized. In this sense, no term or statement can function performatively without the accumulating and dissimulating historicity of force. (51)

For Butler, the fact that success is only ever temporary, creates a kind of structural loophole in the reiterative logic of hegemony; subversion becomes a question of "working the weakness in the norm ... of inhabiting the practices of its rearticulation" (Butler, *Bodies* 237). If Felman reveals the scandal of the performative as speech act, Butler scandalizes our cultural norms and conventions much more deeply—most particularly by unravelling the invisible thread which binds the points of sex, gender, and sexuality in a "compulsory" order. As Parker and Sedgwick note, Derrida and

Butler's renewal of performativity's "specifically Austinian valences ... has enabled a powerful appreciation of the ways that identities are constructed iteratively through complex citational processes" (1–2). As a consequence of this reinvigorating of the category of the performative the speech act is no longer "the *only actual* phenomenon which ... we are engaged in elucidating" (Austin 148). Instead all "ritual, ceremonial, scripted behaviours" (Parker and Sedgwick 2) are now read as performative.

"I love you" is a persistently heterosexualized formula of romance in terms of Butler's analysis of categories of sexuality as performative. She describes heterosexuality as: "a compulsive and compulsory repetition that can only produce the *effect* of its own originality (Butler, "Imitation" 21). According to Butler's constructivist refiguring of performativity, it "must be understood not as a singular or deliberate 'act,' but, rather, as the reiterative and citational practice by which discourse produces that which it names" (Butler, *Bodies* 2). In these terms, "[c]onstruction is neither a subject nor its act, but a process of reiteration by which 'subjects' and 'acts' come to appear at all. There is no power that acts, but only a reiterated acting that is power in its persistence and instability" (9). According to Butler's "volatile logic of iterability" (105), "I" do not own my "I love you"; we are misled by grammar. When I say "I love you," I install myself as the author of that utterance, *at the same time* as I cite "I love you," thus "establishing the derivative status of that authorship." The power of Don Juan's promises for instance is thus "a power accrued through time" which is concealed at the moment that he utters "I promise..." (Butler, *Excitable* 49). "Indeed," as Butler asks, "is iterability or citationality not precisely this: *the operation of that metalepsis by which the subject who 'cites' the performative is temporarily produced as the belated and fictive origin of the performative itself?*" (49; see also 225-6). Assessed performatively, "I" only pretend to have a deliberate and originary ownership of my utterances: "[I]f the 'I' is a site of repetition, that is, if the 'I' only achieves the semblance of identity through a certain repetition of itself, then the 'I' is always displaced by the very repetition that sustains it" ("Imitation" 18). The compulsory and compulsive repetition of "I love you" takes place on a kind of conceptual Möbius strip then, circuitously staging the stabilization and destabilization of the position of the "I."

In effect, this book takes "I love you" as a synecdoche of heterosexuality's insistent and compulsory repetition. "I love you" is uttered as the clarifying conclusion in the paradigmatic narrative of sexual intelligibility which ties a line of causality through the points of sex, gender, and sexuality (a male who is masculine desires a female who is feminine and vice versa.) To this extent, heterosexual romance fictions can be read performatively as an incessant rendition of heterosexuality's promised but never fully achieved absolute intelligibility. As Butler explains, "heterosexuality is always in the process of imitating and approximating its own phantasmatic idealization of itself—and failing" (Butler, "Imitation" 21). Because it suspects its tenuous position, heterosexuality—"as an incessant and panicked imitation of its own naturalized idealization" (Butler, "Imitation" 23)—is propelled into an endless repetition of itself.

Not only can speech act theory help us to recognize that texts are themselves "acts"—that in saying something they are also doing something—but further we can use the analytical tools speech act theory provides to delve more fully into the question of *how* they act. I set out both to identify the interpellative function of the historical romance genre in the context of heterosexual hegemony; and also to find ways to locate and name the enunciative mechanisms by which that interpellation is effected. In the process I aim to suggest new ways to think about *both* the romance genre and performativity. The best example of this is my use of a speech act ("I love you") to define a fictional form (the romance genre). Of course, "I love you" does not operate in isolation from other formulaic speech acts.

In her article "Queer Performativity: Henry James's *The Art of the Novel*"[3] Sedgwick nominates another conventional affective utterance as a "performative": "Shame on you." Her discussion of this phrase's performative status is remarkably pertinent to my analysis of "I love you"; both are phrases which play on the frustrating distinction between description/expression and performance. Sedgwick notes the similarity of "Shame on you" with Austin's core examples. "I love you" shares these similarities: a pronoun matrix (strictly first person) and naming of its illocutionary intent (to declare love). She goes on to demonstrate the "transformational grammar" of "Shame on you"—both in terms of its pronoun positioning ("Shame on *you*" or "*I* love *you*") and in terms of the relational intent of its affect (shame or love). Like "I love you," "Shame on you," represents, in Austin's words, "an appropriate or fitting response or reaction to a certain state of affairs ... [a] case where such a response is natural (or we should like to think so!)" Austin's bracketed exclamation unsettles the notion of a "natural" response by suggesting that being "appropriate or fitting" might have more to do with being conventional than being "natural." The explicit performative is normative before it is anything else. "I love you" is said *only because it is* conventional. Performative utterances are conventional, formulaic, idiomatically prescribed utterances.

Sedgwick argues that "Shame on you" is characterized by a similar indeterminacy. She extrapolates from an explanation of its uncertain constative/performative status to examine the double role shame plays in processes of identity formation. Sedgwick writes of the way in which the language of shame makes, and breaks identity:

> Shame floods into being as a moment, a disruptive moment, in a circuit of identity-constituting identificatory communication. Indeed, like a stigma, shame is itself a form of communication. Blazons of shame, the "fallen face" with eyes down and head averted—and to a lesser extent, the blush—are semaphors of trouble and at the same time of a desire to reconstitute the interpersonal bridge. But in interrupting identification, shame, too, makes identity. In fact shame and identity remain in very dynamic relation to one another, at once deconstituting and foundational, because shame is both peculiarly contagious and peculiarly individuating. (5)

---

3   See also Sedgwick's most recent book, *Touching Feeling: Affect, Pedagogy, Performativity*. This volume includes a number of essays published in earlier versions: "Queer Performativity: Henry James's *The Art of the Novel*," "Socratic Raptures, Socratic Ruptures: Notes Towards Queer Performativity," "Shame and Performativity: Henry James's New York Edition Prefaces," and "Shame in the Cybernetic Fold: Reading Silvan Tomkins" (written with Adam Frank). For the most part, my references in this and later chapters are to these earlier publications.

The same can be said of love. In its most poetic and its most clichéd representations (to play with a handful of Barbara Cartland titles) *The River of Love* floods, or *The Fire of Love* burns into being as *The Enchanted Moment*, emblazoning its participants with all manner of duplicitous bodily effects: blushing, trembling, swooning, melting … all familiar signs of love (and desire). Love is *The Irresistible Force*, but at the same time *Love is the Enemy*, threatening the autonomous and internally coherent individual with its destabilization.

Sedgwick's analysis of the performative force of shame demonstrates how the principal terms and questions of Austin's theory of the performative can produce engaging constructivist accounts of the formation of subjectivity amidst heterosexual hegemony. The following sentence from "Queer Performativity" reads convincingly, whether it names "shame" or "love": "The place of identity, the structure 'identity,' marked by shame's [love's] threshold between sociability and introversion, may be established and naturalized in the first instance *through shame* [love]" (12). I demonstrate a crucial relationship between these two utterances in my analysis of *The French Lieutenant's Woman* in Part III, which argues that normative notions of heterosexual love depend upon a discourse of shame to make sense and to have effects. Sedgwick's work highlights the critical potential of reexamining the processes of subject formation through the lens of performativity theory; her insights are invaluable for reading the representation of these processes in popular fiction and Literature.

Like "Shame on you," the utterance "I love you," as romance's defining performative, is *an instance* in the linguistic and grammatical suturing of formations and assumptions of "identity" through insistent reiteration. Further, "I love you" is circuitously individual and sociable; its grammatical logic figures coupling as an immanent relation. Its strict pronoun matrix can be read as an abbreviated map of popular and psychoanalytic theories or fictions of the acquisition and maintenance of structures of identity or self. In these stories of self, the subject becomes "I" *interrelationally*—through its recognition of an (O)ther (you). Nonetheless, the subject retains its individual integrity through an insistence on its final inaccessibility or unknowability. "Love," which popularly and definitionally can be named but never fully known or understood, mimics the assumed inaccessibility of the meaning or identity of the individual (I)—its self-possession. All sorts of social imperatives— most importantly to do with gender and sexuality—crystallize around the phrase "I love you." It can be seen as exemplary of the fiction or fantasy which facilitates the subject's interpellation into a phallogocentric and heteronormative society. I hope to participate in the elucidation of the connections between the performative and procedures or narratives of subjectification exemplified by the work of theorists like Sedgwick and Butler, but for the benefit of literary studies.

"I Love You" and the Dynamics of Secrecy and Confession

> "Make your confession, you were a woman all along the way."
> "You have guessed my secret." (Henley 446)

Romance narratives are regulated by a dynamics of secrecy and confession. That is to say, this genre takes the strained relations of knowing and unknowing as its impetus and force. Certainly this is not peculiar to romance fiction. One might cite detective fiction as another example of a genre whose plots depend on a "secret." However, there is a distinctive logic to romance fiction's "thematics" of secrecy. In this section, my aim is to build on the analysis of "I love you" offered above to trace this logic, to articulate its assumptions, its rules, and most importantly, its effects. As I show in Part II, one subgenre of popular historical romance fiction, the cross-dressing novel, foregrounds "the relations of the known and the unknown, the explicit and the inexplicit" (Sedgwick, *Epistemology* 3) in fascinating and peculiar ways; however, these preoccupations are common to the genre as a whole. The popularity and the significance of cross-dressing novels are best understood in the context of a broader definition of the romance genre as a fictional form which is about secrecy and confession, veiling and unveiling, concealment and revelation.

What are the implications of describing secrecy/confession as a "theme" of romance at the same time as insisting on the performative dimensions of genres? I am committed to a particular kind of "thematic criticism," the object of which is to ask what a text *does* rather than what it *says*. I identify and interrogate the conjunction secrecy/confession as a controlling "frame" in order to ask how historical romance fiction participates in the inculcation and mobilization of certain meanings about heterosexuality.

Sedgwick explains her critical project in this way: "Repeatedly to ask how certain categorizations work, what enactments they are performing and what relations they are creating, rather than what they essentially *mean*, has been my principal strategy" (27). In her essay, "The More Things Change," Elizabeth Weed cites this sentence as evidence of Sedgwick's "unapologetic thematics" (253). Weed goes on to characterize Sedgwick's approach as a "Foucaultian-inflected use of thematics" (254), which she defines with reference to Nancy Armstrong's essay "A Brief Genealogy of 'Theme.'" For Armstrong, Foucault—particularly in *Discipline and Punish*—reconceptualizes themes as "discursive procedures" which institute and order cultural axes of meaning, rather than as "frames" for meaning(s) which they are simply "about" (41). She writes:

> Michel Foucault offers a way around [the form/content] opposition by inviting us to consider what a text *does*. We can read the text in question as a classificatory project within a larger cultural-historical project. From this perspective, themes are not "about" a reality that is already in place outside the text. Rather themes constitute the world we actually inhabit, as they divide it, for example, into inside and outside, subject and object, self and other, male and female, public and private, as well as the official media, genres and disciplines of knowledge. Indeed, the story of *Surveiller et Punir* (1975) can be read as the story of a theme, or how discipline transformed itself from a residual cultural formation into the master theme of modern culture. The story indicates that, as it underwent this transformation, discipline became virtually indistinguishable from order, or "form," itself. (39)

Weed follows Armstrong to distinguish between traditional and Foucaultian thematics. In a traditional narratological analysis (represented in Weed's essay by Gerald Prince) "theme" is understood to have a "macrostructural relation to the meanings read," whereas within a Foucaultian framework the relation is "constitutive" (254).

Both perspectives define the "theme" as an organizing or controlling category or "frame" over a text's disparate parts. The difference is in their interpretation of the text's relationship to what might be considered "extratextual." For adherents to a traditional approach, the identification of a text's "theme" permits access to a text's meaning; the suasive dimensions of a text are limited to the expression of "the more general or abstract entities (ideas, thoughts, etc.) that a text or part thereof is (or may be considered to be) about" (Gerald Prince qtd. in Weed 254). In these terms the text is understood as a reflective or responsive vehicle in relation to the culture within which it circulates. A "Foucaultian-inflected use of thematics" emphasizes the extent to which a text *participates* in the construction—and, as I will show, the deconstruction—of those general or abstract meanings it might be said to be "about." In the simplest terms, as I stated above, the object of thematic criticism in this sense is to ask what a text or a body of texts *does* rather than what it *says*.

Irene Gammel identifies Foucault as "the most influential recent theorist of western confession" (5). Foucault's analysis of confession in *The History of Sexuality, Volume 1* can be summarized in similar terms to Armstrong's account of his treatment of "discipline" discussed above. What Foucault gives us is the "story" of confession's promotion over time to its current status as the paradigmatic or foundational ritual for the production of truth in the West. To use Armstrong's terms, it moves from being "a residual cultural formation" to being a "master theme of modern culture." Further, like discipline, or more precisely as a technique of discipline, its existence as a theme is inseparable from its operations *as* order or "form." Confession, as historically sedimented cultural ritual in the late twentieth and now early twenty-first century, is no longer confined to the auspices of penance or the church; rather, its reach extends throughout the West's interrelational and social formations and institutions:

> [T]he confession became one of the West's most highly valued techniques for producing truth. We have since become a singularly confessing society. The confession has spread its effects far and wide. It plays a part in justice, medicine, education, family relationships, and love relations, in the most ordinary affairs of everyday life, and in the most solemn rites; one confesses one's crimes, one's sins, one's thoughts and desires, one's illnesses and troubles; one goes about telling, with the greatest precision, whatever is most difficult to tell ... Western man [sic] has become a confessing animal. (59)

Foucault demonstrates that the cultural demand for confession is endemic to the West, passing through innumerable points and determining our relation to "truth" and "identity." To this extent, the ritual of confession is *obligatory* for each and every one of us: "The truthful confession was inscribed at the heart of the procedures of individualization by power" (58–9).

Foucault does not explain the process by which confession changes from being a cultural ritual to being "deeply ingrained in us." He appears to be saying that, by virtue and influence of the sheer propagative force of the confessional ritual as social practice we have consequently *become* "confessing animals." We are so thoroughly inscribed by the ritual of confession that it has become an "internal ruse" (mis)directing our attention away from confession as the effect of relations of power. According to Foucault's formulation, we incorrectly imagine that truth—confession's apparent object—"lodged in our most secret nature," *demands* to surface; that truth "does not belong to the order of power, but shares an original affinity with freedom"; and that power comes into play only when external repressive power prevents the truth from surfacing. Foucault's discussion of confession demonstrates instead that the production of truth is thoroughly imbued with relations of power. As Weed notes, "[t]he difference in Foucault's way of reading has less to do with the objects of his study—discursive formations and institutions versus narrative texts—than with the fact that his thematic has a constitutive rather than macrostructural relation to the meanings read" (254). Confession, along with secrecy as its formal partner, is one of the principal modes through which our subjectification, our constitution as "knowing" subjects, takes place.

Later in his discussion, Foucault shifts his attention to the specific unfolding of the confessional moment itself. He portrays the confession taking place in the context of an immanent hierarchical power relationship between the figure of the one who speaks and the figure of the one who listens: "it is also a ritual that unfolds within a power relationship, for one does not confess without the presence (or virtual presence) of a partner" (61). When approached as a formal or linguistic moment, ("Forgive me Father, for I have sinned…," "I love you") the confession emerges as "a ritual of discourse in which the speaking subject is also the subject of the statement" (61). (The moment of confession is, of course, intensely performative in the Austinian sense.) The secrecy which confession presumes is not, Foucault goes on to say, necessitated by the particular or special value of the secret's contents; rather secrecy and, by implication, confession have a functionally subjective importance for the one who confesses. Secrecy, Foucault comments, derives from the "obscure familiarity and general baseness" of what is to be confessed; there is nothing special about the secret: the value lies in its telling as a secret: "Its veracity is not guaranteed by the lofty authority of the magistery, nor by the tradition it transmits, but by the bond, the basic intimacy in discourse, between the one who speaks and what he is speaking about" (62). The importance of confession, of telling a secret, is not to reveal the truth, but rather to insist on who owns the truth—the primary and individuating bond between myself and what I utter/know.

D.A. Miller's notion of the "open secret" is the best starting point for thinking further about the intimate relation between the confessional mode and processes of individuation and subjectification and their literary representation. In the final chapter of his influential book *The Novel and the Police* Miller elucidates a theory of the "secret" as, in Weed's words, "cultural thematics" (262). This rather detailed discussion of Foucault and Miller is critically important to my argument that the conjunction confession/secrecy manages the progress of historical fictions of heterosexual love and the representation of the heterosexual subject in love.

Based on his observations on the relationship between the reader and the (Victorian) novel, or more particularly observations of his own relationship with Charles Dickens's *David Copperfield*, Miller extends the structure of secrecy to a "general cultural habit" (Weed 262). Rather than focusing on the contents of the secret, Miller attends to the definitional structure of secrecy. He is interested in the way secrecy *works* in the continual definition, maintenance and protection of certain important cultural "knowledges" about the subject. Secrecy in Miller's analysis becomes a general and *necessary* cultural habit—a mechanism in the bolstering and stabilizing of the position of the "I." Echoing Foucault, he writes:

> I can't quite tell my secret because then it would be known that there was nothing really special to hide, and no one really special to hide it. But I can't quite keep it either, because then it would not be believed that there was something to hide and someone to hide it. It is thus a misleading common sense that finds the necessity of secrecy in the "special" nature of the contents concealed when all that revelation usually reveals is a widely diffused cultural prescription, a cliché. ... [S]ecrecy would seem to be a mode whose ultimate meaning lies in the subject's formal insistence that he [sic] is radically inaccessible to the culture that would otherwise entirely determine him. (195)

The "double bind" of secrecy is impossible to resolve in Miller's formulation. Secrecy must be maintained by the subject despite its already being known, because *secrecy functions as the very mechanism which guarantees subjectivity in the first place*.

In his discussion of *David Copperfield*, Miller introduces the notion of an "open secret" to identify the "radical emptiness of secrecy" which emerges once we acknowledge the ways in which the "secret" is formally evacuated of the importance of its contents when it is brought into narrative play (205). He exposes the narrative structure of the Victorian novel whereby the character's secret inside, as opposed to the social outside, is always in some sense an open secret to readers who in turn derive their readerly pleasure from suspending their knowledge:

> The fact the secret is known—and, in some obscure sense, known to be known—never interferes with the incessant activity of keeping it. The contradiction does not merely affect characters. We too inevitably surrender our privileged position as readers to whom the secrets are open by "forgetting" our knowledge for the pleasures of suspense and surprise. (206)

For Miller, the concept of the "open secret" is most clearly exemplified in *David Copperfield* through the character of Miss Mills, whose "love of the romantic and the mysterious" prompts "the fabrication of trivial secrets on the same popular romance principles that make them so easily divined" (205). So, in terms of its *principles*, popular romance becomes the exemplary generic regime of the open secret; love of the romantic operates as the marker for "trivial" secrecy or secrecy for its own sake. There is no need for Miller to explain what these popular romance principles might be. Instead we are assumed to know; his reference to them is exemplary. Popular romance depends on the fabrication of secrets which are easily divined or which are intended to be divined—secrets which aren't meant to be kept. The concluding "secret" of the romance novel (love between the hero and the heroine, a man and a woman) is an "open secret" for the reader who, through generic familiarity with the formula of romance narrative and the assistance of certain "clues" embedded in the narrative, always, in some sense, knows what is happening and will happen. The revelation which concludes and defines the romance narrative—"I love you"—tells the secret we knew all along.

To say "I love you" is, at least in the first instance, to tell a secret, to confess. As I have argued, "I love you," can have the force of a declaration, a promise, a confession …, or indeed can have, and most probably does have, the force of all these things at once. "Love" is the secret which motivates the romance narrative. In its popular definitional mystification, "love" holds the promise of the existence and the truth of the subject (unto itself). When "I" say "I love you," I pronounce myself to know the truth of "love." "I" always remain the authority when I utter "I love you" because love—the ultimate secret—is *the secret I can never quite tell* (or, the promise I can never quite keep). The insistence that love is always and only known subjectively ("How will I know I am in love?" "You'll just know, you'll just know…") is belied by the fact that love is the secret we all know all about. Love stories—anecdotal, on television, in books, films, songs, advertisements, newspapers and magazines, in the greeting card aisle, indeed throughout our culture—furnish us with more information about the circumstances and effects of this utterance than perhaps any other. To this extent it is a secret which we are "trained" to guess. The more time one spends thinking about this phrase, the more difficult it becomes to maintain a distinction between what is narrowly textual or fictional and what is cultural or social. One might argue that it is the gap between the banality and the purported uniqueness of "I love you" which drives its incessant repetition. And further, that it is precisely the necessity to utter, hear, write, and read this phrase over and over again—both in our personal lives and in our fictions—which undercuts the very uniqueness it strives to grasp. "I love you" is a confession and a cliché; the contradiction which appeared to structure this phrase when it first appeared in this book is hopefully beginning to fade and a kind of mutual dependence beginning to emerge.

Romance demands an "open secret." The promised revelation of a (known) secret propels the narrative. We know the nature of the secret; we know where the "I love you" will come from at the end. However, to hold the *promise* of the revelation, to maintain our belief in the uniqueness of each "I love you," we must pretend that we don't know. To this end, it's the promise that counts. We fool ourselves with the hope that *maybe* this time we don't know—the spectre of the "true secret." The peculiar pull of this particular secret is, to a certain extent, love's definitional insistence on its *unknowability*—love holds our cultural promise of the genuine secret or truth. Of course, every "I" (potentially) holds the secret "love." Love is the secret each and every *individual* can hold. Its meaning is "known" subjectively and thus functions as an instance in the maintenance of the West's cult of the individual at the same time as it maintains the cult of the couple.

Analysis of "I love you" as the romantic speech act reveals a contradictory or illogical relationship between the subject's formal insistence on his or her radical inaccessibility, and the necessity to *couple* in order to so insist. Consideration of "I love you" as a confessional moment brings this contradiction into relief. Romantic love is an individualizing secret which cannot exist without the presence, or, to adopt Foucault's phrase, the "virtual presence," of another individual. Whether I confess my love to you, or confess my love for you to another, I cannot help but invoke—even momentarily—my interpellation as a heterosexual subject. As I have discussed in earlier chapters, my interest here is to draw attention to "I love you" as a heteronormative call to order; to expose the instability of this call in and of itself.

While this approach forecloses the possibility of detailed consideration of gay or lesbian utterances of "I love you" in this book, hopefully my work suggests the need for and importance of such a study.

A consideration of the speech act "I love you" in the context of Foucault's "story" of confession and Miller's theory of the "open secret" raises the question of the importance of the dynamics of secrecy and confession in the formation of the heterosexual romantic subject. This suggests the need for more and closer studies of the history of heterosexuality, some of which might consider the constitutive import of both the confessional mode and the narrativization of love.[4] Romance assumes heterosexual love as a secret to be confessed, thus installing it as "natural truth," as that which is "inside" all of us waiting to surface. Part II takes popular romance novels as a representative instance of the process by which hegemonic discourse credits heterosexuality with the status of "truth"; western culture makes heterosexuality an "open secret" in order to secure its promulgation.

Sedgwick's Foucauldian-influenced consideration of the speech act as constitutive of knowledges, ideologies, and institutions (most particularly those to do with gender and sexuality) is an important influence on my theoretical focus in general, and especially on my claims for the cultural potency of the speech act "I love you." As I have already argued, an analysis of the declaration of love as a performative reveals the inherent instability of the heterosexual romantic imperative Western culture issues to its members. This generalized reading of the love story through its defining speech act prefaces and frames the close readings of popular romance novels offered in Part II. In *The Epistemology of the Closet*, Sedgwick cites the following passage from Miller's essay "Secret Subjects, Open Secrets":

> [Secrecy is] the subjective practice in which the oppositions of private/public, inside/ outside, subject/object are established and the sanctity of the first term kept inviolate. And the phenomenon of the "open secret" does not, as one might think, bring about the collapse of these binarisms and their ideological effects, but rather attests to their fantasmatic recovery. (Miller 207; qtd. in Sedgwick 67)

The underlying set of principles which motivates and structures popular romance narratives, *works* to the extent that it enacts the "fantasmatic recovery" of these oppositions and others (e.g. feminine/masculine, heterosexuality/homosexuality), but inevitably *fails* to the extent that their recuperation or revival is only fantasmatic. To simplify, the romance narrative's "purpose" is never quite achieved. This failure helps to explain the romance's peculiar propensity for repetition as a structural necessity which follows from the weakness in its logic. Popular romance novels exemplify the heteronormative obsession with maintaining the binary oppositions which congeal around the categories of sex, gender, and sexuality.

In general terms, the regime of the secret might be said to operate implicitly or covertly in its structuring of the romance genre. As I show in Part II, the cross-

---

4   As Annamarie Jagose notes in her book, *Queer Theory* "[h]eterosexuality has yet to be adequately theorized and much of the initial work completed to date has been undertaken by gay scholars" (133). She cites the work of Henry Abelove and Jonathan Katz as examples of this early work.

dressing novel is remarkable to the extent that it makes the "thematic" importance of secrecy explicit—in more senses than the obvious. In these terms, analysis of cross-dressing novels enables an explication of the ways romantic texts in general figure, refigure (and disfigure) the heterosexual subject and the heterosexual couple. Sedgwick's theory (or "unapologetic thematics") of the closet is a vital influence on this project. This is not simply because to mention the "closet" in this context cannot help but invoke that domestic space—the wardrobe—which houses and embodies the cross-dresser, but because I am persuaded and excited by the explanatory power and interpretive capacity of Sedgwick's analysis of those definitional nexuses most involved in the processes of subjectification.

Sedgwick's extension of Foucauldian (and, less explicitly, of Austinian) philosophy and analysis has been crucial in articulating "the prestige, the promise of epistemological force, the 'sex appeal,' of sexuality in our century" ("Socratic Ruptures" 131). In *Epistemology of the Closet* she characterizes "homo/heterosexual definition" as the "presiding master term" of the twentieth century. Much of her interrogation of this master term takes off from her emphasis on the importance of the closet:

> [W]hat I have been arguing for several years now is the installation, at the beginning of the present century, of two very specific and philosophically anomalous kinds of speech acts, "closetedness" and "coming out," in the most centrally indicative relation to notions of truth and self (which is among other things to say, following Foucault, to notions of sexuality) across our present cultures. ("Socratic Ruptures" 131)

In these terms, the "closet" is the site around which a whole series of meanings coagulate. It is the pivotal site for the definition and redefinition of some of the West's most treasured categorial and relational notions.

Sedgwick highlights "the internal incoherence and mutual contradiction of each of the forms of discursive and institutional 'common sense'" which prevail in our culture on the subject of sexual definition:

> The first is the contradiction between seeing homo/heterosexual definition on the one hand as an issue of active importance primarily for a small, distinct, relatively fixed homosexual minority ..., and seeing it on the other hand as an issue of continuing, determinative importance in the lives of people across the spectrum of sexualities. ... The second is the contradiction between seeing same-sex object choice on the one hand as a matter of liminality or transitivity between genders, and seeing it on the other hand as reflecting an impulse of separatism—though by no means necessarily political separatism—within each gender. (*Epistemology* 1–2)

The closet is "internal and marginal to the culture" (56); it is at once a potent site for gay and lesbian individuals and communities *and* a volatile emblem for a definitional crisis felt by the whole society. The closet then is a metonymic signature for the anxiety experienced by a culture "at once pervasively homoerotic and intensely homophobic" (Weed 254). Sedgwick's analysis reveals the failure of heteronormative discourse to produce a stable rhetorical framework; a vocabulary and a grammar of "common sense" which *makes sense*. To recapitulate in slightly different terms:

those speech acts which Sedgwick argues exist "in the most centrally indicative relation to notions of truth and self" ("Socratic Ruptures" 131) produce a coherent subject only as they undermine that coherence.

Early in *Epistemology of the Closet* Sedgwick articulates one of the book's key theoretical assumptions: "the relations of the closet—the relations of the known and the unknown, the explicit and the inexplicit around homo/heterosexual definition— have the potential for being peculiarly revealing, in fact, about speech acts more generally" (3). Much of this book is concerned with the examination of "I love you" as *the* romantic speech act. What might the "relations of the closet" have to tell us about this speech act? The force of "I love you" depends upon a logic of open secrecy; this claim indirectly supports Sedgwick's arguments about the explanatory or interpretive force of those speech acts with which she is preoccupied: "closetedness" and "coming out." It is important to remember that Sedgwick's formulation of the closet and its speech acts relies not just upon Miller's formulation of the "open secret," but also upon her readers' culturally inherited familiarity with open secrecy and its narrative operations. If "closetedness" describes a speech act of silence, then "coming out" might be said to name a speech act of "confession," the revelation of a private or an inner truth. Sedgwick performs the stunning move of installing the closet—a site which in many ways *belongs* to gay and lesbian culture and politics— at the center of heteronormative meanings, ideologies, and institutions. This is impressive and useful because it refuses the arbitrary distinction between what is marginal and what is internal to culture, by repositioning what might be located in the margins to the very center of the hegemonic culture which attempts to exclude it. "I love you" is one of those speech acts about which her "epistemology of the closet" has something to tell us. Might "I love you" be classified as an utterance spoken from the closet, that linguistic and social cathexis so brilliantly mapped by Sedgwick? "I love you" doubly enacts those two foundational speech acts she strategically calls "closetedness" and "coming out." She writes: "Knowledge, after all, is not itself power, although it is the magnetic field of power. Ignorance and opacity collude or compete with knowledge in mobilizing the flows of energy, desire, goods, meanings, persons" (4). Sedgwick's speech act theory and Foucauldian-inflected epistemology highlight the extent to which the conjunction knowledge/ignorance informs the structural and the semantic dimensions of contemporary culture and its texts.

"I love you" in popular and literary romance novels is an insistent claim that knowledge is individual, intuitive, expressible, and more particularly, that knowledge about sexuality is private, personal, uncorrupted by power or politics. Sedgwick indirectly demonstrates that this ostensible immunity from power and politics is a social fiction, an illusion. As Miller writes: "the secret subject is always an open secret" (205). Further, the logic of iterability which rules the circulation and repetition of "I love you" serves to destabilize its apparent "meaning." The ubiquity of this phrase and the stories it rules is at once an effect and a constitutive element of the crisis around homo/heterosexual definition which Sedgwick identifies.

On one level, my analyses of historical romance novels aim to articulate the processes by which "I love you" interpellates its subject, and object, into a compulsive narrative trajectory which struggles to cement the romance plot as a life imperative for each and every one of us. In its simplest rendition this plot (or "plotting"), which begins with the exclamation "It's a girl/boy!" fetishizes courtship as life's one true adventure, and concludes with a marriage—a happy ending. The individual (the hero or heroine of our paradigmatic plot) is subsumed within that most overvalorized of relational units, the couple, and the reproduction of the heteronormative life narrative is guaranteed as this new couple, will, in due course, exclaim "It's a girl/boy!" themselves. So, this book insists not just on the performative force of individual fictional texts, but on the performative force of fictions generally; it suggests that an implicit theory of genre is embedded in the idea of a performative act even in its earliest formulation. At the same time, however, I have neither the expertise nor the inclination to develop a study of precisely how it is—linguistically, psychologically, sociologically—that we learn and use conventional stories to organize and interpret our speech (and behavior). This project is motivated to make sense, at least in part, of the pull romance fictions—whether we read novels by Barbara Cartland or not— exert on our everyday lives. I am guided by the sense that our personal experiences and stories of love cannot be disentangled from the generic fictions of romance which prevail in our culture. Catherine Belsey is similarly concerned to justify her decision to study desire by reading fictional texts, rather than in some other way. This strikes me as a particularly important and worthwhile concern for any academic study of cultural discourse. Following Belsey then: "What are the materials of this study? Experience? Perish the thought! Texts, then. But *which* texts? Second, what is to be my critical framework? ... I do not believe that we have access to other people's experience. I am not even sure we have access to our own. But more important, experience, like sexuality, surely does not exist in the raw, in its natural state, outside the order of language and culture" (10).

PART II
Popular Historical Romance Fiction: Cross-Dressing Novels

Chapter 3

Speech Acts and Costumes:
Georgette Heyer

Georg Lukács begins his famous study of the historical novel by discounting from his consideration those "historical novels" in which "history is ... treated as mere costumery: where it is only the curiosities and oddities of the *milieu* that matter, not an artistically faithful image of a concrete historical epoch" (19). In this and the following chapter, I identify a subgenre of popular historical romance fiction which revels in its status as "costumery": the cross-dressing novel. In the only book-length study of popular historical romance published to date, Helen Hughes states that disguise is one of its most frequently used and important "motifs." Yet her discussion of disguise is brief, and focuses on the concealment of a character's social status or class. While Hughes notes that cross-dressing is one common manifestation of the disguise "motif," she does not follow this observation through to examine the treatment of gender and sexuality in these novels. This chapter looks closely at three cross-dressing novels by Georgette Heyer, an enduringly popular—if critically neglected—writer who published more than forty historical novels between 1921 and 1975: *These Old Shades* (1926), *The Masqueraders* (1928), and *The Corinthian* (1941). As Hughes points out, the publication of *These Old Shades* in 1926 marked a turning point in the development of popular historical romance. In the late 1920s, the genre began to focus on the love story at the expense of adventure, as it increasingly came to be seen as a subset of "women's fiction." The turn to the love story signals also the beginning of popular historical romance fiction's detailed and ongoing exploration of the patterns and privileges of heterosexuality. It is, as this chapter demonstrates, no coincidence that *These Old Shades* is a cross-dressing novel. This subgenre exemplifies and crystallizes some of the most pertinent and enduring aspects of popular historical romance fiction's representation of heterosexual love.

Romance fiction is, as I have already argued, defined by the drama of secrecy and confession encapsulated in the speech act, "I love you." This drama gains an additional layer of intrigue when the heroine first attracts the attention of the hero in the guise of a boy. Cross-dressing novels hinge on the representation of a redoubled scene of confession: the revelation of the heroine's true sex and the declaration of love. This scene is pivotal in each of Heyer's cross-dressing narratives, just as it is in Pam Rosenthal's *Almost a Gentleman* (2003) and Margaret McPhee's *The Captain's Lady* (2004). For this reason, there is a strong line of continuity running from Heyer's novels to the most recent examples of the subgenre; however, I don't want to suggest that the cross-dressing novel is a static form. To the contrary, there are significant differences between Heyer's cross-dressing novels and later examples of the form, such as Laurie McBain's *Moonstruck Madness* (1977) and Kathleen A. Woodiwiss's

Ashes in the Wind (1980). Further, the cross-dressing novels of the last decade have moved away from some of the conventions followed by Woodiwiss and other romance writers in the 1970s and '80s. The analyses of individual novels included in this chapter and the next address some of the developments in the subgenre over the last eighty years or so. I am, however, less struck by evidence of change in the cross-dressing novel than by the extent to which the basic narrative structure laid down by Heyer remains the foundation for writers contributing to the subgenre today. The cross-dressing novel's resilience follows from its capacity to keep pace with changes in the broader romance marketplace, most notably in the characterization of the hero and heroine, and through the inclusion of erotic content, without drifting too far from its moorings in conservative assumptions about sex, gender, and sexuality.

The historical romance genre recites a familiar and powerful narrative of naturalization for heterosexual hegemony, but it doesn't do this with ease. In broad terms, popular romance fiction is most sympathetically described as a lively and long-running conversation between writers and readers about the norms of gender and sexuality. Historical romance directs this conversation to thorny questions about the status of gender as an historical or natural category, and the impact of historical and cultural context on sexual identity. The genre's attention to such questions is heightened in cross-dressing novels. As I will show, this subgenre, while often deeply sexist and homophobic, nevertheless adds up to a thought-provoking investigation of the terms of reference for popular historical romance and, more complexly, of the premises of heterosexual hegemony. Tania Modleski insists on "the importance of seeing both progressive *and* regressive elements in popular texts" ("My Life as a Romance Writer" 67). Like Modleski, I don't think it's possible to account for the paradoxes and pleasures of romance genres without taking popular fiction's uncertain politics as a starting point. My interest in popular historical romance fiction in general takes off from an initial refusal to dismiss it as what Lukács terms "mere costumery"—a fictional form which simply uses "history" as a stage for drama and doesn't seek to ask bigger questions about the past and our relationship to it. This genre uses settings in the past as the impetus to ask difficult questions about the qualities and progress of heterosexual love. How and when the hero and heroine say "I love you" is the key to unravelling the often contradictory and unsettling erotics of historical romance novels. In the cross-dressing novel, this phrase becomes the meeting point for a quite confusing range of emotions and responses, from the perspective of both the hero and the heroine. Does the speech act "I love you" modulate into something other than heterosexuality when spoken in a cross-dressing novel, or do these books show heteronormativity to be a more insecure regime than it might at first appear? My goal is not to recuperate popular historical romance novels as homoerotic, but rather to trace the logic driving their heteroerotic function. Imagining one sexual possibility necessarily involves imagining others; cross-dressing novels make this process explicit.

Quite early in Heyer's career, a review of *Beauvallet* (1930) described her brand of historical novel as "really just fiction wherein the course of action doesn't grow from the necessity of character in history, but the need of a plot all dressed up in costume" (qtd. in Fahnestock-Thomas 85). By the 1950s, reviewers typically labelled Heyer's novels "costume pieces" or "costume romances." In a gorgeous example of the kind of self-mocking comedy Heyer excelled at, the eponymous heroine of *The Grand Sophy* (1950) denies the idea that "there are more important things to think of than one's dresses." She replies, "What a stupid thing to say! ... Naturally there are, but not, I hold, when one is dressing for dinner" (48). The cross-dressing subgenre both intensifies and questions the passion for costume which characterizes popular historical romance. Janice Radway notes the significance of descriptions of characters' clothing in romance; however, she argues that they "almost never figure significantly in the developing action" (193). Instead she explains the genre's careful attention to dress as one of the most important devices in its achievement of a "mimetic effect." Radway places similar emphasis on verisimilitude in her discussion of historical romance's lavish descriptions of "domestic architecture and home furnishings." While Radway is certainly right when she explains that these characteristics of popular romance fiction draw on and reinforce stereotypes of femininity, I am convinced that there is something altogether more complex going on with popular historical romance's fascination with dress and dissemblance. Heyer's inclusion of "[a]ll the details of dress and fashion" (Rosemary Carr Benét qtd. in Fahnestock-Thomas 143) certainly has, in Radway's terms, a "mimetic effect." Likewise, for A.S. Byatt and Jane Aiken Hodge, Heyer's careful attention to historical detail facilitates her readers' escape into an imaginary world. But, can the regularity and richness of descriptions of characters' clothing in Heyer's novels and in popular romance more generally be adequately explained by their mimetic function? And do these descriptions always (and only) work in the service of dominant discourses about gender and sexuality, or might they sometimes work for quite another purpose?

A review of *Venetia* (1958) recommended the novel to "those who want a costume story or a tale of love" (qtd. in Fahnestock-Thomas 184). Stella Bruzzi, in her study of costume in cinema, insists that "clothing exists as a discourse not wholly dependent on the structures of narrative and character for signification" (xvi). From this perspective the "costume story" can counter or complement the "tale of love," or, as I will argue, it can do both. Bruzzi refutes the assumption that the sole function of costumes is to assist with narrative development and characterization, as "a means of understanding the body or character who wears them, not an end unto themselves" (xiv). Instead, her approach to studying costume in film points to the performative force of clothing in its focus on the degree to which clothing is "able to impose rather than absorb meaning" (xiv). While the details and subtleties of Bruzzi's study are tied to the study of cinema, her guiding premises have a potentially broader compass. As my readings of popular (and in later chapters, literary) historical romance novels illustrate, descriptions of clothing are often crucial to the building of characters and the progress of narrative. The frequency with which reviewers describe historical romance novels as "costume dramas" attests to the genre's delight in detailed descriptions of clothing and accessories. From the outset, the label "costume dramas"—and the less friendly "bodice rippers"—suggests that, despite Radway's claim to the contrary, costume does "figure significantly in the developing action." However, the role of costume in popular historical fiction is never straightforward. Instead, while references to costume are frequently the impetus for efforts to shore up heterosexual hegemony, they are just as frequently the entry-point for competing discourses about bodies and desires.

Cross-dressing novels, from Heyer to today, have used gender disguise to represent the truth (in multiple senses) of the hero and heroine's love. They insist—over and over again—that there is an entirely predictable and indisputable relationship between an individual's sex, their gender, and their sexuality. At the same time their disguise plots fail to close off the disruptive or progressive possibilities of cross-dressing. Desire, in these novels, does not behave according to the apparently simple binary logic which dominates normative constructions of gender. Instead the response of the hero to the cross-dressed heroine shows up the complexities and paradoxes of such logic. This is most evident in the circuitous course the novels chart from the hero's attraction for a "boy" to a happy ending for heterosexual love.

This chapter and the next interrogate the flexibility and the relevance of contemporary theories of gender masquerade in relation to a body of texts against which they have not yet been tested, beginning with a reading of Georgette Heyer's three cross-dressing novels. Chapter 4 examines a cross-section of cross-dressing romances published since 1980. Both of these chapters continue to bring Austin's idea of the speech-act together with recent reconceptualizations of performativity.

Recent practitioners of performativity theory are not so much interested in speech as in cultural behaviors and practices more generally. In Judith Butler's view, for instance, "performativity is not just about speech acts. It is also about bodily acts" (*Undoing Gender* 198). Despite the greater interpretive possibilities such a widening of focus might suggest, most literary and cultural critics who make extensive use of the idea of performative behavior focus on the relationship between gender and costume—on "cross-dressing," "masquerade," "transvestism," and "drag."[1] My own work shares this fascination with the performative force of gendered dress, but where it differs from most studies of cross-gender disguise is in its attention to the relationship between masquerade and heterosexuality, rather than homosexuality. This interpretive priority enables a reconsideration of some of the most influential claims which have been made about the meaning and force of cross-dressing over the last fifteen years or so—most memorably by Butler and Marjorie Garber. I do most of this work in the next chapter when I present a theoretical analysis of cross-dressing in contemporary heterosexual romance as a practice which both confirms and complicates normative categories of gender and desire. The unpicking of Heyer's novels in the final section of this chapter anticipates and builds support for this claim.

---

1   Annamarie Jagose makes a similar point to this in her discussion of the "hypercirculation" of Butler's notion of performativity. She names Judith Halberstam, Cathy Schwichtenberg, and Paula Graham as examples of critics who use the notion of performativity to "concentrate on those theatricalised stagings of gender which self-consciously interrogate the relationship between sex, gender and desire" (86). I would add Ann Pellegrini's book, *Performance Anxieties*, to this list.

Speech and Costume: Historical Romance Fiction and Georgette Heyer

In 2002, Germaine Greer revealed on British television that "her sexual fantasies are stalked to this day by Heyer's Byronic heroes." On the same programme, A.S. Byatt called Heyer's novels "wonderful." Watching this programme, Kate Fenton, who confesses to being a "Heyer user" herself, "nearly fell off [her] chair." Fenton is not the first critic to express her surprise that "thinking women" can also be Heyer fans. In 1970, Marghanita Laski wrote that she could find no explanation for Heyer's popularity with "well-educated middle-aged women" (283). Whereas she found their "appeal to simple females of all ages ... readily comprehensible," Laski simply could find no way to account for why women like her might turn to Heyer. (In a letter to her publisher, Heyer described the critic as "that awful Laski woman" (qtd. in Hodge 185), so at least their disdain was shared.) Laski suggests that she might understand the attraction if the novels had any sex in them, but she can find none. Instead, she describes Heyer's characters as costumes without bodies underneath: "Even if Miss Heyer's heroines lifted their worked muslin skirts, if ever her heroic dandies unbuttoned their daytime pantaloons, underneath would be sewn-up rag dolls" (285). For Byatt, one of the distinctive pleasures of Heyer's novels is "the absence of sex-in-the-head." She praises "Georgette Heyer's innocence and lack of prurience" for allowing us to "retreat into this Paradise of ideal solutions, knowing it for what it is, comforted by the temporary actuality, nostalgically refreshed for coping with the quite different tangle of preconceptions, conventions, and social emphases we have to live with" ("An Honourable Escape" 265). What then is "stalking" Germaine Greer's sexual fantasies? The lack of explicit sex scenes in Heyer's historical romance novels does not make them devoid of any discourse about sexuality. To the contrary, as I read them, Heyer's novels are ambivalent, contradictory, and fascinating stories about the "tangle of preconceptions, conventions, and social emphases" which construct the heterosexual romantic subject.

Heyer's commercial success—described as "phenomenal" by Byatt ("The Ferocious Reticence" 34)—began in earnest in 1926 with the sales of *These Old Shades* in Australia. Heyer played a vital role in the history and the development of twentieth-century historical romance fiction. Described by Byatt as "one of the great best-sellers" (29), Heyer is most well known for her virtual invention of the Regency romance novel: a "comedy of manners" set during the reign of the Prince Regent (1810–1820) in England. Heyer's novels—themselves imitations and adaptations of established adventure and romance plots—inspired a whole industry of romancers, virtually all of whom "[covet] the accolade 'in the tradition of Georgette Heyer'" (Mussell xiii). Heyer began her career writing "cloak and dagger" romances like those popularized by writers such as Baroness Orczy (*The Scarlet Pimpernel*) and Rafael Sabatini (*Scaramouche*). By the end of the 1920s she had adapted the genre to focus on social comedy and the romantic plot.

In a talk for the British Library Centre for the Book in 1996, Carmen Callil said, for her, Heyer "gave out mixed messages" (479): "she was of severely masculine appearance, and many of her novels describe a mannish heroine such as she: a woman who spends her life among men, and who wants to be—and often is—like them. In some of her early novels, her women dress like men too ... She was an obsessive, meticulous researcher and writer, yet she called her novels 'another bleeding romance'" (479). Heyer's biographer, Jane Aiken Hodge, provides plenty of evidence that the author preferred the company of men, was ambivalent about her novels, and dismissive of the fans who adored them. At least three troublesome binaries tangle together in discussions of Heyer's fiction and life: masculine/feminine, history/romance, and Literature/popular fiction. Any attempt to produce an author profile of Heyer involves negotiating a number of confusions of category: Was Heyer a historical novelist or a romance writer? Are her novels best classified as popular fiction or Literature? Are her books openly critical of normative constructions of gender or do they reinforce them? For the most part, these three questions have driven the research on Heyer published thus far. As explained in Part I of this book, my own research is propelled by a somewhat different (if related) question. It's self-evident that Heyer's historical romance novels are tales of heterosexual love, but as Stephanie Burley asks in her reconsideration of the "cultural work" (127) done by contemporary popular romance, "what kind of heterosexuality is this?" (146)

Heyer's novels certainly give out "mixed messages" on a number of fronts. In addition, her letters to her publishers are peppered with ambivalence for her status as a writer of popular fiction. In 1943, she wrote:

> Spread the glad tidings that [*Friday's Child*] will not disappoint Miss Heyer's many admirers. Judging from the letters I've received from obviously feeble-minded persons who do so wish I would write another *These Old Shades*, it ought to sell like hot cakes. I think myself I ought to be shot for writing such nonsense, but it's unquestionably good escapist literature and I think I should rather like it if I were sitting in an air-raid shelter, or recovering from the flu. Its period detail is good; my husband says it's witty—and without going to these lengths I will say that it is very good fun. (qtd. in Hodge 8)

Heyer's exasperation with the demands of the "Trade" (160) and the "dim-wits" who were devoted to her novels poses a problem for popular fiction scholars used to speaking up for the field. "Not unnaturally," she wrote, "[fans] expect me to be Romantic and I'm nothing of the sort" (71). Perhaps Heyer's refusal to identify herself happily as a romance writer explains, at least in part, the dearth of research published on her novels. Despite her extraordinary and enduring popularity and the key position she occupies in the history of popular genres in the twentieth century, Heyer has attracted the attention of remarkably few researchers. The lack of published studies of Heyer is even more surprising when we consider the many volumes of scholarly output available about her near contemporary Agatha Christie. Mary Fahnestock-Thomas's recent anthology, *Georgette Heyer: A Critical Retrospective*, goes some of the way towards redressing the balance by bringing together in one volume Heyer's short fiction and essays, reviews of her novels (1921–1997), obituaries, citations from reference books, articles, and excerpts from dissertations and books.

Fahnestock-Thomas writes that the collection "is not intended as a scholarly effort," but aimed at admirers of Heyer's fiction like herself, who "believe that the pure pleasure her works have given us is worth far more than any scholarly seal of approval" (2). Similarly, Jennifer Kloester's *Georgette Heyer's Regency World*, while based on her doctoral research, was promoted on its publication in 2005 as "A must-have for every Heyer fan!" Kloester's book is published by William

Heinemann, an imprint of the Random House Group. Jane Aiken Hodge's 1984 biography, *The Private World of Georgette Heyer*, was re-released under the same imprint in April 2006. In 2004, Random House launched their reissue of Heyer's historical novels under their Arrow Books imprint in the United Kingdom, Australia, New Zealand and South Africa. Random House has moved away from the mass-market paperback format of their 1990s Mandarin paperbacks towards a distinctly more literary style. Heyer's name and the title are printed in white in an understated elegant font, over details from eighteenth- and nineteenth-century paintings. The covers of the reissues feature testimonials from British literary novelist Margaret Drabble ("My favourite historical novelist"); romance writer Katie Fforde ("Georgette Heyer achieves what the rest of us only aspire to do"); and chick lit author India Knight ("Georgette Heyer is unbeatable"). This repackaging of Heyer signals an attempt by Random House to stamp her novels anew with the markers of literary respectability at the same time as signalling her significance in the popular romance canon. Arrow's publishing director, Kate Elton, explains the relaunch as an attempt to position Heyer alongside literary authors such as Philippa Gregory and Tracy Chevalier: "The packaging of her books was unrepresentative of what they are like. The books had jackets that were really downmarket, absolutely not like her" (Kean). In the United States, Heyer has been published by Harlequin since 2000, and is thus immediately classified as a romance writer. Her significance to the genre's history is signalled by Harlequin's inclusion of forewords by contemporary romance writers in their reissues, such as Anne Stuart (*The Masqueraders*), Catherine Coulter (*The Grand Sophy*) and Stephanie Laurens (*These Old Shades*).

The recent shift in the marketing of Heyer signals the need for more thorough investigation of her position in the broader literary field. While a detailed author profile is beyond the scope of this book, the attempt by Random House to reshelve Heyer across the Literature and popular fiction stacks lends weight to my claim that genre cuts across the broader distinction between popular fiction and Literature. The few critics who have published work on Heyer share a reluctance to place her firmly on one side of the Literature/popular fiction divide. In her examination of Jane Austen's influence on Heyer, Barbara Bywaters concludes that "Heyer merges the forces of high art and the appeal of popular fiction in her mastery of the elements of the romance formula" (508). In a similar vein, E.R. Glass and A. Mineo argue that Heyer's unusually complex use of history distinguishes her from lesser contributors to the genre and classify her novels as "middlebrow" (422) (she's not as good as Austen and not as bad as Cartland). Karin E. Westman explains the "vexed position" (166) Heyer occupies between Literature and popular fiction as a function of her classification as a writer of "women's fiction." Gender hierarchies and literary hierarchies clearly intersected in the critical reception of Heyer's historical romance novels during her lifetime. Diana Wallace makes the same point, but with a more positive inflection: "We need to read both 'serious' and 'popular' novels together if we want fully to understand the range of meanings that history and the historical novel have held for women readers in the twentieth century" (5). Over the course of her career, reviewers praised the depth and accuracy of her historical research while mocking her "frothy" romantic plots (see Fahnestock-Thomas 54–253); for instance, they frequently contrasted the masculine rigor of her careful cataloguing of the historical record with her feminine preoccupation with courtship rituals and happy endings. For most reviewers, the frippery dominated the serious history and Heyer was typically classified as a writer of "amusing light fiction" (127) and the occasional "seriously conceived historical novel" (129). In the complex global romance market, it is clearly no longer quite as easy to pass her over as a "purveyor of romantic froth" (Hodge 7).

All but two of Heyer's historical romance novels have remained in print since the time of their first publication. Her role as a genre-innovator is clear. Heyer remains the "standard-setter" (Ramsdell 201) for writers of Regency period romance. Her impact on readers is more difficult to quantify; for many commentators the first step towards gauging the genre's social force is theorizing its escape function. In her essay, "My Life as a Romance Reader," Tania Modleski insists that "in our culture *all* women imbibe romance fantasies from a variety of sources" (48). Modleski drives home the point that popular romance fiction is one such source by telling the story of her own life-long "addiction" to a genre which she finds both irresistible and disturbing for its representation of love between men and women. It falls beyond the reach of my expertise to trace the complex psychological processes by which romance novels initiate or fuel the fantasies which manage our affective and sexual relationships. Nevertheless, reading cross-dressing novels provides evidence that at least this subgenre does not offer a coherent model for living as a heterosexual woman. In her readers' guide to romance fiction, Katherine Ramsdell states that, if a novel is to qualify as a romance, it must be "written in such a way as to provide the reader with some degree of vicarious emotional participation in the courtship process" (5). Ramsdell writes of romance fiction as though it offers instruction in love for its readers: "They want to know exactly what it felt like to be living (and loving) during that particular period in history. In short they want to escape into and actually experience the period" (113). Popular romance novels are a key cultural reference point for thinking through what it means to say "I love you"; the escapist function of romance is, in these terms, tied to its performative aspects. Does the genre's capacity to draw readers into its imaginary worlds follow from the familiarity and predictability of its narrative structures or is some degree of unfamiliarity and strangeness necessary to facilitate "escape"? Ken Gelder offers one answer to this question. He identifies the proximity of romance fiction and readers' lives as a possible explanation for the genre's "remarkable popularity": "romance can indeed sit closer to women readers' actual lives and aspirations than one might at first imagine" (52). However, this suggestion does not gel with standard explanations of Heyer's appeal, which always emphasize the distance between reader's lives and the idiosyncratic world depicted in the novels.

In *Twentieth Century Romance and Historical Writers*, a bio-bibliographical guide to popular and literary fiction, S.A. Rowland describes Heyer's novels in this way:

> Her distinctive, essentially inimitable style (though many tried) combines remarkable historical accuracy with high quality literary artifice in plot, characters and social code. No plagiarist could equal Heyer's precision on fashion, and the material world of Regency London, nor the slang of characters drawn from contemporary records. (Vasudevan 310)

It is significant that two of the aspects of history (and fiction) isolated in this passage are fashion and slang. Period costume and dialogue are the stock-in-trade of historical romance novels. Umberto Eco's narrator in *The Name of the Rose*, refers to "those bad novelists who, introducing a French character, make him exclaim 'Parbleu!' and 'La femme, ah! La femme!'" (5). Heyer could easily be described as just such a "bad novelist" (indeed, she often described herself in such terms), if her work was not so consistently applauded for its historical accuracy. Rowland's description of Heyer's fiction in such contradictory terms is fairly typical. Reviewers and critics commonly describe Heyer's novels as historically accurate, yet remark that the world they portray is definitively "Heyer's"; her books offer both "accuracy" and "artifice." Rowland contends that Heyer is distinctive (and "inimitable") because of her creation of an "artificial world," a "unique world of artifice," which values "birth, decorum, and manners" above all else: "Characters are either Quality or are willing to serve, and society is run happily by males born to privilege and duty while females are confined to the domestic and romantic spheres. Contrary to recorded history, no voice is allowed to challenge these restrictions." At the same time, Rowland insists that Heyer's world can be applauded for its "remarkable historical accuracy" (310): Heyer is "[e]ssentially a writer of adult fairytales in a credible historical setting" (311). This paradoxical combination of "history" and "romance," realism and fantasy, defines and names the *historical romance* genre. From a reader-response perspective, such as Radway's or Hughes's, this paradox works in the interests of verisimilitude, or, to extrapolate only a little, in the interests of "escape."

For Hughes, the appeal of historical romance is the genre's combination of "verisimilitude" and "fantasy." In her terms, this "mingling" of "distance" and "reality" facilitates the consumption of historical romance novels as "surrogate experience." Their function, she argues, is "wish-fulfilment":

> The major themes of romance are adventure and sexual love, with a range of behaviour and experience being portrayed. Well-known stories, reassuring in their familiarity, are used and re-used. For essentially the romance is written to entertain: it frees the reader from "inhibitions and preoccupations" by drawing him or her into its own world. (3)

History provides the setting, or sets the scene, for the recitation and recirculation of familiar stories; it functions as a "backdrop" for fiction. There's little dispute that popular historical romance novels entertain readers by providing a "holiday from reality," but do they also contribute to our ideas about that reality? Taking up this question involves attending to the performative aspects of texts, and considering their capacity to define and redefine the key indices through which we read the world.

Popular fiction does not simply confirm or authorize already existing assumptions and attitudes about sex, gender, and sexuality; instead, popular novels take part in a wider process of continual confirmation, and authorization of cultural norms. In these terms, Heyer's novels do not merely re-present or reflect essentially extratextual contemporary mores and values, but rather they are also moments in the continuing naturalization of precisely those things which they describe or define as "natural." As my analyses of *The French Lieutenant's Woman* and *Possession* illustrate, I hold the same view about Literature. That is to say, this book examines the particular discursive mechanisms by which popular historical romance novels attempt to render heterosexual love timeless, universal, utterly unconstructed and uncorrupted by history. At the same time, reading cross-dressing novels exemplifies Butler's point that "Norms do not exercise a final or fatalistic control, at least, not always" (*Undoing Gender* 15).

These Old Shades, *The Masqueraders*, and *The Corinthian*

It is Terrific...
It is a Classic Heyer. (This means it is a lot of froth about nothing...)
It is EXACTLY what the Fans like.
It is in my best manner. (Heyer, Letter to Louisa Callender)

These Old Shades opens with a detailed description of its hero's lavish dress:

He walked mincingly, for the red high heels of his shoes were very high. A long purple cloak, rose-lined, hung from his shoulders and was allowed to fall carefully back from his dress, revealing a full-skirted coat of purple satin, heavily laced with gold; a waistcoat of flowered silk; faultless small clothes; and a lavish sprinkling of jewels on his cravat and breast. A three-cornered hat, point-edged, was set upon his powdered wig, and in his hand he carried a long beribboned cane. (1)

This passage introduces a novel which is intensely preoccupied with descriptions of dress: the colors and textures of exquisite fabrics, fine tailoring, bejewelled and beribboned accessories, the details and peculiarities of fashion. *These Old Shades* could be read as a series of descriptive vignettes of its prettily dressed characters, linked together by a lightly sketched tale of love and adventure (as, indeed, could most of Heyer's novels). However, paying attention to the costumes in *These Old Shades* reveals a somewhat differently nuanced story than that which is foregrounded by the events of the narrative of love and adventure. This novel is as preoccupied with how clothing is worn, who wears what when, and who dresses (or redresses) whom as it is with achieving a happy ending for heterosexual love. The apparent trivialities and flourishes of dress have enormous symbolic and narrative importance in this novel. Indeed, the romantic plot of *These Old Shades* is propelled by the display and the performance of gender, by the dressing, undressing, and redressing of characters as feminine, masculine, or foppish. This novel is a "costume drama": it is *about* the performative force of gendered clothing and accoutrements. While "true" masculinity and femininity are exposed throughout the novel as the open secrets of foppery and female cross-dressing respectively, the disguise plot fails to close off the disturbing or disruptive possibilities of gender masquerade. The "naturalness" of femininity, masculinity, and heterosexual love is both reinforced and confounded by a plot which delights in the artifice of costume.

The hero described above, Justin Alastair, His Grace the Duke of Avon, is a man of fashion, a fop. Avon is almost always introduced into a scene with just such a detailed description of his elegant and foppish costume. Other characters "[draw] in a quick breath of wonderment" (44) or stand "staring open-mouthed" (207) on the two occasions when he descends a staircase. He is the beauty of this novel:

"The Duke was always magnificent ..." (44). The heroine never quite achieves the same head-turning splendor as the Duke. On the only occasion when she descends a staircase the bevy of men below fail to immediately exclaim her beauty: "'But look at me!' she said reprovingly" (255). Defined by a certain "to-be-looked-at-ness," the Duke is also the character who looks more closely, and thus sees things more clearly, than any other.

Avon's foppery is quickly exposed as a clever diversion from his "natural," and all-the-more-dangerous, masculinity. In the novel's opening scene, Avon is walking alone down a dark Paris side-street, "glancing neither to left, nor to right, apparently heedless of possible danger," when a figure rushes from an alley and collides with him:

> The figure clutched at that elegant cloak, cried out in a startled voice, and tried to regain his balance. His Grace of Avon swirled about, gripping his assailant's wrists and bearing them downwards with a merciless strength belied by his foppish appearance. His victim gave a whimper of pain and sank quivering to his knees. (1–2)

The fop is only feminine—and hence weak—on the surface; he is a "real" man underneath. The body who hurtles into and disturbs this pretty scene—"a body hurled itself upon him" (1)—is the very figure who will most disturb Avon's foppish persona. Avon learns that his "victim" is running from his violent older brother, Jean de Bonnard, who has been beating him. He gives de Bonnard the diamond pin from his cravat in exchange for the boy: "I purchase your brother, body and soul" (4). Before this exchange, Avon notices a number of things about the boy whom he has so easily overpowered: his youth, his "great violet-blue eyes," and his distinctive copper-red curls ("ruffled into wild disorder" (3)). As will be clearer by the end of my discussion of cross-dressing novels, physical weakness, apparent youth, expressive eyes, and unruly hair are signifiers of femaleness which, within the rhetoric of this subgenre, it is very difficult to conceal. The terrified boy, Léon, who clutches at Avon's "elegant cloak," and pleads for his help is in fact the heroine of the novel, Léonie. It is significant that Léon seizes Avon's "elegant cloak" rather than his body, because it is a narrative of (re)dress which will ultimately "save" this "pretty child" (5). Similarly, the fact that Léon is bought by Avon with a fashion accessory initiates a plot in which the hero will come to own or possess this youth by "fashioning" him ("I will make him my page. So entertaining to possess a page, body and soul" (5)). Avon must make his page's appearance correspond with his "true" self—he must make Léon over into Léonie—in order to conclude or consummate his affection for him. However, as we shall see, Avon is a reluctant hero; he is not "happy" about engineering Léon's feminization. He likes him better as a boy.

Avon takes Léon home with him and introduces "his new possession" (4) to his friend Hugh Davenant. Hugh is distinctly troubled by the prospect of a young and innocent boy living in the care of a man like Avon, and says quietly, "You are not the man to care for a child of his age" (6). The *double entendre* in the following conversation between Hugh and Avon suggests just what might happen to a youth in the care of such an "inhuman taskmaster" (6):

Always a faint undercurrent of sarcasm ran beneath the surface of the Duke's smooth voice. ... "The question Is—Hugh will of course have the answer ready—what next to do with Léon?"
"Put him to bed," said Davenant.
"Naturally—And do you think—a bath?" (7)

This chapter repeats the image of Léon, "unfledged innocence" (7), in (the Duke's) bed: Avon twice directs his lackey to put Léon to bed, and the chapter concludes with him remarking to Hugh that Léon is surely asleep, leaving the room and himself going "slowly up to bed" (11). The thinly veiled inference that what Avon might next do with Léon is "put him to bed" pictures, however briefly or fleetingly, a sexual relationship between a man and a boy. Hugh complains of Avon's "importunate" behavior and states grimly that "[i]t would be very distressing if that innocence left him—because of you" (8). In reply to Hugh's question, "Why do you want him?" Avon remarks that "Titian hair has ever been one of—my ruling—passions" (9). The homoerotic excess of this scene—Hugh's homophobia and Avon's duplicitous speech—begins something which the narrative must work very hard to contain, or conceal, if it is to reach a happy ending for heterosexual love. Indeed, the romantic cross-dressing plot *must* stage a homoerotic relationship between a man and a "boy," in order to *be* romantic; without suggestions of erotic tension between the hero and heroine the romance plot simply cannot proceed. If the hero thinks that the heroine is a boy, then his desire for "him," must be retrospectively rescripted as a desire for "her." This retrospective logic is a standard *modus operandi* in the romance genre: the happy ending draws our attention back to all those hints in the text that, despite appearances, the hero loved as he should all along. However, the retrospective logic in this novel is ineffective, its ending is "unhappy" to the extent that Avon is reluctant to accept that Léon is not a boy. While I would suggest that the failure of the happy ending to be fully successful is generic to the romance, this novel, more than any of the others I discuss here, foregrounds the genre's rhetorical shortcomings. Léon is much more entertaining—and attractive—to Avon as a boy than as a girl.

From the first chapter, it is clear that Léon is not what he seems: wide-eyed, slight and utterly dependent on Avon, he is anything but a strapping working-class lad. Hugh in fact makes this explicit when he suggests that Léon is "of gentle birth. One can tell that from his speech, and his delicate hands and face" (8). Hugh, of course, is altogether less "omniscient" than our hero, and fails to see immediately that Léon's uncertain class-status is not his only "mystery." Readers of the Mandarin and Arrow editions of *These Old Shades* know that Léon "becomes the ravishing beauty Léonie" from the moment they read the back cover; Avon's announcement that Léon is Léonie is not a surprise. For Avon and readers alike, Léon's femaleness is an "open secret." In this context, the narrative pleasure of the "open secret"—of "'forgetting' our knowledge" in order to better enjoy the novel—is not so much, as in D.A. Miller's analysis, the pleasure of suspense or surprise, but rather it is the pleasure of having known all along, having guessed the "truth," or more specifically, having been able to "read" the markers of gender. This pleasure is not peculiar to the cross-dressing novel, but is generic to the romance. As Miller says, we defer our pleasure in order to be surprised by characters' confessions and revelations, but is there not a correlative delight in having already guessed the character's secret, in having been a good (romance) reader?

Avon—the best "reader" in the novel—forgets what he knows because he does not want to know. He may have "known from the very first," (98) but he believes in Léon's masculinity nonetheless: "She is more a boy to me than a girl" (82). It is significant that it is Avon who first declares Léon's femaleness: "There never was a Léon. A Léonie, perhaps" (64). There are frequent references in the novel to Avon's "omniscience": "It is my business always to know" (198). Avon reveals the truth about Léon to three other characters before confronting the "boy" himself. Léon's femaleness becomes as much Avon's secret as the cross-dresser's own. Both hero and heroine have something to confess: Avon that he has allowed this "little comedy" to go on for his own pleasure, and Léonie that she has been disguised as a boy for seven years.

Avon finally sets Hugh straight in Chapter 8: "Hugh Davenant is Amazed."

> "And all the while you knew he was a girl."
> "You are becoming rather involved," remarked Avon.
> "She, then. You knew she was a girl. Why have you allowed her to keep up the pretence? What do you mean by her?" (89–90)

Nobody, however, is more "involved" than Avon himself. He polices Hugh's pronouns, enforcing a constative rule of language: the word must be true to the referent. However, it is Avon who most persistently ignores this rule—"I call her Léon" (80). What exactly does he *mean* by her? Léon is simultaneously boy and girl for him; he insists that "[t]here never was a Léon" (64) but can only think of his page *as* "Léon." He allows Léonie to continue her masquerade, precisely because he likes her better in disguise. He continues to chide Hugh for his errors of reference:

> "Hugh—" Avon tapped the table with his fan. "Your painful anxiety impels me to inquire—what do *you* mean by her?" ...
> "I've an affection for Léon, and if I allowed you to take her innocent as he is—"
> "Careful, Hugh, careful!"
> "Oh, *she,* then! If I allowed that—I—"
> "Calm yourself, my dear. If I did not fear that you would mutilate it I would lend you my fan. May I make known my intentions?"
> "It's what I want!" ...
> "It will surprise you to hear that I am fond of Léon."
> "No. She will make a beautiful girl."
> "You will at least be surprised to hear that I had not thought of Léonie in the light of a beautiful girl." ...
> "When shall you—put an end to her boyhood?"
> "When we arrive in England. You see, I am deferring the moment as long as may be."
> "Why?"
> "One reason, my dear, is that she might feel shy of me in her boy's raiment when once I knew the secret. The other—the other—" He paused, and studied his fan, frowning. "Well, let us be honest. I have grown fond of Léon, and I do not want to exchange him for Léonie." (86–8)

The unspoken question in this dialogue is a question of propriety: Are Avon's "intentions" strictly honourable? If Hugh is not surprised to hear that Avon is fond of Léon, then he must be surprised to hear that he has never thought of his page as a girl (despite having known this to be the case from the very beginning). His "keen affection" (76) for Léon does not follow from him really being a "beautiful girl," but from him being a boy. The homoerotic implications of Avon's honesty are only slightly deflected by his claim that he is only admitting a "fatherly emotion, believe me" (76). It is not fatherly love which makes him delay ending Léon's masquerade for as long as he can, but something altogether less explicable within the terms of a conservative heterosexual romance. Avon teases and torments Hugh for his failure to correctly name the cross-dresser according to anatomical sex, only to confess his own disobedience: "I have grown fond of Léon, and I do not want to exchange him for Léonie."

Throughout their discussion, Hugh is as disturbed by Avon's new fan as he is by his circuitous speech. The fan is a gift from a friend ("I send you this pretty trifle ... we rival the ladies now in this matter" (87)) which Avon opens, shuts, taps, waves, and flutters throughout the chapter: "handling the chicken skin like a woman" (88). Hugh dismisses Avon's new affectation ("Foppery!" (87)) and punctuates his enquiries after Léon with demands that Avon "Put away that damned fan!" (89) Avon insists, however, that "The fan expresses his emotions," and persists with his new frippery, playing the flirt and calling Hugh "dear," "beloved," "irresistible." There is a kind of heteronormative logic in the notion of a feminine man being attracted to a masculine girl—"opposites attract." However what is also interesting about this scenario is the extent to which that which attracts the other is not "natural" but contrived; one cross-dresser desires another. When Avon explains to Léon what he must do to become a woman, he says, "you shall ... learn to curtsy, to flirt with your fan, to simper, to have the vapours—" (100). So, in order to be "feminine," Léon must learn her foppish hero's habits and affectations and hence become *like* him. He, in turn, must "[throw] down his fan" (219) in order to become a "masculine" hero for his now "feminine" love object.

In Chapter 26, "Léon and Léonie," Avon finally does what he has been so reluctant to do and confesses to Léon that he knows "his" secret. When his master begins to "play with his fan, ... his mouth rather grim, ... Léon rack[s] his brains to think how he could have offended his master." Léon does not in fact become Léonie, even in his own thoughts, until Avon declares it so:

> My infant, it has become time to put an end to the little comedy you and I have been playing ... I am very fond of Léon, my child, but it is time he was Léonie ... You see, I have known from the very first. (98)

Léon does not voluntarily confess his secret, rather his confession must be forced from him. He has, it seems, "no doubt ... forgotten" (64) that he is really a girl. Unlike the heroines of Heyer's later novels and all but two of the novels I discuss in the next section, Léon does not want to be a girl. Instead, he is passionately opposed to the idea: "'I won't, I won't! ... Let me be Léon! Please let me be Léon! ... I do not want to be a girl! ... I don't w-want to be—a girl! ... I will not! I will not! ... Never, never!'" (99).

Avon cajoles his page into staying with his sister, Fanny, from whom he will "learn to be a girl" (100). Fanny quickly rids Léonie of her breeches and coerces her into a low-cut, green silk gown. Léonie is then left alone in her room where she addresses her new self in the mirror and acknowledges her femaleness for the first time: "'You are not Léon: that is very certain. Only one little bit of you is Léon.' She bent forward to look at her feet, shod still in Léon's shoes" (117). Once she steps into dainty slippers, we can assume, there will be nothing left of Léon at all. In fact, she forgets her adventures so quickly, that when Avon suggests she pretend he is the Duchess of Queensbury and show him her curtsey, she is not so much unable to curtsey as unable to imagine him a woman: "But you cannot be a duchess, Monseigneur. ... That is ridiculous. You don't *look* like a duchess! Let us pretend you are the Duke of Queensbury" (132). At the novel's conclusion, Léonie asks Avon what he was wearing at a soirée: "'Thus the female mind,' murmured his Grace. 'I wore gold, infant, and emeralds'" (333). The two protagonists are, at least on the surface of things, correctly re-gendered—the too pretty boy has become a girl, the fop has discarded his fan—to star in a finale in which love is declared and a betrothal made. Still, Avon maintains to the very last that he is "no hero ... no fit mate"; (336) his "sincerity" remains in question.

These Old Shades introduces many of the devices and contrivances typical of the romantic cross-dressing plot: a passion for costume; a simultaneous belief in and denial of the effectivity of disguise; a heroine who passes as a male to everyone but the "knowing" hero (whether he "knows" it or not); uncontainable homoerotics; and a troubled retrospective logic to secure an equally troubled "happy ending."

In her essay "Costumes of the Mind: Transvestism as Metaphor in Modern Literature" Sandra Gilbert compares the treatments of transvestism by male and female modernist writers. Her argument is, in brief, that whereas male modernists tend to represent transvestism in terms of an opposition between true self and false costume, women (most particularly Virginia Woolf) deny the existence of a true self beneath the false costume, believing instead that the true self male modernists describe is also false, another costume. She begins her essay by comparing two very famous statements about costume; the first from *Orlando* and the second from W.B. Yeats's "Sailing to Byzantium," both published in 1928:

> There is much to support the view that it is clothes that wear us and not we them ... we may make them take the mould of arm or breast, but [clothes] mould our hearts, our brains, our tongues to their liking. (Woolf 117, qtd. in Gilbert 391)

> An aged man is but a paltry thing,
> A tattered coat upon a stick, unless
> Soul clap its hands and sing, and louder sing,
> For every tatter in its mortal dress. (Yeats qtd. in Gilbert 391)

Gilbert identifies these as opposing statements about the nature of costume explicable in terms of each writer's gender: "For Woolf, we are what we wear, but for Yeats, we may ... have to undo the last button of what we wear in order to dis-cover and more truly re-cover what we are" (391–2). While Yeats maintains the "traditional dichotomy of appearance and reality," Woolf intervenes in that opposition to suggest that appearance constitutes reality. Gilbert further argues that male modernists, including Yeats, typically oppose "false costume" to true clothing, or to nakedness; they assume the existence of a proper (or "natural") relation between reality and appearance, bodies and clothes, "sex" and "gender." (This might be described as a "constative" view of representation.) Female modernists, in contrast, consider all clothing or costume to be "false costume," and recognize the falseness of the "true" nakedness privileged by the male modernists. (This might be described as a "performative" view of language and culture.)[2]

It is a fascinating exercise to ask how a third statement about costume, also published in 1928, might bear out or trouble the oppositional terms of Gilbert's argument. The following passage from Heyer's novel, *The Masqueraders*, discusses Robin Tremaine's success playing the role of Kate Merriot in polite London society:

> With her petticoats he cast off all Miss Merriot's mannerisms. Kate had a tripping step: Robin a clean, swift stride; Kate was languorous: Robin never; Kate fell into charming attitudes: Robin's every movement was alert and decisive; Kate could adopt a melting siren's voice: Robin's speech was crisp, just as his eye was keen where Kate's was languishing. The truth was he was a consummate actor, and if he played a part he became that part, heart and soul. (245–6)

Certainly, this passage has less the temper of a maxim or a statement of truth than its more literary counterparts, nevertheless it can be similarly assessed as a summary of the way Heyer defines and describes transvestism. The two views of costume which Gilbert identifies and opposes exist simultaneously and paradoxically in this passage and indeed throughout all three of Heyer's cross-dressing novels. The gestures, mannerisms, and moods which belong to "femininity," are "cast off" with Kate's petticoats, with her underwear. By implication, Robin becomes Robin again only when he is naked. When dressed as Kate, he *is* Kate, "heart and soul": "He seemed to know *by instinct* how to flirt his fan, and how to spread his wide skirts for the curtsey" (42, my emphasis). Flirting with a fan and curtsying are, of course, two of the skills Léon must learn if he is to become a woman in *These Old Shades*. In these terms, to be a "woman" or a "man" is to play a part, to act, regardless of the actor's anatomical sex: when wearing breeches, Léonie becomes Léon; when wearing petticoats, Robin becomes Kate. In these terms, the stereotypical gestures and behaviors of "femininity," do not follow from femaleness, but rather are directly

---

2   Gilbert goes on to examine the rhetorical use to which women writers put transvestism. She frames this discussion in terms of Woolf's description of writing novels as a "tunnelling" (412) process. She writes: "For the male modernist, in other words, gender is most often an ultimate reality, while for the female modernist an ultimate reality exists only if one journeys beyond gender" (394). Gilbert appropriates Woolf's notion of "tunneling" to describe a kind of journey of discovery, a utopian search for a place or a time beyond or before gender. For Gilbert, representations of transvestism by women writers can be read as moments of just such a journey: "many of whom wish either to identify 'selves' with costumes or to strip away all costumes (and selves) to reveal the pure, sexless (or third-sexed) being behind gender and myth" (412–13) Transvestism is about shedding layers to discover the deepest and truest self. Gilbert fails to articulate what is *similar* about the male and female texts she discusses: cross-dressing is an established literary trope for getting to the "truth" of characters and selves.

linked with the wearing of costume: "clothes wear us and not we them." To be gendered is to *perform* gender. Léonie has been dressed as Léon for so long, that she has "forgotten" how to be anything else. Robin is a skilled masquerader who can peruse his closet and take on any persona at will. At the same time, however, Léon's breeches and Kate's petticoats are "false costume." The "truth" is that Robin is a "consummate actor"; he is a man pretending to be a woman. Léon cannot conceal his femaleness from Avon, because he cannot help being "feminine": he is emotional, weak, "as conceited as a girl." In the end, petticoats "suit" him better than breeches. Heyer's cross-dressing novels couple a belief and a delight in the capacity of clothing to perform gender, with an insistence that masculine and feminine apparel is a "true" expression of male- or femaleness. Gender is undecidably performative and expressive. In a sense, the latter position permits and legitimates the former: if it all comes right in the end, then it's okay to play dress-ups, to make believe, until then. These novels betray a certain anxiety over where the "truth" of gender resides—in the body or in clothing/costume. The convoluted logic of the passage cited above, and of the three novels it summarizes, identifies the very paradox which propels the romantic cross-dressing plot.

A review of *The Masqueraders* dismissed the novel for its superficial characters and derivative plot: "The characters are charmingly dressed dolls. And the plot could not be described as original." Robin Tremaine is not the only cross-dresser in the novel. His sister, Prudence, masquerades as Kate Merriot's brother, Peter. In J.S. Bratton's article "Irrational Dress," she describes an 1835 William Collier play, *Is She a Woman?*, in which a brother and sister swap costume and lifestyle. The brother dresses in elaborate women's clothing and dabbles in the "feminine arts," and his sister shoots and hunts. The siblings are both happy in their new roles and remain cross-dressed until the end of the play. Bratton identifies an early precedent for Collier's play: *Love's Cure; or, The Martial Maid* (c.1625). The plots of the two plays are virtually identical, except that *Love's Cure* concludes with brother and sister falling in love with a woman and a man respectively. They are thus "cured" of their aberrant behavior and clothed in their "proper" attire. *The Masqueraders* tells just such a tale: Robin and Prudence Tremaine, "dissemblers since they were children" (back cover), are "cured" by love. Robin falls for a "damsel in distress" the masqueraders rescue from a rake at the beginning of the novel, and Prudence for Sir Anthony Fanshawe, a London gentleman.

The Tremaine family motto is "I contrive," and the novel opens with Prudence and Robin travelling to London disguised as Mr. Peter and Miss Kate Merriot. Kate is described as a "prodigiously lovely lady" (3), and Peter as a "prodigiously modish young buck" (272). Descriptions of them throughout the novel are extremely lavish, over-the-top even. "Pretty picture" follows "pretty picture" (214) of this charming pair: Miss Merriot sits in a window-seat, "supporting her fair head on one delicate hand," and presents an "enchanting profile to the room" (213), wears her "fair ringlets *en demie toilette*" (2), or comes "all powdered and patched and scented; a fair vision in pale blue taffety" (37); Mr. Merriot strikes a "truly masculine attitude, with a foot on the window seat, and an elbow resting on that bent knee" (213); he wears his dark hair "confined demurely at the neck by a black riband" (3); and stands in a "modish coat of brown velvet, with gold lacing, and a quantity of Mechlin lace at his throat and wrists" (3). Such excessive displays of gender are not peculiar to this novel, nor to romantic cross-dressing novels in general; rather they are a distinguishing feature of popular historical romance. The heroine descending the stairs, or flouncing into a room, laced, frilled, and beribboned, circulates as *the* image of popular historical romance. A hyperbolic economy of display organizes the costume romance.

What I find particularly enjoyable about Heyer's fiction is the extent to which it parodies itself while insisting upon the legitimacy of the narrative order it undermines: characters who are not "feminine" or "masculine" enough explicitly and repeatedly question their suitability as heroes or heroines of a romance; references to "Romance" and the necessity for a "happy ending" abound; descriptions of characters are excessive, garish, comic. The conservative logic of these novels is troubled: internally incoherent, discordant, displaced by its own excesses. Heyer's representations of gender and desire are performative to the extent that their whole drama is bound up in whether they privilege artifice or "nature," in whether they belong to a rhetoric of expression, or a system of tropes.[3]

The first description of Sir Anthony Fanshawe, a magnificently presented gentleman with a studied disinterest in his surrounds, echoes the opening description of Avon in *These Old Shades*:

> The large gentleman paused on the threshold and put up his quizzing-glass, through which he blandly surveyed the room. He was a very large gentleman indeed, with magnificent shoulders and a fine leg. He seemed rather to fill the room; he had certainly a presence, and a personality. He wore a tie wig of plain brown, and carried his hat under his arm. The hilt of his sword peeped out from between the folds of his greatcoat, but in his hand he held a cane. (16)

Like Avon, Sir Anthony's apparent nonchalance conceals an unusual attentiveness; again, it is the hero's "business to know." Robin is immediately alerted to Sir Anthony's difference and repeatedly warns his sister: "The gentleman with the sleepy eyes sees things, I'll warrant you" (23); "He displays already a most fatherly interest in my little sister, ... We are like to be undone by it" (32). Unlike Avon, whose interest in Léon is also described as "fatherly," Sir Anthony does not guess Peter's secret immediately. Instead, it is his growing "interest" in a young *man* which rouses his suspicions. Soon after they first meet, Sir Anthony offers Peter lodgings at his London house: "Prudence flushed in sudden surprise, and looked sideways at the gentleman. This was unexpected; it seemed Sir Anthony was developing a kindness for her" (25). Later in the novel, Peter questions Sir Anthony about his offers of friendship: "I wonder that you should so greatly desire my company, Sir Anthony" (99). The too-attentive gentlemen replies: "I believe ... I have an odd liking for you, little man. One of these strange twists in one's affections for which there is no accounting" (99). Prudence has nothing to fear from other male characters, not just because they are less observant or clever than Sir Anthony ("the disguise was deep enough to hoodwink a dozen ... rattlepates" (51)), but because they are not attracted to her. Robin explains his fear of Sir Anthony not in terms of his remarkable powers

---

3   I am deliberately echoing the tenor and phrasing of Diane Elam's comments about the ambiguous linguistic status of "I love you." See Chapter 1.

of observation, but in terms of his "affection" for Peter. Similarly, when Robin later asks the hero how he guessed, he responds: "I should find it hard to tell you, Robin. Some little things and the affection for her I discovered in myself" (164). While other male characters remain thoroughly duped by Prudence's masquerade, the hero must make sense of his "odd liking" for Peter Merriot. The only imaginable or permissible explanation is that Peter is a girl.

The romantic hero will always see through false costume. If, like Sir Anthony, the hero does not expressly guess the cross-dressed heroine's secret immediately, when he does finally realize or learn the truth, he *also* realizes that he has in fact known inarticulately or subconsciously all along. The retrospective effect of Sir Anthony's *Aha-Erlebnis* is to explain away any confusion about his desire for Peter. In Chapter 18, "The Large Gentleman is Awake," Sir Anthony confronts Peter/Prudence with his new (and reassuring) knowledge: "I've had suspicions of your secret since the first night you dined with me here ... Of late I have been as certain as a man may be of so wild a masquerade" (153). His certainty follows a series of events and conversations which have intensified and made public his interest in Peter, including the "odd liking" admission cited above, and a duel in which he stuns polite society by playing the role of champion for another man. Homosexual desire is both abnormal ("strange," "odd") and always already heterosexual (the boy is really a girl). Indeed, in both of the novels discussed thus far, homosexual desire precedes and enables heterosexual desire. Homosexuality is imagined and pictured as a developmental stage towards, or infantile form of, heterosexuality.

The "happy" conclusion of the cross-dressing plot hinges on the success of a redoubled confessional scene. Prudence has suspected Sir Anthony knows her secret since the duel. Finally unmasked, she tells him her real name:

> "Prudence ..." Sir Anthony repeated and smiled. "I don't think you were very well-named, child." He looked down at her, and there was a light in his eyes she had never seen there before. "Will you marry me?" he said simply.
> Now at last there came surprise into her face, on a wave of colour. She rose swiftly to her feet, and stood staring. "Sir, I have to suppose—you jest!"
> "It is no jest!"
> "You ask a nameless woman, an adventuress to marry you? One who had lied to you, and tricked you! And you say it is no jest?"
> "My dear, you have never tricked me," he said amused. [...]
> "I don't understand you. Why do you offer this?"
> "Because I love you," he answered. "Must you ask that?" (153–4)

Sir Anthony has only suspected the truth since she first dined with him (some time after they first meet and become friends), but she has "never" fooled him. The mechanism of the open secret is laid bare. The distinction between knowledge and ignorance is not clear cut. Instead, there are gradations of knowing and levels of secrecy: Sir Anthony now knows absolutely what he must have known implicitly. He can account for the "strange twist in his affections" without difficulty and confusion. He developed a "kindness" for Peter not because he is "odd" (queer?), but because he sensed, felt or unconsciously discerned the truth: Peter was lovable or desirable because "he" was always a "she." Of course the reader has "known" all of this from the beginning: Prudence is really romantic, Sir Anthony's eyes are not really sleepy, and Prudence will marry Sir Anthony.

Sir Anthony and Prudence are not the only "happy couple" at the end of this novel. Another tale of secret courtship and romance runs parallel to theirs: Robin woos and marries Letitia Grayson, the "damsel in distress" Mr and Miss Merriot rescue and befriend at the beginning of the novel. Robin attends a masquerade ball dressed as a man and presents himself to Letty as *l'Inconnu* (the Unknown): "Miss Pink Domino [Letty] should feel Romance at hand on such an introduction" (64). Later when both Peter Merriot and *l'Inconnu* ask her to dance, Letty replies: "Mr Merriot, I have to choose *l'Inconnu* because I am a female, and they say the silly creatures love a mystery" (69). Too-romantic Letty (like the apt-named Lydia in *The Corinthian*) is a foil for the prudent heroine:

> "I believe I've fallen into a romantic venture, and I always thought I was not made for it. I lack the temperament of your true heroine." [...]
> "Do you?" [Sir Anthony] said. "Then who, pray tell me, might stand for a true heroine?"
> "Oh, Letty Grayson, sir. She has a burning passion for romance and adventure." (254)

In the terms of this novel, a truly "feminine" woman is necessarily "romantic." Letty, unlike Prudence, is a silly frippet, prone to tears, fainting fits, and a sucker for a good Romance; that she could ever pass as "masculine" is unimaginable.

l'Inconnu leaves the masquerade ball before the traditional unmasking, answering Letty's protests with a gorgeous summary of the romantic cross-dressing plot: "To unmask would be to kill romance" (65). It is precisely when Prudence is "unmasked," or reinscribed as "feminine," that the romance can be "happily" concluded. When Prudence begins to feel an "odd delight in [Sir Anthony's] masterful treatment of her," her "feminization," is nearly complete. "Masculine" and "feminine" are hierarchically opposed in Heyer's cross-dressing novels according to a long list of binary opposites: large/dainty; strong/weak; intelligent/foolish; serious/silly; languorous/alert; decisive/fickle; coquettish/gallant; and so on. In *The Masqueraders*, Prudence is remarkable because she eschews the lesser qualities of the "weaker sex"; she is a better woman to the extent that she is "masculine." Sir Anthony ponders his attraction to Prudence (still cross-dressed) in exactly these terms:

> She stood still before him, a slim figure in dove-gray velvet, one hand fingering the black riband that held her quizzing-glass, and her tranquil eyes resting on his face. Even though he was angry with her for her obstinacy he could find it in him to admire the firm set of her mouth and the clean-cut determination of her chin. She had spirit, this girl, in the man's clothes, and with the man's brain. Ay, and she had courage too, and a calmness of demeanour that pleased. No hysterics there; no sentimentalism; no wavering that one could see. Bravery! He warmed to the thought of it. She made nothing of this masquerade; she had faith in herself, and for all the restfulness that characterized her, that slow speech, and the slow smile she had, the wits of her were quick, and marvellously resourceful. (224)

Of course, this description of Prudence echoes the introductory description of Sir Anthony cited at the beginning of my discussion of this novel. Sir Anthony is attracted to Prudence because she is like him. Unlike the too-feminine woman, the cross-dresser *can* pass as a man. Similarly, the cross-dressed heroine of *The Corinthian*, Pen Creed, apologizes to the hero because she is less than feminine. He quickly dismisses her concerns: "As a boy you would have been in no way remarkable; as a female, believe me, you are unique" (66). These novels insist upon the heroine's happy return to, or acceptance of, "femininity," while privileging her "masculinity." Nevertheless it is the heroine's "femininity" which must appear to define her.

Prudence declares to Sir Anthony that she "can never be in a flutter," and he corrects her with a kiss:

> He bent his head over hers; she had a wild heart-beat, and put out a hand with a little murmur of agitation. It was taken in a firm clasp: for the first time Sir Anthony kissed her, and if that first kiss felt awry, as a first kiss must, the second was pressed ruthlessly on her quivering lips. She was held in a hard embrace; she flung up an arm around Sir Anthony's neck, and gave a little sob, half of protest, half of gladness.
>
> The horses moved slowly on; the riders were handlocked. "Never?" Sir Anthony said softly.
>
> She remembered she had said she could never be in a flutter. It seemed one was wrong. "I thought not indeed." Her fingers trembled in his. "I had not before experienced—*that*, you see. [...] You give me the happy ending I never thought to have." (255–6)

Prudence is more like Letty than it first seemed. From the beginning, Sir Anthony inspired in her a "disinclination to simulate" (33); heterosexual desire makes her feel "feminine" and propels her into "true clothing": "And so we all live happily ever after. Who'd ha' thought it?" (282). My emphasis on the normalizing force of the happy ending does not mean to imply that Heyer's plots are straightforward or rhetorically coherent. In a letter to her publisher, she confessed the "secret of [her] Art": "On no account must the story be About anything in particular, or hold water for half a minute." The plots of these novels, and indeed of cross-dressing novels in general, are fascinating precisely because they simply don't "hold water." Still, to quote another Heyer letter, it "All Comes Right in the End" (qtd. in Byatt "Ferocious Reticence" 34). Or does it?

There are naturally other aspects of Heyer's fiction on which I might have based my examination of her representation of heterosexuality: her debt to Jane Austen (Bywaters; Glass and Mineo); the intriguing story of her suppression of some of her early novels (Westman); or her idiosyncratic take on the people and places of Regency London (Kloester). My discussion is obviously limited to her cross-dressing novels, but a more thorough and longer study of Heyer's *oeuvre* would show that gender and sexuality are unstable and contentious categories in all of her novels. In her extraordinary study of British conservatism between the world wars, Alison Light argues that "masculinity" and "femininity" were anything but fixed notions in the popular fiction of the period. Instead, she shows, especially in her analysis of Christie's "conservative modernity," that ideas about gender were "constantly in the process of being revised and discussed across the range of popular genres" (163). Light cites Heyer's work as one of the more "obstinate manifestations of Toryism," but speculates that even writers like Heyer, P.G. Wodehouse or Angela Thirkell "do not emerged unscathed from what we call modernity" (215). Heyer's genre innovation takes on a new cast when viewed from this perspective: "Far from being stuck in the mud of the past, conservatism seems to have improvised rather well in the modern period, making something homely and familiar from the brand new." Light's insistence on the contradictoriness of British popular writers resonates with my readings of *These Old Shades* and *The Masqueraders* as it does with my ideas about her last cross-dressing novel, *The Corinthian*.

In her essay "Cross-Dressing in Wartime: Georgette Heyer's *The Corinthian* in its 1940 Context" Kathleen Bell takes quite a different approach to explaining Heyer's use of gender disguise to the one I've presented in this chapter. She sees the heroine's costume as a reflection of "a time when the suitability of women in wartime work, as well as femininity itself was the subject of political debate" (464). Bell's argument falls down for me when she expressly denies the erotic valences of the cross-dressing plot. She argues that the relationship between the heroine, Pen Creed, and the hero, Sir Richard Wyndham, is "signally lacking in erotic interest" (464–5). I am not satisfied by Diana Wallace's discussion of *These Old Shades* and *The Masqueraders* for the same reason: on the one hand, she argues that masquerade is "used to explore gendered identity as socially constructed and potentially fluid" (35), and even goes so far as to suggest Heyer's novels "look forward" to Butler's notion of performative gender; on the other, she concludes her discussion by refusing to look closely at the "spectre of homosexuality raised by cross-dressing" (42). For Wallace, Heyer "defuses such possibilities by revealing the cross-dressing to the *reader* very early on" (43). In my analysis, the operations of open secrecy activate rather than neutralize the homoerotic potential of cross-dressing novels. These novels *are* haunted by the idea of same-sex desire; therefore, to focus on gender at the expense of analysis of the representation of sexuality can produce only a partial reading.

The hero of *The Corinthian*, Wyndham, is an exquisite dandy, known amongst the *ton* for his invention of a neckcloth style, the Wyndham Fall. He first meets Pen Creed when his "sleepy gaze" takes in a figure in boy's clothes climbing from a first-floor window "by means of knotted sheets" (25). Unlike the heroes of *These Old Shades* and *The Masqueraders*, Sir Richard sees (or rather feels) through Pen's disguise at once, when he helps her down from the window: "Sir Richard, his chin tickled by curls and his arms full of fugitive, made a surprising discovery" (26). There is clearly a body beneath Pen's breeches, but the hero is in no hurry to see her in a dress. In fact, he is less bothered by the mismatch of sex and attire than by her poorly tied cravat: "Are you under the impression that you have tied that—that travesty of a cravat in a Wyndham Fall?" (31). While Westman acknowledges that the "doubt" surrounding the heroes' knowledge of the heroines' sex in *These Old Shades* and *The Masqueraders* "adds a layer of erotic interest to their encounters," (464) she concludes that the "relationship Pen and Richard achieve is asexual" (471). This strikes me as an extraordinary deduction to make from an affair which begins with the image of the hero's "expert fingers" working "with the crumpled folds round [the heroine's] neck" (31) (I don't think I need to belabor the point about the symbolism in play here) and concludes with this scene:

> "My darling!" he said. "Oh, my precious, foolish little love!"
> The coach lumbered on down the road; as it reached the next bend, the roof-passengers, looking back curiously to see the last of a very odd couple, experienced a shock that

made one of them nearly lose his balance. The golden-haired stripling was locked in the Corinthian's arms, being ruthlessly kissed.

"Lawks a-mussy on us! whatever is the world a-coming to?" gasped the roof-passenger, recovering his seat. "I never did in all my born days!"

"Richard, Richard, they can see us from the coach!" expostulated Pen, between tears and laughter.

"Let them see!" said the Corinthian. (233)

The conclusion of *The Corinthian* is, of course, a comic scene. Pen draws attention to the happy couple's scandalous behavior through laughter. The heavy-handed comic effect of this scene is somewhat different to the more subtle parody of Heyer's two earlier cross-dressing novels. The late twentieth-century novels which I will discuss in the next section take up, one might say, where Heyer left off. They stage, over and over again, an embrace between two males, to deliberate comic effect. (They never, however, conclude with that embrace.)

In the July 1996 edition of *Romantic Times Magazine*, the monthly "theme spotlight" column focuses on novels which feature a heroine disguised as a male. The columnist, Kate Ryan, discusses the theme's appeal, authors and readers offer their thoughts, and there is a long recommended reading list. Ryan writes that what fans really love "are the hilarious antics that ensue during any sort of cross-dressing charade." Similarly, for reader Jocelyn Cazier it is "*very* hilarious keeping up with the disguises," and romance writer Jude Deveraux recommends a novel in which "the skinny heroine's long legs looked so fabulous in tights, she had all the men drooling over her and hating themselves for doing it. It was hilarious!" (29). The romantic cross-dressing plot makes heterosexual love the most *serious* of things by refiguring anything else as *funny*, to be laughed at. Interviewers Osborne and Segal ask Butler to clarify her argument that the figure of the homosexual or the homosexual couple exposes heterosexuality as an "inevitable comedy." She replies: "I think that every sexual position is fundamentally comic. If you say 'I can only desire X,' what you've immediately done, in rendering desire exclusive, is created a whole series of positions which are unthinkable from the standpoint of your identity. Now, I think that one of the essential aspects of comedy emerges when you actually end up occupying a position that you have just announced to be unthinkable. That is funny. There's a terrible self-subversion in it" (114). The vocabulary and rhetoric of romance fiction is a discursive moment in the naturalization and idealization of compulsory heterosexuality and its institutions. Further, the romance plot might be read as a persistent retelling of the successful or "happy" interpellation of a heterosexual subject. The cross-dressing plot dramatizes only to cover over—or to attempt to cover over—other possibilities of sexual definition and exchange by enforcing a fixed model of gender on a "sexual field" which concedes the mutability of gender.

The romantic cross-dressing plot tells a story of concealment; its triumphant "happy ending" attempts to hide those textual elements which might otherwise have disturbed it. We might take a further step and characterize this plot as a story of deferral: the cross-dressing plot is told over and over and over again and each "happy ending" effects but a temporary closure in this continual narrative of anxiety, panic, and phobia. In theory, if this plot was ever successful in its attempts to finally expel its demons—if its ending was ever truly felicitous—then there would be no need to tell it again. This subgenre is beset by an anxious cycle of echo and answer, which—once we begin to look at more recent examples of the cross-dressing plot—only becomes more fraught, more bizarrely persistent in its demands for closure and normalization. Each retelling of the cross-dressing plot reproduces the conditions for another (and another) retelling.

Chapter 4

Performativity and Heterosexuality: Judith Butler and the Cross-Dressed Heroine 1980–2005

Popular romance writer Jo Beverley has identified cross-dressing as "one of the classic ingredients of historical romance."[1] Romance novelists like Beverley employ the cross-dressing plot—over and over again—to refigure the stability and the truth of normative constructions of gender and desire. At the same time, the figure of the cross-dresser circulates in contemporary critical theory as a kind of signature for the transgression of norms of gender and sexuality; and even, in a more generalized sense, as a signature for transgression *per se*. In her well-known book *Vested Interests: Cross-Dressing and Cultural Anxiety* Marjorie Garber insists that "*transvestism is a space of possibility structuring and confounding culture*: the disruptive element that intervenes, not just a category crisis of male and female, but the crisis of category itself" (17). Garber celebrates the cross-dresser as a marker—if not *the* marker—of those crises of meaning which challenge Western binary thinking. Garber's notion of "category crisis" does not name a threat which is *external* to hegemonic culture, but rather a vulnerability which is *internal* to it. My interest here is specifically in those "crises of meaning" which disrupt the binary oppositions male/female, masculine/

---

1   Beverley wrote this during an on-line newsgroup discussion about cross-dressed heroines. This discussion took place simultaneously on two newsgroups: Romance Writers (RW-L@sjuvm.stjohns.edu) and Romance Readers Anonymous (RRA-L@kentvm.kent.edu) in late 1995 and early 1996. The thread began when I posted a message asking people to suggest titles of novels featuring heroines disguised as males. Shortly after this discussion petered out, the newsgroups' collectively generated recommended reading list appeared in Kate Ryan's "Theme Spotlight" column in *Romantic Times Magazine*. When attempting to generate a thematic bibliography of popular romance fiction, it seems that fans' memories might be the best resource. While researching and writing this chapter, I have been nagged by a sense that projects such as my own are defied by the genre they attempt to classify. These novels are too numerous and too fast-moving for scholarly researchers who are not themselves fans. Each title—and there are millions of them—only kisses the retail shelf for a brief moment before being kept, loaned, swapped, sold and resold in an informal network of friends, second-hand bookstores, op shops, school fetes and garage sales. Public libraries provide only fragmented collections as they regularly turn over their titles in order to keep up with both the volume of new releases and their apparently insatiable readers. This massive genre is categorically unwieldy. Given the peculiar difficulties of popular romance studies, I am indebted to the subscribers to RW-L and RRA-L without whom the early research for this chapter would not have been possible.

feminine and homosexual/heterosexual.[2] In Garber's terms, the transvestite exposes the inherent failure of hierarchical binary oppositions to adequately describe or represent cultural formations and institutions. What happens then when the cross-dresser is employed—and repeatedly employed—as a representative for the intrinsic stability and immutability of meaning?

Garber gets carried away by the transgressive capacity of transvestism. We need a less euphoric account of cross-dressing which recognizes how often gender masquerade consolidates the very categories and norms which Garber argues it overthrows. While recent feminist and queer theories have championed the cross-dresser *as* threat, as self-consciously subversive, popular historical romance employs the cross-dresser to *dispel* threats to normative ideas about gender and sexuality. I'm frustrated by the simple opposition between progressive and conformist practices of gender which dominates academic discussions of cross-dressing. In popular historical romance novels of the last twenty-five years, the cross-dressed heroine is a complex negotiation of the binary logics of gender. While, ultimately, I think her ideological function is to prop up heteronormative forms and formulas, this role is not achieved without compromise or digression. Throughout these novels, the woman in the guise of a boy stands *uncomfortably* between conformity and progression. Despite her early rejection of the radical potential of heterosexual transvestism, Judith Butler's theory of performativity provides the most subtle and nuanced set of terms and ideas for reading the cross-dressed romance heroine.

Butler provides a stunning account of the linguistic and discursive processes by which leading ontologies gain, maintain—and may even lose—their grounding. As I will show, the very questions which continue to preoccupy Butler are played out in the pages of popular historical romance fiction. In broad terms, this genre worries over the questions of "life" and "survival" for women which Butler sees at the center of feminist theory (*Undoing Gender* 205). More specifically, the novels I discuss in this chapter articulate the troubled relationship she describes between sex, gender, and sexuality, in their portrayal of the cross-dressed heroine's femaleness, her femininity, and her desire for the hero. As Butler explains, "Theory is an activity that does not remain restricted to the academy. It takes place every time a possibility is imagined, a collective self-reflection takes place, a dispute over values, priorities, and language emerges" (175–6). I don't think I'm stretching the point to apply this argument to a popular genre; to the contrary, the only way to make sense of the continual revisiting of the same character types and plot devices by romance writers and readers is as

---

2   While these oppositions are my focus here, the cross-dresser, in these novels and more generally, also invokes crises of meaning around categories of race and class. Questions of the relationship between class and gender surface in all three of Heyer's cross-dressing novels. Léonie's gentle features, for instance, suggest both femininity and "good breeding." While they are not my primary focus, issues of race and class could certainly figure in analyses of a number of the novels I discuss in this chapter. The heroine of Kathleen Woodiwiss's *Ashes in the Wind* (1980) disguises herself as a "mulatto." Zenia Stanhope in *The Dream Hunter* (1994) masquerades as a Bedouin boy. The soft skin and polished turn of phrase of the grubby cabin boy in Margaret McPhee's *The Captain's Lady* (2005) are clues to her class more than her sex.

evidence of an ongoing "collective self-reflection" about the "values, priorities, and language" which inform the genre.

The key issue for writers and readers of cross-dressing novels is the problem of the hero's attraction to a "boy." As I showed in my critique of Georgette Heyer's novels, in the romantic cross-dressing plot the pronouncement "I love you" is concomitant with the pronouncement of the heroine's "true" sex. The happy ending is achieved when the cross-dressed heroine is re-dressed as a woman and both she and the hero are re-installed as unambiguously, and happily, heterosexual. The redoubled confessional scene depends upon a retrospective logic which rewrites the attraction of the hero for the cross-dressed heroine, of man for "boy," as always already heterosexual. Valerie Traub observes that "[m]ost critics would agree that the device of cross-dressing involves the suggestion of homoeroticism" (107). The romantic cross-dressing plot might be read as an anxious—because ultimately unsuccessful—denial of this suggestion. These novels cannot help but picture, however fleetingly or accidently, an erotic relationship between a man and a boy. My intention is not to "out" the popular romance novel or its characters. Rather, despite or, indeed, because of these "accidental" couplings, these novels return, again and again, to cross-dressing as a device with which to reform the cross-dresser as unambiguously heterosexual— despite their ambiguous gender status. The premises and motivations of cross-dressing in popular romance fiction are unswervingly heteronormative. Nevertheless, these novels cannot help but give away the game as they demonstrate our culture's primary confusion about exactly what it means to be, or to love, a woman.

How to Do Things with Clothes: Judith Butler and Performativity

For Judith Butler, gender is inherently "unstable." She says: "I'm interested in the problem of cross-identification; I'm interested in where masculine/feminine break down, where they cohabit and intersect, where they lose their discreteness" (Cheah and Grosz 24). Her model of performativity underpins my analysis of the representation of the cross-dressed heroine in historical romance novels. However, using Butler to read examples of "heterosexual drag" is not a straightforward process. She insists that "one can't understand performativity fully as a strategy" (40), but resists its application to the study of popular heterosexual texts (or those which would never self-identify as "queer"). If, as Butler herself argues, the meaning or effect of any performative act neither originates with nor belongs to its "actor," then her subtle distinction between texts which are appropriate for analysis by performativity theorists and those which are not simply doesn't hold. My claims in this chapter, and throughout this book, rest on performativity theory's capacity to identify and explain moments of self-subversion in a conservative genre.

What is most impressive about Butler's theory of performativity is its capacity to describe the structural weakness which inheres in the production and reproduction of heterosexual hegemony; to name those processes and effects which normative discourse attempts but fails to hide (or secret away). "Performativity" describes the discursive process by which ontological categories are constructed; for Butler, its appeal seems to be its long-established (Austin, Felman, Derrida) capacity to further describe the self-de(con)structive tendencies of that process. That is to say, taking her cue from speech-act theory's enactment of the performative's penchant for self-destruction—which began, as I discussed in Chapter 1, with Austin's self-effacing play in *How to Do Things With Words*—Butler describes the reproduction (or "reiteration") of cultural norms as a process both for and against itself. To describe gender as "performative" is to draw attention to the fact that the normative production of gender categories depends on the repeated imposition of a false logic; a "constative" logic which insists that gender simply "states" or expresses a referential truth: "That the gendered body is performative suggests that it has no ontological status apart from the various acts which constitute its reality" (*Gender Trouble* 136).

The only way to grasp the details of Butler's theory of gender performativity is to maintain a hold on the two principal notions of the "performative." On the one hand, the term describes a particular type of sentence, a *conventional* utterance which performs what it names: a "speech act." Classic examples of the explicit performative in this sense include "I dare you…," "I promise…," and "I pronounce you (husband and wife)," all of which bring about what they name: a dare, a promise, a marriage. As I have discussed in some detail, "I love you," can be described in terms of this definition of the "performative." On the other hand, contemporary critical theorists "credit a performative dimension in all ritual, ceremonial, scripted behaviours" (Parker and Sedgwick 2). To refer to, or to practise, "speech-act theory," is both to invoke an ancestor of what we now call "performativity theory," and to engage with (or return to) a particular and limited type of that theory. If speech-act theory is interested in conventional speech acts, then performativity theory is interested in conventional *acts*. For Butler, "performativity is not just about speech acts. It is also about bodily acts" (*Undoing Gender* 198). The enactment of gender norms is the leading example of performativity in these terms.

Since the publication of Butler's *Gender Trouble* and the numerous interpretations and applications of its theory thereafter, transvestism has emerged as the leading trope of performativity.[3] Cross-dressing continues to circulate in contemporary critical theory as the exemplar of "performativity," of the subversive dimensions of performativity theory, despite Butler's repeated insistence that this celebration of transvestism is based on a misreading of her argument. In an interview with Peter Osborne and Lynne Segal, significantly titled "Gender as Performance," Butler refutes the "voluntarist interpretation" of her notion of "performativity," referring explicitly to misreadings of her emphasis on drag in *Gender Trouble*. She says, "the problem with drag is that I offered it as an example of performativity, but it has been taken up as the paradigm for performativity. One ought always to be wary of one's examples" (111). Butler offers this somewhat self-critical maxim in response to the suggestion that she may well not have been clear enough in *Gender Trouble*.

---

3   It is important to make a few remarks about my use of the term "cross-dressing." Marjorie Garber prefers "transvestism," and Judith Butler uses the more explicitly theatrical term, "drag." I mostly use the term "cross-dressing" in this chapter because I think that the verb "to cross" brings into relief the conceptual problems which attend any discussion of the practice of gender masquerade, however it is named.

Osborne and Segal point out that some of the popularity of the book followed from the "voluntarist interpretation" Butler rejects:

> A lot of people liked *Gender Trouble* because they liked the idea of gender as a kind of improvisational theatre, a space where different identities can be more or less freely adopted and explored at will. They wanted to get on with the work of enacting gender, in order to understand its dominant forms. (111)[4]

To equate "performativity" with "performance," is to miss the most productive and incisive dimensions of Butler's work: "the [latter] presumes a subject, but the [former] contests the very notion of the subject" (112).

Butler's "subject" is not an actor who simply moves in and out of character as they step in and out of costume. Rather, her conception of a performative subject is emphatically anti-volitional; anti-sovereign. She reconceives of subversive agency in terms which refuse the possibility of a subject existing outside the matrices of power. Her work can be read as a rejection of the conceit of the first-person; there is, for Butler, no "I" which precedes acts—verbal or otherwise. The authority of the maxim "My word is my bond"—a favorite of Austin's—follows not from any original or primary relationship between the speaker and the (speech) act: "the binding power of the act [only] *appears* to be derived from the intention or will of the speaker" (*Bodies* n.5, 282). In fact, as Derrida demonstrates in "Signature Event Context," performative force is a function of the "citationality" of the act. Butler takes off from Derrida's insight: "Indeed, is iterability or citationality not precisely this: *the operation of that metalepsis by which the subject who 'cites' the performative is temporarily produced as the belated and fictive origin of the performative itself?*" (*Excitable* 49).

In *Bodies That Matter* and *Undoing Gender* Butler expressly dissociates herself from the "Butler" that so many people seem to have (mis)read, and insists that she means "performativity" to denote much more than the theatricality of gender categories. Musing on her treatment as an "unruly child" (the author of "trouble") by the academic community in the preface to *Bodies*, she writes:

> Matters have been made even worse, if not more remote, by the questions raised by the notion of gender performativity introduced in *Gender Trouble*. For if I were to argue that genders are performative, that could mean that I thought one woke in the morning, perused the closet or some more open space for the gender of choice, donned that gender for the day, and then restored the garment to its place at night. (x)

Which is, as we shall see, more or less what the cross-dressed romance heroine does. In these "costume dramas," the dictum "Clothes Make the Man" appears to be

---

4 It is interesting to note that the voluntarist misreading persisted despite Butler's fairly explicit disclaimers against this interpretation in *Gender Trouble*: "To enter into the repetitive practices of this terrain of signification is not a choice, for the 'I' that might enter is always already inside: there is no possibility of agency or reality outside of the discursive practices that give those terms the intelligibility they have" (148).

upheld; the heroine always passes as a man.[5] Butler continues: "Such a wilful and instrumental subject, one who decides *on* its gender, is clearly not its gender from the start and fails to realize that its existence is already decided *by* gender" (x). The relationship between costume and gender identity remains under debate in academic circles. As my readings of the cross-dressing subgenre illustrate, this debate is not confined to universities, but is alive and well (although less explicitly) in the pages of popular fiction.

One binary which is placed under considerable stress by conventions of characterization and plot in cross-dressing romances is the opposition of real to false or fake gender. The relationship of bodies to their performance of gender, of biological sex to cultural practices, is raised as a problem for analysis throughout this genre. For instance, when the heroine of Norah Hess's *Devil in Spurs* (1990), Jonty Rand is injured and rips her shirt and breast bindings, Cord McBain sees her naked breasts and cannot believe he hasn't "seen it before": "'You didn't for a simple reason,' his inner voice pointed out. 'Ever since you've known her, you've been conditioned to believe she was a male'" (186). Sylvia Andrew's *Lord Trenchard's Choice* (2002) approaches the issue of gender conditioning from a slightly different perspective. The friends of cross-dressing Jossie Morley debate the best way to counter the impact of her father's decision to "bring Jossie up as a substitute son" (32); they work together to rectify a false gender assignment. Pam Rosenthal's *Almost a Gentleman* (2003) is particularly interested in the question of the "*body below the costume.*" The heroine is unsurprised that she is able to pass as a man for three years: "All dress was masquerade, all manners a game of hide and seek" (86). In *Undoing Gender*, Butler reframes her theory of gender performativity in terms of the opposition of real and fake gender. She offers four propositions as a summary of her account of gender performativity and her use of drag as an example early in her career:

(A)   What operates at the level of cultural fantasy is not finally dissociable from the ways in which material life is organized.

(B)   When one performance of gender is considered real and another false, or when one presentation of gender is considered authentic, and another fake, then we can conclude that a certain ontology of gender is conditioning these judgments, an ontology (an account of what gender *is*) that is also put into crisis by the performance of gender in such a way that these judgments are undermined or become impossible to make.

(C)   The point to emphasize here is not that drag is subversive of gender norms, but that we live, more or less implicitly, with received notions of reality, implicit accounts of ontology, which determine what kinds of bodies will be considered real and true, and which kind will not.

(D)   This differential effect of ontological presuppositions on the embodied life of individuals has consequential effects. And what drag can point out is that (1) this set of ontological presuppositions is at work, and (2) that it is open to rearticulation. (214)

---

5   Kate Ryan writes in her "Theme Spotlight": "Romance readers agree that 'Clothes Make the Man,' especially in the proper historic context." (28).

This final point is at the center of my argument about cross-dressing in popular historical romance fiction. The use of gender disguise in romance exposes the presuppositions through which gender is communicated and read *and* opens the possibility that gender norms are subject to change. However, this adoption of Butler's terms is not only made possible by this latest work, but can proceed from the earliest versions of her theory of performativity.

Butler first offers drag as a "subversive bodily act" in *Gender Trouble*, to the extent that cultural practices such as drag, cross-dressing, and butch/femme stylization "parody" normative assumptions about gender. She suggests "that drag fully subverts the distinction between inner and outer psychic space and effectively mocks both the expressive model of gender and the notion of a true gender identity" (137). In these terms drag upsets the causal logic of what she calls the "heterosexual matrix" (and later "heterosexual hegemony"):[6]

> that grid of intelligibility through which bodies, genders, and desires are naturalized. … a hegemonic discursive/epistemic model of gender intelligibility that assumes that for bodies to cohere and make sense there must be a stable sex expressed through a stable gender (masculine expresses male, feminine expresses female) that is oppositionally and hierarchically defined through the compulsory practice of heterosexuality. (n.6, 151)

The heterosexual matrix imposes a relationship of causality, of logical continuity, of expression, between a person's anatomical sex, gender identity, and sexual desire. Butler's innovation is to expose this relationship as always already unstable; to expose the structural discontinuity which inheres in the hegemonic model; to realize, that is, the performative character of gender. These points are also made, albeit with an entirely different vocabulary, within the pages of cross-dressing novels. The heroines who pass as boys are able to do so not because gender is a *performance*, but because it is *performative*. Their deliberate masquerades rely on the citational workings of gender; they rely, that is, on the common index of physical and behavioral characteristics which regulate gender to fool their audience.

Gender is "performative" to the extent that those acts—verbal, gestural, stylistic—which announce a person's gender do not so much express, as produce the effect of an inner "truth." The production of gendered bodies "along the culturally intelligible grids of an idealized and compulsory heterosexuality" (135) depends upon a series of exclusions of, and prohibitions about, what not to be. Butler discusses the way in which this process effects a *"false stabilization* of gender in the interests of heterosexual construction and regulation of sexuality within the reproductive

---

6   Butler later rejected the term "heterosexual matrix," preferring instead "heterosexual hegemony." She justifies this in the following way in her interview with Segal and Osborne: "The heterosexual matrix became a kind of totalizing symbolic, and that's why I changed the term in *Bodies That Matter* to heterosexual hegemony. This opens the possibility that this is a matrix which is open to rearticulation, which has a kind of malleability" (119). Butler's phrasing in this passage suggests that she still thinks of "heterosexual hegemony" as a "matrix"; the term "matrix" retains a specificity which distinguishes it from the term "hegemony." I therefore don't follow Butler's lead in this matter and continue to use both terms where appropriate.

domain" (135, my emphasis). I focus on the falseness of that stabilization, its capacity to pretend coherence, to persist and to seduce despite its instability. As I will argue, the cross-dressing plot tells the story of this troubled logic, as it reiterates the narrative of "an idealized and compulsory heterosexuality" which regulates and polices the limits of intelligible bodies.

Butler offers her theory of performativity in opposition to the "expressive model" of gender; a model which persists despite the "gender discontinuities" which Butler argues "run rampant within heterosexual, bisexual, and gay and lesbian contexts" (136). What is most remarkable about the history of the constative/performative distinction in speech-act theory is its capacity to persist, to continue to "make sense," despite its theoretical unsustainability. The tenuousness of an expressive, or "constative" model of speech or behavior emerges once we begin to consider those utterances or practices which simply do not fit into such a model. Austin's attempts to produce a lexicon of those utterances which expose the "descriptive fallacy" of traditional linguistic philosophy fails to the extent that "performative" comes to describe much more than just exceptions to the rule; the performative/constative distinction is subsumed by a "general theory of illocution." There is a similar interrogative logic at work in Butler's discussion of drag. What parodic displays and enactments of gender do, for Butler, is draw attention to, or expose, the extent to which non-parodic instances of gender are also performances, dramatizations. In Butler's analysis drag is not simply related to gender as a copy to an original; rather drag subverts the very notion of an original or an originating gender: "*In imitating gender, drag implicitly reveals the imitative structure of gender itself—as well as its contingency*" (137). In these terms consideration of drag informs and complicates our understanding of gender identity. It is an example of those kinds of acts which cannot be easily subsumed under the categorical and classificatory headings of a hegemonic discourse.

How can literary studies scholars use Butler's theory of gender performativity to read representations of gendered bodies? What are the implications of Butler's approach for those of us committed to critical heterosexual studies? Butler describes the workings of "heterosexual performativity" in *Bodies That Matter*:

> To claim that all gender is like drag, or is drag, is to suggest that "imitation" is at the heart of the *heterosexual* project and its gender binarisms, that drag is not a secondary imitation that presupposes a prior and original gender, but that hegemonic heterosexuality is itself a constant and repeated effort to imitate its own idealizations. That it must repeat this imitation, that it sets up pathologizing practices and normalizing sciences in order to produce and consecrate its own claim on originality and propriety, suggests that heterosexual performativity is beset by an anxiety that it can never fully overcome, that its efforts to become its own idealizations can never be finally or fully achieved, and that it is consistently haunted by that domain of sexual possibility that must be excluded for heterosexualized gender to produce itself. In this sense, then, drag is subversive to the extent that it reflects on the imitative structure by which hegemonic gender is itself produced and disputes heterosexuality's claim on naturalness and originality. (125)

Following this passage, Butler feels "obliged to add an important qualification"—she is disinclined to admit the subversive possibilities of "heterosexual drag." However, this reluctance is belied by her argument that "heterosexual hegemony" cannot help but reveal the tenuousness of its claim to originality and naturalness: "The repetition of heterosexual constructs within sexual cultures both gay and straight may well be the inevitable site of the denaturalization and mobilization of gender categories" (*Gender* 31). Must this repetition be from within "non-heterosexual frames," or might instances of, to use Butler's suggestive terms, "hyperbole, dissonance, internal confusion, and proliferation" confound heterosexual constructs in contexts which can only be characterized as heterosexist and homophobic?

Butler argues that those "forms of drag that heterosexual culture produces for itself"—exemplified in her discussion by films such as *Tootsie*, *Victor, Victoria* and *Some Like it Hot*—invoke other identificatory and sexual possibilities only to close them off (*Bodies* 126). It is significant that, in all three of these films, a heterosexual romance plot effects the necessary closure of the narrative and the consequent stabilization of the sexual field. The trope of masquerade is *both* performative and romantic, and, perhaps more crucially, it is performative *of* romance. The narrative trajectory of these films is so familiar, that the cross-dressed figure in a heteronormative context signals the beginning of a recuperative tale of heterosexual love disguised as something altogether Other. That is to say, from Shakespeare to Georgette Heyer to Jo Beverley, the cross-dresser is an archetypally romantic figure.

For Butler, *Tootsie* & Co. illustrate heterosexuality's capacity to "concede its lack of originality and naturalness but still hold onto its power. ... Indeed, one might argue that such films are functional in providing a ritualistic release for a heterosexual economy that must constantly police its own boundaries against the invasion of queerness, and that this displaced production and resolution of homosexual panic actually fortifies the heterosexual regime in its self-perpetuating task" (126). There are two competing models of power at work in Butler's analysis at this point. First, her theory of performativity, a Foucauldian-influenced model of culture and cultural productions, emphasizes the extent to which hegemonic discourses produce the very subjects, categories, *and* narratives they endeavor to exclude. Butler's notion of performativity is useful precisely because it enables analysis not just of explicitly subversive re-enactments of gender, but also of those normative reenactments which might be said to subvert or undermine themselves. Second, her efforts to distinguish between drag performances which are "subversive" and those which are not betrays the assumption of a kind of "repressive hypothesis." Do heterosexual drag performances and texts succeed in their efforts to "repress" or, to use Butler's words, "contain" the "anxiety over a possible homosexual consequence" (126), or is this an anxiety which, in the final analysis, they can never overcome? As the long passage cited above suggests, this is actually a "Butlerian" argument: heteronormative narratives cannot help but betray the instability of their logical foundations. Must we uncover the contradictions and incoherences of heteronormative narratives, only to perform a regulatory maneuver ourselves by emphasizing the success of the closure and normalization which invariably concludes such narratives? Or might we emphasize instead the extent to which that success is only ever "provisional," a "false stabilization" of the sexual field (again, my terminology deliberately echoes Butler's)? If heterosexual hegemony is, in some sense, always already anxious about its claims to naturalness and originality, and if it is this incurable anxiety which propels its perpetual repetition, then does it not always risk a kind of self-betrayal? If, as Butler insists, "hegemonic heterosexuality is itself a constant and repeated effort to imitate its own idealizations," then the question is not so much one of subversion, but of "self-subversion"; of the extent to which hegemonic discourse cannot help but fail in its efforts to seal up and secure the coherence and continuity of its own logic.

Butler's reconceptualization of the notion of "performativity" argues that the conditions for change inhere in the mechanisms which function to sustain the status quo. In these terms, it becomes theoretically possible to conceive of even the most normative of cultural moments or practices as (inevitably) self-subversive. The romance narrative is all about idealizing (or "romanticizing") heterosexual relations and institutions; it is precisely "a constant and repeated effort to imitate its own idealizations." Its ubiquity is symptomatic of hegemonic heterosexuality's failure to ever fully approximate its own ideal. My interest here is bent towards disclosing the instability of heterosexuality's self-sustaining logic. Though the subversive effect may be fleeting, nevertheless, there is much to gain, I would suggest, from directing our interpretive energies towards heterosexuality's Janus-faced structure; the cross-dressing plot enforces the status quo in a time of crisis but is nevertheless always implicated in that crisis.

This survey of cross-dressings novels published between 1980 and 2005 is offered as a case study of what Butler has called "a critical form of heterosexuality studies, one that does not take its norms to be established or beyond criticism, one that asks how sexuality and gender are interrelated within heterosexuality, and how heterosexual definition is, as Sedgwick has taught us, bound up with homo definition" (Butler, "There is a Person Here" 23). The textual analyses in the next section address two interrelated questions: (1) how does this subgenre understand gender? and (2) how does it conceive the relationship between gender and heterosexuality? My argument supports Butler's sense that rethinking heterosexuality from this critical perspective exposes it as "usually more queer than it is willing to know" (23).

Cross-Dressing Novels

Kate Ryan's *Romantic Times Magazine* "Theme Spotlight" column, "Disguised as a Male," generalizes about the fate of the cross-dressed heroine:

> [T]he heroine who is disguised as a male wins the power and independence she desires through disguise. But what she discovers is that love comes in many forms. And her true love will love her in any form. Just like the Emperor in his new clothes, the heroine learns that appearances can be deceiving and that freedom, the truth, and true love can only be found by being true to who you are—gender and all! (28)

This passage is riven by a crucial contradiction: love is not fussy about its object *at the same time* as it is only heterosexual. On the one hand, the hero will love the heroine "in any form"; he will love her disguised as a boy or man. On the other hand, the heroine will only find "true love" when she is undisguised, when she reveals who she is, "gender and all!"; the hero will love her only as a woman. In all of the novels I discuss in this chapter, the object of the hero's desire hovers undecidedly between the cross-dressed heroine's "masculinity" and her "femininity," between "homosexuality" and "heterosexuality."

"Masculine" and "feminine" circulate as terms polarized along the lines of a whole series of fixed oppositions. This subgenre, and historical romance fiction more broadly, treats gender norms as historical constructs. The heroines invariably adopt masculine constume because living as a boy or young man allows them a degree of mobility and independence denied them within the context of their historical period. The concomitant malleability of gender norms is, however, strictly controlled by the demands of a heterosexual romance plot. While "masculinity" and "feminity" are explicitly critiqued as oppressive categories across this subgenre, "heterosexuality" and "homosexuality" are not subject to the same open analysis. As my analyses show, the auspices of heteronormativity require the maintenance of hierarchical gender oppositions in the face of challenges posed by the heroine's play with gender expectations.

Before she decides to adopt the guise of a boy, Georgiana Raithwaite, the heroine of Margaret McPhee's *The Captain's Lady* (2004), "rankle[s]" (314) at the options available to her. She knows that the appropriate feminine response to her overbearing father is to be "obedient and unquestioning" (313), but is frustrated by the limits of gender: "Not for the first time, Georgiana wished that she'd been born a man. The feeble weapons of women were not those she would have preferred to use. But they were the only ones available to her" (314). The heroine's capacity to pass as a male is typically accounted for by her possession of certain "masculine" characteristics. These characteristics are often described as evidence of her "spirit" or "passion." But, as it turns out, within the terms of a heterosexual romance plot, the heroine cannot help being "feminine." By the end of *The Captain's Lady*, Georgiana accepts that some differences run deeper than costume—they follow from biology. She cannot save herself from the novel's villain, but must wait to rescued by Lord Nathaniel Hawke: "From deep within she drew a tiny spark of courage and fanned it with thoughts of all Nathaniel had done to save both her reputation and her life. The flame burned brighter" (517). Paradoxically, the characterization of the heroine as a "spirited" woman frustrated by the inequities of gender both functions as a critique of gender and leads to the essentialization of the hierarchical gender binary. Georgiana is a better woman because she has "masculine" traits and tendencies, but Nathaniel can still bring a "blush" to her cheeks (522). Georgiana's realization that she is in love with Nathaniel follows the acceptance of an essentialist view of the relationship between sex and gender. Nathaniel, somewhat conversely, first desires her because her capacity to pass as a grubby cabin boy distinguishes her "from any other female he knew" (407).

Mapping the trajectory of the hero's desire for the cross-dressed heroine is never an easy task. In all of the cross-dressing romances I examine, the hero is attracted to the heroine *both* because she is "feminine" and because she is "masculine." Cord McBain, the hero of Norah Hess's *Devil in Spurs*, makes this explicit when he notices that the only "manly" thing about his "sissy" ward (the cross-dressed heroine, Jonty Rand) is his "spirit": "He liked that spirit in him" (165). Cross-dressing novels invariably stage an erotic relationship between a man and a boy, a relationship which is conditioned as much by phobia as it is by desire.

Cord is the most obviously panicked hero discussed in this chapter: he desires Jonty, is horrified by his desire, and reassured of his normality when he learns Jonty is a woman. In the following scene the nature of his desire ranges from homoerotic to homophobic to safely heterosexual in a moment:

> He came to Jonty's curled, sleeping form and hunkered down beside it. He hung there a minute, breathing in the smell of clean flesh, gazing at the sleep-flushed cheeks, the long lashes laying shadows on them. His chiseled lips softened, and unconsciously he laid a gentle hand on the cap of tousled curls. Why was it, he wondered, that he always had the wish to punish and protect the boy at the same time? Then the picture of this same boy being held in [Jim LaTour's] arms flashed in front of him, and he jerked his hands out of the silky hair as though repulsed. (68)

Heterosexuality is the "open secret" of this passage. It is the "truth" and the "happy ending" of Cord's desire that Jonty is *properly* "feminine." Her "silky hair," long lashes and soft features tell us this as much as the fact that a man wants to protect her. Yet, for Cord at this moment, Jonty is a boy, and a boy that he likes for his "spirit." The hero's desire is persistently bifurcated along opposing, if coexisting, lines. And there lies the rub: any attempt to "map" the erotics of the cross-dressing plot is already circumscribed by a heteronormative economy of desire. The very term *cross*-dressing implies and presumes the existence of an original or proper state of dress which the cross-dresser has come from and may return to—hence, the rhetorical appeal of cross-dressing to a genre (and industry) which has a vested interest in upholding that "original" state of gender (and desire) as ideal.

Sedgwick describes a culture beset by a kind of anxiety of indecision: homoerotic as it is homophobic. Western culture cannot resolve the question of an anxiety tempered by desire, or a desire tempered by anxiety. Pictured in these terms, the hero of the cross-dressing plot is troubled both by anxiety and desire, neither of which is reducible to the other. Jack Melville, in Mona Gedney's *Lady Diana's Daring Deed* (2000), is confused by the "thrill of pleasure" when he briefly touches hands with Trevor Ballinger during a card game: "He ... regarded the young earl uneasily, wondering just what force was at work here" (68). Cord spends much of *Devil in Spurs* taunting Jonty for being a "men lover," attempting to "knock such unnatural leanings out of [him]" (44), and bashing any man whom he suspects of "hankering" after the boy. At the same time Cord is in no doubt that he is himself aroused by Jonty: "Why was it that this green-horn kid made him lose control to such an extent?" (69). Lord David Hervey, the hero of Rosenthal's *Almost a Gentleman*, is thoroughly unsettled by his attraction to exquisite London dandy, "Phizz" Marston: "The *only trouble* was that if he attended the next Almack ball he might encounter that young man again. ... *I think he wanted me as much as I wanted*—as I want—*him. And we could both burn in hell for it*" (27). How does one name Cord's and David's phobic passions?

Performativity names the double process by which hegemonic systems of meaning reauthorize themselves only as they reimagine and reproduce the possibility of other systems of meaning. In turn, the unavoidable tendency of hegemony to trip itself up necessitates the continual restaging of its definitive acts as *felicitous* acts. This brings us to the consideration of the performativity of popular narratives. The structural insecurity performativity theory describes is precisely that which motivates and propels the incessant reiteration of those narrative formulas which strive to naturalize, normalize, and legitimate the hegemonic. This might describe a cycle of denial or triumph depending on which way you look at it: ritual narratives such as those I am discussing direct their energies towards the happy ending as an anxious denial of the infelicity of this perpetual arrival at happiness; or, the happy ending is a triumphant gesture for a system of meaning which remains intelligible and powerful despite betraying its own weaknesses.

As I argue in my discussion of Heyer's cross-dressing novels, throughout this subgenre, the revelation of the heroine's "true" gender is concomitant with the declaration of love; for instance, the revelation that Jonty is actually a girl reconstitutes Cord's desire for her as safely heterosexual. In Patricia Potter's *Swampfire* (1988), the hero discovers that his young travelling companion is a girl when she runs crying from him:

> [Y]oung Sam was crying as if his heart were breaking. And the sound was not that of a boy. Connor's grip loosened as he eased Sam to the ground, feeling the slim womanly body under the rough clothes ... A girl, for God's sake. A slip of a girl. And she had fooled them all. ... A confusing surge of protectiveness flooded him. ... He tipped her face up to look at it, and she reached, almost desperately, for his lips. When they met, Connor could feel the trembling and it birthed a hunger and desire he hadn't expected. As he pressed his lips to hers, there was a sweetness and longing that did more to arouse him than any experienced passion ever had. His arms tightened around her and reason left both of them. There was only need. (127–9)

The long sex scene which follows this kiss is couched in terms of an uncontrollable passion: Samantha arches her body towards Connor in an "instinctive response as old as life itself," his "manhood stretch[es] toward her" of its own accord (129). Connor is—as he shortly announces—now passionately in love with a woman who he believed only moments ago to be a boy. Connor's special interest in Sam up until this moment was, it seems, motivated by heterosexual desire all along. Their now unbridled passion reads as the culmination of a long (if secret) courtship.

In Rita Mae Brown's *High Hearts* (1986), the hero, delirious from a gunshot wound, declares his love to Jimmy Chatfield, the young soldier nursing him. He discovers the boy's secret soon after his recovery, but his earlier declaration acts as proof that he knew all along: "Something in the boy tugged at the corners of his heart" (185). Similarly, the hero of Jude Deveraux's *Velvet Song* (1984) makes love to his "soft" (55) squire when he is ill with a violent fever. The novel ends "happily" with the hero spanking his new wife soundly for all of the trouble her masquerade caused him. When David, in *Almost a Gentleman*, first learns that Mr Marston is a woman, he feels as if he is "waking from a dream" (69): "*A woman. A beautiful woman. The person I've been burning and aching for all this week is a woman. ... And so Stokes— dear, good Stokes—was right about me after all. For I clearly ain't no Nancy-boy*" (68–9). Importantly, this confessional "scene" need not be explicitly narrated in order to be an organizing "moment" in the cross-dressing novel: "I love you" need not follow immediately from the heroine's undressing in the diegesis in order for there to be a constitutive relationship between the two "acts." Instead, this scene is most often envisioned or imagined retroactively. It takes place over time and is condensed into a "scene" by the retrospective logic I have already discussed in some detail. This is, of course, a familiar romantic device which effectively installs the happy ending as a *fait accompli*: "I have loved you from the moment I saw you."

In Kathleen A. Woodiwiss's *Ashes in the Wind* (1980) the happy ending is the cumulative effect of a long and involved plot. The heroine, Alaina MacGaren, is cross-dressed for the first half of the novel and the hero, Cole Latimer, is fooled by the heroine's disguise. The heroine is forced to marry the hero at the end of Part One, and Part Two tells a familiar "marriage for convenience" tale. As I will discuss shortly, Alaina's clothing remains the focus of the second part of the novel; she must be "properly" dressed as a woman before they can be happily married.

Ashes in the Wind is set during the American Civil War. Alaina is framed as a confederate spy and flees her plantation home, Briar Hill, to travel to her uncle's home in New Orleans disguised as an ill-educated boy. When "Al" arrives in New Orleans, he is befriended by "Yankee" doctor, Cole Latimer, who gets him a job working at the local hospital. The novel begins with a long description of Al, just arrived in New Orleans:

> Halfway down the once elegant staircase from the promenade deck, a slender lad stood … Beneath a battered slouch hat pulled low over his ears, wary grey eyes stared out of a begrimed face. Overlarge garments emphasized the smallness of his frame, and the baggy trousers were gathered about his thin waist with a rough rope. He wore a loose cotton jacket over a voluminous shirt, and though its long sleeves were rolled back several times they still flopped over the narrow wrists. … His claim to years appeared no more than a dozen, yet the deliberateness and quiet reserve in his manner belied his apparent youth. (4)

The signals of gender incongruity in this passage are familiar from Heyer's novels and remain typical in novels of the last twenty-five years: slenderness, delicate frame and face, expressive eyes, narrow waist and wrist, disguised hair, apparent youth belied by mature behavior. This description is soon paralleled by a vision of a "tall figure," Cole, whose gender is unquestionable: "wide shoulders," "lean waist," angular facial features (9). Unlike Al, Cole is "a man, completely and totally. It showed in his walk, his speech, his gestures" (24). Within the context of this subgenre, it is clear from these very first descriptions that this uncertain boy and rugged man are "meant for each other."

Cole is further remarkable because of his eyes, which "fringed with dark lashes, seemed capable of piercing to the lad's innermost secrets, causing a chill of fear to go through him" (10). Alaina is similarly disturbed by Cole's eyes early in their marriage: "those thoroughly blue eyes locked on her and slowly raked her. She had forgotten how brilliant and clear they were. In some magical way they seemed capable of stripping the lies from whatever passed between them" (356). The frequent descriptions of Cole's special sight throughout the novel are belied by a plot in which he does not see, or cannot consciously recognize, the truth about Al despite the numerous clues before him. For example, Cole lifts Al onto a horse and declares "You're as soft as a woman" (17); notices his slim frame, delicate feet and "soft" temperament; witnesses Al's aunt and uncle's shock when they first see him; lives in the same house as Al and works closely with him every day at the hospital; and has sex with a mysterious woman and does not detect the lie when Alaina's tall, curvy cousin, Roberta, claims to have been the thin, "boyish" girl he slept with. (He immediately marries Roberta.) Most tellingly, Cole twice sees Alaina dressed as a woman but fails to recognize her as Al.

Alaina dons "widow's weeds" to attend a friend's funeral in New Orleans and rouses Cole's curiosity:

> Though he roweled his memory with cruel spurs of will, he could put no face or name to the woman, yet there was an elusive familiarity about her, something about the way she moved with a bold, almost boyish grace. (153)

The widow attracts Cole because he both recognizes and does not recognize her as either the boy, Al, or as the woman with whom he recently spent a night of consuming passion. Cole finally puts all the clues together when he surprises Alaina in his and Roberta's room where she has been lovingly fingering his wife's luxurious clothes. (Alaina covets Roberta's clothes as much as she desires her husband.) Cole tears Alaina's gown from her as she attempts to run from the room, the first of many "bodice-ripping" scenes in the novel:

> There was only the briefest meeting of soft, bare bosom against hard, furred chest before Alaina tore away with a gasp. … This was *not* Roberta! The form was too small, too slim, too light. He reached out a hand, brushing her hair, and immediately it all came back to him. The short hair! The slim body! His mind rebelled in disbelief. (199)

Cole is deceived by Alaina until he feels and sees her naked body. He can now recognize the object of his love and desire, but cannot be satisfied or happy until he gains control over her clothing.

In Part Two of the novel (after Roberta has died and Cole marries Alaina) he effectively redresses Alaina as a good woman; he makes her body correspond with her clothing by insisting she accept the wardrobe he has purchased for her. Alaina covets, but initially refuses to wear the finery he has purchased for her, assuming that he has married her for convenience rather than love. Cole is outraged by Alaina's refusal to be well-dressed and literally cuts the clothes she is wearing from her, only to be aroused by her naked body: "'You are woman, Alaina,' he murmured huskily" (383). Once the two declare their love, of course, Alaina begins to wear the neglected outfits and the novel can end "happily."

In the contemporary cross-dressing novel, "true" nakedness is opposed to false costume. In contrast to Heyer's heroines, the cross-dressers in these novels never *become* boys or men. Clothing *performs* gender to the extent that the heroine can pass as a man, but this performance is always an "act." In contrast to Heyer's distanced semi-parodic narration, these novels are typically focalized through a heroine who is unhappy in disguise and longs to be properly dressed. They present, over and over again, the scene of dressing in lavish detail. The unhappily dressed heroines are forever opening wardrobes and closets to run their eyes and hands over their beloved dresses and gowns. The heroine of Virginia Henley's *Seduced* (1994), Tony Lamb, sails to France with the hero, Adam Savage, to buy fashions to trade in the Indies:

> If only she could have chosen clothes for herself, she would have been in paradise. She was careful not to let Savage see her looks of longing as she viewed and selected her purchases. Her eyes sparkled at the delicately exquisite materials of the gowns and undergarments spread before her in such colorful array. Silks, gauzes, muslins, satins, laces, pongees, poult-de-soies, tulles, and taffetas in every imaginable hue and design took her fancy and she ordered one of each. (288)

In the cross-dressing subgenre, particulars of costume (fabric, style, color, make-up, hairstyles, shoes, gloves) are treated as innate carriers of meaning, both for the actor and the spectator(s). The heroine of *Devil in Spurs*, Jonty, has been dressed as a boy her whole life, yet "she longed so much to wear pretty, feminine dresses, to feel sheer muslin petticoats and camisoles next to her skin" (89). Tony "[s]ometimes … absolutely lusted for frills and ribbon" (231), as does Chastity in Beverley's *My Lady Notorious* (1993): "She couldn't suppress a laugh of delight at the selection of pretty gowns before her. It had been so long since she'd seen such delicious confections. … She shivered with pleasure as [the chemise] slithered over her skin" (155). Zared Peregrine in Jude Deveraux's *The Conquest* (1991) has lived as a boy since childhood. But all she wants are "the most feminine things": pretty gowns, roses and long hair (242). Zenia Stanhope, the heroine of Laura Kinsale's *The Dream Hunter* (1994) has lived in the desert with her mother her entire life—disguised as a Bedouin boy, "Selim": "she would never be among her own people or have a proper dress as English ladies wore. The thought of the dress made fresh tears roll down her cheeks" (21).

Cross-dressing romances insist upon a natural or causal relationship between anatomical sex and "true clothing," between femaleness and feminine frills and flounces, between maleness and strongly tailored lines and heavy fabrics. In two novels set in the Regency period, *My Lady Notorious* and *Seduced*, the heroes flout the dictates of fashion and refuse to be fops. Their masculinity is affronted by the effeminacy of the dandy. Despite the explicit critique of gender norms, in the end, within the terms of these novels "feminine" or "masculine" clothing "expresses" an absolutely natural and perfectly intelligible "truth." To be fooled by a cross-dresser is simply to read gender "correctly."

When Jonty is injured and rips her shirt and breast bindings, Cord sees her naked breasts and cannot believe he hasn't "seen it before": "'Ever since you've known her, you've been conditioned to believe she was a male'" (186). However, Cord has *desired* Jonty all along; his discovery that Jonty is a woman rewrites his attraction as always already heterosexual. Similarly, in Catherine Coulter's novel *Lord Harry's Folly* (1980) the hero, Lord Jason Cavander, realizes that Lord Harry Monteith and Miss Henrietta Rolland are one and the same person when he injures her in a duel and removes her bloody shirt and breast bindings. Her body finally "makes sense." Harry had previously struck Jason as "a complex puzzle whose pieces simply do not fit together" (136). It is only when he sees Harry's partly naked body—"the gentle inward curving to a slender waist, the soft smoothness of the white skin"—that his "benumbed mind [is jarred] into the undeniable truth. Lord Harry Monteith was a girl!'":

How strange that looking down at her now, everything made sense; the myriad parts he had thought about so fancifully now fit perfectly together. ... Curling ringlets were working themselves loose from the black ribbon at her neck, and the thick pomade no longer held the curls back from her forehead. ... It was often said that the clothes made the man. He was now inclined to believe, rather, that one saw what one expected to see. Lord Monteith dressed as a gentleman, talked like a gentleman and partook in all the gentleman's sports. Everyone had accepted him as such. Now, gazing down at her undeniably feminine face, he was forced to admit that she had pulled the wool over everyone's eyes. (166)

Once Cord and Jason see Jonty's and Hetty's naked bodies, they are suddenly able to see the women's "undeniable" femininity. This new-found perception and, indeed, the heroines' success playing men, depends upon an *unsustained* distinction between female- or maleness and femininity or masculinity; between anatomical sex and gender display. Harry's masculinity is read as a sign of maleness, despite his appearing "deuced unusual" (136). On the one hand, femininity or masculinity is a consequence, or an expression, of female- or maleness to the extent that one *means* the other: Hetty's body gives away her "femininity" as much as it gives away her femaleness—one equals the other. On the other hand, a distinction must be maintained between the two in order for the plot to work; femaleness can be concealed *and* it cannot be concealed.

In *My Lady Notorious*, *The Conquest*, Coulter's *Night Storm* (1990), Johanna Lindsey's *Gentle Rogue* (1990), and Laura Kinsale's *The Prince of Midnight* (1990) the hero is never fooled. The heroine deceives everyone *except the hero*; it is precisely his "business to know." The heroine of *The Conquest*, Zared Peregrine, has been disguised as a boy since infancy to protect her from the Howards, a rival wealthy family with whom the Peregrines have been feuding for generations. The novel is set in mid-fifteenth-century England and tells of crumbling castles peopled with handsome knights, pretty maidens, and vengeful ghosts. Zared is captured by Tearle Howard's men early in the novel and Tearle is amazed to realize that he is the only one who can see through her disguise: "Tearle could only gape at the men. Couldn't they see that they held a girl? Couldn't they tell the difference between girls and boys?" (17). In these novels, the truly "masculine" man can always tell the difference between boys and girls; heterosexual desire will always recognize its object. Zared escapes and travels to a tournament with her older brother, Severn, where she is immediately besotted by the "beautiful" knight, Colburn. Unlike Tearle, Colburn is both deceived by Zared's disguise and fails to be aroused by her when she helps him bathe. Zared misreads Tearle's special ability to see through her costume as evidence that he is less-than-masculine: "he'd known she was female, but that was probably because he was half-female himself" (35). Tearle sets about proving his masculinity to her by disguising himself as the "Black Knight" at the tournament and besting Colburn: "I am made of sterner stuff than you imagine. In fact, I think that now I am made of steel. Do you know of a sheath where I could hide my sword?" (257). Tearle's masculinity is put in question by his desire for a cross-dressed woman even though he knows her to be a woman. The ribaldry of his "medieval" pick-up line brings into (comic) relief the cross-dressing plot's excessive loyalty to the heterosexual matrix; however, the "humor" of his sexual overture cannot disguise its implied violence.

The heroines of *Night Storm* and Johanna Lindsey's *Fires of Winter* (1980), the only cross-dressers in the examples of the subgenre selected for this chapter who don't long for "feminine" clothing, are violently redressed by the heroes. Both women are coerced into "true clothing." Contrary to generic precedent, neither Eugenia Paxton (*Night Storm*) nor Lady Brenna (*Fires of Winter*) have to dress as a man to protect themselves or others; they are cross-dressers by choice. Eugenia does, however, make a vain attempt to fool the hero with her disguise: "Alec knew women, knew how they felt down to the fragile bones in their wrists, and he wondered just who this girl was trying to fool" (24). The cap which Eugenia wears to hide her long hair becomes an object of hatred for the hero, whose early fantasies about her begin with him pulling off her "ridiculous cap." He is determined to see the body he desires dressed in suitable clothing and sets out to ensure that Eugenia becomes too aware of her "femininity" to keep up her masquerade. In the most disturbing scene in this truly offensive novel, Alec ties Eugenia to a bed, rips off her clothing and rapes her: "When I'm finished with you, Mr. Eugene, you're going to wonder why you ever wanted to ape a man, you'll relish your womanness so much. You'll probably burn all your breeches" (128). In *Fires of Winter*, Lady Brenna is also raped by her hero, Garrick Haardrad: "I will master you in the one sure way a man dominates a woman. I will have you" (105). Both women enjoy the rape despite themselves—Brenna has a "traitorous body" (123). Their first sexual experience violently and effectively installs their femininity. Their newly awakened sexual desire for the hero teaches them to (want to) be "women." While rape scenes are much less common in more recent examples of the genre (see Modleski, "Romance Reader" and Ramsdell), the assumption persists that desire for the hero will put an errant heroine back in her place. For instance, the heroes of both *Lord Trenchard's Choice* (2002) and *Almost a Gentleman* (2003) set out to make the heroine "want" to dress as a woman again. Following her rape, Eugenia asks Alec for sex in exactly these terms: "I want to be a woman now, Alec" (192). Alec is delighted with the progress of his seduction:

> She would soon want to accept the fact that she was a woman—his woman. She would want to wear her woman's clothes, she would want to bear his children, she would want him to care for her. She would come to accept what she was meant to be. He would see that it was so. (231)

However, it is precisely Eugenia's disguise which most provokes and excites Alec's interest in her: "Here he was, randy as a mountain goat, for a female dressed as a man" (164). Garrick is similarly impressed by Brenna in male clothing: "Her slim form was made for pleasure, not wielding a sword" (88). Nathaniel Hawke, in *Lord Trenchard's Choice*, finds it difficult to look away from Georgiana's legs in culottes (357). In this subgenre, it is the cross-dressed woman's disguise which attracts the hero *differently* or makes him "love" her; cross-dressing is a narrative trope which triggers and facilitates a heterosexual romance.

In *Undoing Gender*, Butler thinks through the political and personal implications of her theorization of gender performativity in some detail. In particular, she considers the upshot of one's awareness that "I am always constituted by norms that are not of my making" (15). For Butler such self-understanding necessitates an attempt to "understand the ways that constitution takes place" (15). Popular romance fiction, and especially the cross-dressing novel, pursues both of these issues with a particular focus on gender. In short, the analytical self-reflection in this subgenre comes down to two questions: (1) What are the implications of the heroine's (and to a lesser extent the hero's) recognition that gender norms are a social construct? (2) How then does the heroine come to own (and welcome) her gender? The experience which makes the movement from the first to the second of these questions possible is invariably falling in love with a man; the progress of heterosexual love involves a stabilization of gender.

Butler writes, "The staging and structuring of affect and desire is clearly one way in which norms work their way into what feels most properly to belong to me" (15). Much of her discussion in *Undoing Gender* builds on a metaphorics of doing (and undoing):

> If gender is a kind of doing, an incessant activity performed, in part, without one's knowing and without one's willing, it is not for that reason automatic or mechanical. On the contrary, it is a practice of improvisation within a scene of constraint. Moreover, one does not "do" one's gender alone. One is always "doing" with or for another, even if the other is only imaginary. What I call my "own" gender appears perhaps at times as something that I author or, indeed, own. But the terms that make up one's own gender are, from the start, outside oneself, beyond oneself in a sociality that has no single author (and that radically contests the notion of authorship itself). (1)

The idea of "doing" advances her theorization of gender and sexuality as simultaneously subjective and social categories: "I cannot be who I am without drawing upon the sociality of norms that precede and exceed me" (32). For Butler, defining gender and sexuality must begin from recognition of the "constitutive sociality of the self" (19). She considers what it means to talk about "*my* sexuality or *my* gender" if "[n]either of these is precisely a possession, but both are to be understood as *modes of being dispossessed*, ways of being for another, or, indeed, by virtue of another" (19). She writes, "Let's face it. We're undone by each other. And if we're not, we're missing something" (19). I think that such claims resonate with popular texts about heterosexual relations as much as they do with self-consciously queer texts. As I hope this book illustrates, to shy from applying the extraordinary analytical tools Butler gives us to tales of heterosexual love and romance would be to miss an opportunity to track the operations of heterosexual hegemony over the very terrain where they seem most straightforward.

When Lord David Hervey and Mr Philip "Phizz" Marston first meet in *Almost a Gentleman*, both are almost "undone" by the experience. David is "astonished and rather shaken by the feelings that had seized him" (10), but is in no doubt that his attraction to the elegant young dandy is sexual: "He wasn't the sort of man for an exotic passion. But there was no denying that he'd felt something—a bolt of strange cold lightning had flashed through him when he'd returned the young man's gaze" (11). Philip (Phoebe) is similarly unsettled by David: "*Tonight I met the first gentleman ever ... to make me feel, to make me* want *to feel like a woman*" (22, italics and ellipses in original). Of course, this novel is a radically different kind of text to *Undoing Gender*. Nevertheless, its deployment of a metaphorics of doing and undoing (e.g. 6, 9, 22, 82, 121) resonates in quite remarkable ways with Butler's use of these terms to rethink gender performativity. In particular, this novel uses an opposition of doing and being to think of the body as, in Butler's terms, the "site where 'doing' and 'being done to' become equivocal" (21). After meeting David, Phoebe considers the future of her masquerade for the first time: "Oh, her disguise was clever enough; she'd *done* a good job of turning her unusual looks into those of an exquisitely well-realized dandy … She was so convincing as a man because she didn't ever want to *be* a woman again" (22, my emphasis). Gender is something Phoebe "does," but only until her performance of the role of Mr Marston clashes with the return to femininity triggered by her desire for a man. When David unmasks Phoebe and offers her his help, Phoebe feels "As though there were nothing more natural than my soliciting aid from someone who has the power to expose and undo me" (82).

To a degree, the stabilization of gender positions which follows the revelation of the heroine's sex and the mutual declaration of love between the hero and heroine are examples of what Butler describes as the "regulatory operation of power that naturalizes the hegemonic instance" (*Undoing Gender* 43). The conclusions of cross-dressing novels invariably effect a reinscription of a "restrictive discourse on gender that insists on the binary of man and woman as the exclusive way to understand the gender field." However, while Butler goes on to say that such regulatory maneuvers within heterosexual hegemony "[foreclose] the thinkability of its disruption," I don't see evidence for this in popular historical romance fiction. To the contrary, the degree to which these novels open gaps through which to re-examine heterosexuality is, for me, precisely what makes them so fascinating.

Annamarie Jagose offers Kath Weston's critique of Butler's focus on performativity as an example of the kind of "serious misreading" which predominates in discussions of Butler. She argues that Weston's critique fails to the extent that she equates performativity with "voluntary theatricality"; a misreading which begins with her title: "Do Clothes Make the Woman?" (89). Jagose cites a passage from *Bodies That Matter*—"fortuitously rendered in the same vocabulary"—in reply to Weston's leading question: "The publication of *Gender Trouble* coincided with a number of publications that did assert that 'clothes make the woman,' but I never did think that gender was like clothes, or that clothes make the woman" (231; qtd. in Jagose 89). In these terms, recent cross-dressing novels can start to look like a bad reading of Butler. Cross-dressing plots are singularly unable to reconcile a belief in the effectivity of gender disguise with a demonstrated faith in a causal relationship between anatomical sex, appearance, and behavior. In these novels, "clothes make the woman" (or the man) both in the sense that they control how any given body will be read by others and also because, in the genre's own terms, a "properly" gendered costume completes the process of becoming a "woman." In Chapters 4 and 6, I examine the representation of the "figure of woman" in literary historical romance novels. As my discussions of Sarah Woodruff and Christobel LaMotte make clear, the nature of the relationship between a woman's body and her "performance," between her sex, her gender, and her sexuality, is a preoccupation which runs through this genre. Studying cross-dressing novels helps to bring issues at the heart of historical romance fiction into sharp relief.

PART III
Literary Historical Romance Fiction:
Victorian Romances

Chapter 5

"Who is Sarah?": History and Heterosexuality in John Fowles's *The French Lieutenant's Woman*

The woman had no face, no particular degree of sexuality. But she was Victorian; and since I always saw her in the same static long shot, with her back turned, she represented a reproach on the Victorian age. An outcast. I didn't know her crime, but I wished to protect her. That is, I began to fall in love with her. Or with her stance. I don't know which. (Fowles, "Notes" 136)

In the introduction to his well-known essay "Notes on an Unfinished Novel" John Fowles tells of the "pregnant female image" (137) which inspired him to write *The French Lieutenant's Woman*. His tale of the novel's "birth" has been taken up with some enthusiasm by commentators on Fowles's work who frequently retell it in their discussions of the novel. Fowles writes that the novel "started as a visual image. A woman stands at the end of a deserted quay and stares out to sea. That was all" (137). The image first appeared to him one morning when he was still half asleep and persisted in his thoughts until he began deliberately to invoke it. Peter Conradi writes that Fowles "has given a valuable account of the novel's genesis. He was imaginatively solicited by the figure of a woman staring out to sea" (59). Discussions of *The French Lieutenant's Woman* reveal an unspoken consensus about the significance and usefulness of this anecdote to Fowles's readers. As I see it, this consensus has two aspects. First, Fowles's story is to be treated as a "gift" which grants us special access to the author's thoughts—his dreams no less—and thus to the novel's meaning. Second, the most important thing "Notes on an Unfinished Novel" tells us is that Fowles is in love with his heroine. However, the introduction to "Notes" can be read as more than simply an anecdote of artistic inspiration or as a kind of love story between author and character. I read it, rather, as an unintentional condensation of the novel's thematic preoccupations, its generic and historical assumptions, and its narrative logic and force. The interpretive agreement about this text is my starting point for thinking of ways to read this fascinating novel differently than prevailing assumptions about how to read it have previously allowed or encouraged. The most important thing Fowles's essay does is to highlight the importance and the mutually constitutive force of romance, history and heterosexuality in *The French Lieutenant's Woman*.

Katherine Tarbox's introduction to her chapter on *The French Lieutenant's Woman* typifies the use to which "Notes" is most commonly put in academic discussions of the novel:

> As Fowles tells it, the vision of Sarah Woodruff came to him early one morning as he
> lay asleep. He saw her as she first appeared to Charles Smithson: at the end of the Cobb,
> looking accusingly into the sea. He fell in love with that face. Fowles was working on
> another project (several projects, as a matter of fact) at the time, but the vision was so
> intrusive and compelling that he was forced to lay aside his other work and follow the
> mysterious Sarah wherever she might lead. So into Fowles's life she came, in much the
> same way she came into Smithson's: commanding interest and attention, and pushing
> rivals aside with a look. That the author and his protagonist are both in love with the
> heroine is one of the many eccentric features of this eccentric novel. (60)[1]

There is, undoubtedly, a weird narrative trajectory in Fowles's essay which sees him
falling in love with, impregnating, and finally marrying his heroine: he "began to
fall in love with her" (136); characters are like "lovers" to whom he is the "active
partner—the writer—and only something like love can provide the energy" (137);
his "seed germinates" (138) and the "not literally—pregnant female image" (137)
which appeared to him can give birth to a novel; writing, after all, "is like ... making
love; a natural process, not an artificial one" (138); finally he is "condemned to a
marriage of sorts—I have the woman on the quay (whose name is Sarah) for better or
for worse" (144). This brings into play precisely the kind of gender opposition I have
argued informs and persists in the grammar of the romantic speech act: "I (masculine
subject) love you (feminine object)." Yet commentators on this novel persist in
talking about Sarah as the "active partner" in her "*affaire*," to use Fowles's term,
with the writer; she is the temptress, the muse, the fallen woman, the whore. There is
an oddly retroactive temporality at work in Tarbox's paraphrase of the introduction
to "Notes" according to which Fowles's "vision" was of "Sarah" rather than simply
"a woman." In these terms, Sarah Woodruff has an autonomy and an agency which
precedes and indeed is the origin for Fowles's naming and representation of her.
Sarah seduces—or to use Conradi's word "solicits"—author and character alike.
"Commanding interest and attention," Sarah is the instigator of both relationships.
In effect, according to the rhetoric of this passage, Sarah is responsible for the
production of the novel in which she features.

In Tarbox's paraphrase of Fowles's story of the novel's genesis, "Sarah" first
appears to Fowles "looking accusingly into the sea. He fell in love with that face."
Fowles writes:

> The woman had no face, no particular degree of sexuality. But she was Victorian; and
> since I always saw her in the same static long shot, with her back turned, she represented
> a reproach on the Victorian age. An outcast. I didn't know her crime, but I wished to
> protect her. That is, I began to fall in love with her. Or with her stance. I don't know
> which. (136)

Tarbox so conflates Fowles with Charles Smithson, the visual image with Sarah,
"Notes" with the finished novel, that each begins to take on the characteristics of
the other. This is, however, a conflation that Fowles's rhetoric (both here and in the
novel) encourages; the visual image is both *this* woman and *any* woman: "perhaps

---

1   See also Barnum 52–3; Onega 9. Fowles has also written of the "single image" which
inspired *A Maggot*; see Balsamo 138.

Charles is myself disguised. … Modern women like Sarah exist, and I have never understood them" (*French* 85). She is a historical character, and yet history is irrelevant to her characterization.

This is the first of two chapters about *The French Lieutenant's Woman*.[2] It argues that the characterization of Sarah Woodruff as a woman who defies the Victorian age is crucial to her function as a romantic heroine. This chapter lays the groundwork for the next in which I seek to elucidate the joint importance of two speech acts to the structure of this historical novel: "I love you" and "Shame on you!"

"Who is Sarah?": The Role of the Heroine

The French Lieutenant's Woman tells the story of Charles Smithson and Sarah Woodruff; throughout the novel, readers are positioned to share Charles's and the narrator's fascination with Sarah, rather than to identify with the heroine. One of the most frequently cited sections of this much discussed novel is the narrator's intrusion at the beginning of Chapter 13. At the conclusion of Chapter 12, the reader is cast as a spy of sorts, or indeed as a "peeping tom," watching Sarah through her bedroom window. This is, importantly, not the first or last time Sarah is "spied" upon in the novel. In a crucial sense, she is frequently figured as the object of a manifold gaze, sometimes censoring, sometimes desiring, oftentimes both:

> Later that night Sarah might have been seen—though I cannot think by whom, unless a passing owl—standing at the open window of her unlit bedroom. The house was silent, and the town as well, for people went to bed by nine in those days before electricity and television. It was now one o'clock. Sarah was in her nightgown, with her hair loose; and she was staring out to sea. A distant lantern winked faintly on the black waters out towards Portland Bill, where some ship sailed towards Bridport. Sarah had seen the tiny point of light; and not given it a second thought.
>
> If you had gone closer still, you would have seen that her face was wet with silent tears.

---

2   *The French Lieutenant's Woman* is a widely discussed novel. In contrast to my emphasis here, studies of the novel aim most often to read it in terms of the principal philosophical and political influences on Fowles's life and work, especially existentialism (see Pohler 57) and Jungian psychoanalysis. These studies often involve comparative analysis of *The French Lieutenant's Woman* with Fowles's other novels and with his 1964 philosophical volume, *The Aristos*: see Balsamo, Conradi, Eddins, Ferrebe, Lynch, and Tarbox. Most of these references focus on Fowles's commitment to existentialist philosophy. Carol Barnum's *The Fiction of John Fowles: A Myth for Our Time* is the most detailed Jungian analysis of Fowles's novels. The popularity of focusing on the relationship between the novelist and his novel has also produced a number of comparative studies of the published novels and Fowles's manuscripts (Smith; Mansfield). For other critics, the most important thing to notice about *The French Lieutenant's Woman* is its "metafictional" structure. The key proponent of this argument is Linda Hutcheon (see also Holmes, "The Novel"; Onega). These critics tend to emphasize the "postmodernist" qualities of Fowles's fiction. For the most extensive analysis of Fowles's fiction as postmodernist, see Salami. A number of critics argue that *The French Lieutenant's Woman* sets out principally to upset the opposition between realism and romance (Binns; Johnson; Brown). I will be steering clear of much of this material in order to focus on theoretical questions which have fallen outside the scope of the most common approaches to the novel.

> She was not standing at her window as part of her mysterious vigil for Satan's sails; but as a preliminary to jumping from it.
>
> I will not make her teeter on the window-sill; or sway forward, and then collapse sobbing back on to the worn carpet of her room. We know she was alive a fortnight after this incident, and therefore she did not jump. (83–4)

We learn certain important things about Sarah in this passage; however, I would argue that the most important thing that we "learn" here is that there is only so much we can see and know about Sarah; in the book's own terms, what we don't know is much more important to her status as the novel's heroine. If Sarah is not staring out to sea in the hope that she might see her lost lover's ship returning, then why does she stare so? Why is she so miserable? More pertinently this passage suggests a relationship between history and fiction which guarantees Sarah's unknowability, her mystery. Not only does Sarah "exist" in a time distant from our own, before electricity and television, but she is the product of her author's imagination ("I will not make her teeter on the window-sill …") and he can tell us as little or as much as he likes about her; we are ripe for teasing. We cannot pass by her window (the narrator tells us she "might have been seen—though [he] cannot think by whom") but must rely on the narrator (the "novelist") to describe the scene for us and to tell us his character's thoughts. However—and here's the rub—Sarah is a mystery even to the narrator/"novelist."

Chapter 12 finishes with the question, "Who is Sarah? Out of what shadows does she come?" (84) and Chapter 13 begins with the response, "I do not know" (85). This intriguing shift from narrative to something like literary criticism is followed by the narrator's musings on the relationship between the novelist and his characters. Analysis of this part of the text reveals some clues to the nature of Sarah's narrative function. The narrator states that the novelist "stands next to God" (85), but not in the sense that we might imagine. Rather, "[t]here is only one good definition of God: the freedom that allows other freedoms to exist. And I must conform to that definition" (86). The distinction between an "omniscient and decreeing" (86) God and the narrator's non-interventionist divinity is couched in terms of a broader opposition, that between the Victorian age and our own: "If I have pretended until now to know my characters' minds and innermost thoughts, it is because I am writing in … a convention universally accepted at the time of my story: the novelist stands next to God. He may not know all, yet he tries to pretend that he does" (85). The new novelist, the argument runs, is entirely more honest, more liberal, more responsible to the degree that he acknowledges his shortcomings and foibles. The novelist of the late twentieth century writes "in the new theological image, with freedom our first principle, not authority" (86). The novelist, that is, is no puppeteer. His original intention, so he says, was to "tell all" about Sarah at this stage ("*Chap. Thirteen—unfolding of Sarah's true state of mind*" (85)); his plan, that is, was to write as a nineteenth-century novelist might have done. Instead he finds himself "suddenly like a man in the sharp spring night, watching from the lawn" (85). He casts himself in exactly the same position or rôle as that into which he has only just cast his readers: a spectator, a voyeur fascinated by what he might see through a woman's open bedroom window, but only able to see so much: "But I am a novelist, not a man in a garden—I can follow her where I like? But possibility is not permissibility.

Husbands could often murder their wives—and the reverse—and get away with it. But they don't" (86). The relationships between writer and heroine and reader and heroine are thus aligned and, perhaps more importantly, heterosexualized.

The image of a woman at her bedroom window (the particular setting of this episode is not, of course, insignificant) seems to have prompted a number of interrelated questions for the "novelist": How can or should he write (and indeed, how can we read) about the mid-nineteenth century, or more particularly, how can or should he write about a Victorian woman? What is the writer's relationship to his characters? What does it mean to be a twentieth-century novelist writing about a historical period to which he can have no direct access? How can he best negotiate the relationship between history and literature? The question that this chapter prompts me to ask is of a somewhat different kind: Why is it Sarah, most particularly, who inspires this metafictional break in the story?[3]

In her book *Romancing the Postmodern* Diane Elam insists on the centrality of the "figure of woman; for within the postmodern romance the figure of woman is what allows the work of re-membering to be performed" (16). This is a fascinating argument to bring to bear on Fowles's novel and the representation of its title character. Elam writes:

> Postmodernity's re-membering of the past is performed through a re-engendering of the historical past as romance. That is to say, the figure of woman is what allows the past to be represented (via the en-gendering of romance), but she is also the figure whose very inscription reveals, through the play of gender, the impossibility of accurate and complete representation. (16)

Postmodern fiction's negotiation with the past is enabled by inhabiting the tropes and adopting the terms of romance. That is to say, romance, whose metonymic figure is (a mysterious) "woman," provides the means by which postmodernity can re-present the past. Elam runs this argument against what she calls a "realist discourse on romance as 'women's literature.'" "If romance evokes an unrepresentable other side to history," she writes, "realism displaces the problem of unrepresentability onto gender" (16). Realism dismisses romance as just "female fantasy." In a now familiar theoretical move, Elam suggests that this dismissal fails to the extent that romance is the constitutive outside of realism; "female fantasy" is foundational and thus necessary to what would exclude it.

Elam maps the opposition realism/romance onto the opposition modern/postmodern; both oppositions whose terms, as she carefully demonstrates, are not mutually exclusive. For Elam, "[r]omance by virtue of its complex relationship to both history and novelistic realism, will have been the genre to address postmodernity in narrative fiction" (1). From this perspective, postmodernism does not follow, nor is it simply opposed to, modernism. Romance, she insists, has been postmodern all

---

3   At one point in Chapter 13, the narrator refers specifically to Charles's disobedience: "When Charles left Sarah on her cliff-edge, I ordered him to walk straight back to Lyme Regis. But he did not; he gratuitously turned and went down to the dairy" (86). Nevertheless, Sarah's "mystery," not Charles's supposed impertinence, triggers the narrator's self-analysis.

along. It's a question of a "counter-discourse" on history and representation being, to use Elam's delightful pun, "delayed in the post":

> [R]omance, as a signature of the possibility of postmodernism, is always present to *modernist* discourse. Postmodernism, that is, does not simply come after modernism but is a counter-discourse on history and the real which modernism must repress in order to establish itself as a statement of the real. History is always a consideration, but what it might mean to the historical is a point of contestation. Thus, the relationship between postmodernism and romance does not allow for any straightforward historical narrative. Postmodernism is not a perspectival view on history; it is the rethinking of history as an ironic coexistence of temporalities. (3)

The flip-side of this analysis is that the more straightforward, the less ironic, lingers in the postmodern as a signature of the modern. For Elam, this is precisely the importance of the figure of woman in "postmodern romance," a generic category in which she includes the work of Walter Scott and George Eliot. Of course, if we accept the argument of *Romancing the Postmodern*, then *all* historical romance is to some extent characterized by the "postmodern."

As I explained in Chapter 1, rather than use the term "postmodern romance," I prefer the looser generic category of "historical romance fiction." This approach allows me to discuss novels by Georgette Heyer and Norah Roberts alongside those by Fowles and A.S. Byatt without overstretching the limits of my nomenclature. Anachronism, after all, is foundational throughout this genre. The "ironic coexistence of temporalities" which Elam points out is not peculiar to the high end of the genre. Instead the bringing together of "history" with "romance," which, for me, accurately names this genre, produces the kinds of conflicts and confusions which Elam uncovers not just in books by Eco, Fowles or Sontag, but also in novels which I cannot comfortably call "postmodern." The idea that the "figure of woman" enacts the temporal collapse necessary to the writing of historical fiction is as relevant to the study of popular fiction as it is to the study of literature. The cliché of the spirited heroine, the woman ahead of her time, provides simple evidence of this.

Fowles has been described as both a modernist and a postmodernist, and with comparative enthusiasm and confidence.[4] Following Elam (and despite her preference for the term "postmodern romance") any clean distinctions between modernity and postmodernity, realism and romance, become less easy the more we think on them. In any case, it is not my aim to answer the question of Fowles's modernism or postmodernism, but rather to suggest that his combination of literature and history in *The French Lieutenant's Woman* is nothing if not troubled by the competing discourses which inform him. Fowles's ironic, "postmodern," treatment of genre—his playful (or precocious) literary historiography—proceeds on the basis of a less ironic, more "modern" treatment of gender and sexuality. Historical romance is precisely the genre within which realism and romance can be said to lock horns. Fowles begins "Notes on an Unfinished Novel" with the information that his next book "(provisionally entitled *The French Lieutenant's Woman*) is set

---

4   For references to Fowles's "modernism" see Walker and Lovell. For references to his "postmodernism" see Salami, Onega, and Balsamo.

about a hundred years back." His next sentence denies the importance of this setting: "I don't think of it as a historical novel, a genre in which I have very little interest" (136). Fowles's interest, we can discern from the tale of the mysterious female image which follows his denial, is to "re-engender the past as romance."

Referring specifically to the work of Scott and Eco's *The Name of the Rose*, Elam generalizes about the fate of women in "postmodern romance":

> History is preserved from fantasy and its anachronisms only by the becoming-fantastic of the female. The fantastic returns as the gendered complement of the real historical male that sought to exclude it. Woman, that is, may permit the past to be represented as romance, but the price of this is that she herself cannot be adequately represented. ... [T]he past is brought back within the ambit of representation only at the price of woman's expulsion from it. (16)

Her analysis of the extent to which the "figure of woman" has enabled negotiations of literature and history allows us to contextualize Fowles's novel in more productive ways than an emphasis on the specialness or uniqueness of his characterization of Sarah does: "Woman, in a sense, phrases history and its uncertainty in her simultaneous status as excluded from history and yet most fiercely historical" (17). Once we recognize that the figure of the unrepresentable or mysterious woman is itself a trope of historical romance, from Scott through to Eco, the significance of "Notes" and of Fowles's characterization of Sarah is less a question of Fowles's eccentricity than of his mobilization of a powerful and entirely predictable metaphor.

In his discussion of "Notes on an Unfinished Novel" Conradi writes that Fowles is "solicited" by the woman on the quay. His choice of verb is noteworthy: "[Fowles] was imaginatively solicited by the figure of a woman staring out to sea" (59). Fowles is momentarily installed as the client of a Victorian prostitute. Such a relationship, however fleetingly pictured, can be posed only by virtue of the dissemination of the "figure of woman" *across* history. Sarah exceeds history and representation; as a catalyst for romance, she is rendered absolutely knowable. She is the "figure of woman" who enables Fowles's negotiation of the past and the present, his ironic intertexts, and unreliable narration—those features of the novel most often cited as evidence of his literary accomplishment and his postmodernity.

If, as I have argued throughout this book, "I love you" is the linguistic or verbal signature of romance, then the image of a mysterious woman might well be its visual equivalent. *The French Lieutenant's Woman* opens with an epigraph from Thomas Hardy's poem "The Riddle":

> Stretching eyes west
> Over the sea,
> Wind foul or fair,
> Always stood she
> Prospect-impressed;
> Solely out there
> Did her gaze rest,
> Never elsewhere
> Seemed charm to be. (7)

This poem effectively circumscribes or marks the limits of the narrative which follows; the "riddle" of this novel is the "figure of woman." In the opening paragraph of "Notes on an Unfinished Novel" Fowles suggests that, while he cannot pinpoint its origin, the image of the woman on the quay most probably represents the cumulative effect of years spent collecting books and prints from past centuries.

Hardy's poem represents only one "source" for Fowles's characterization of Sarah and for her narrative function. In her essay about the translation of *The French Lieutenant's Woman* into film, "Feminism and Form in the Literary Adaptation," Terry Lovell describes Sarah as a "composite figure, reminiscent of a good many Victorian heroines" (116). Lovell notes particularly Sarah's resemblance to Hardy's Tess and to Jane Eyre. She goes on to argue that Fowles's "modernism permits him to lift these figures out of the narrative and subject them to critical scrutiny alongside the literary conventions which produced them and their predecessors, and the historical contexts, Victorian and contemporary, which they reference" (116). While approaching the question from a different direction to Elam, Lovell also recognizes that the mythic figure of woman facilitates novelistic negotiations of history and literature. Lovell's analysis falls short of Elam's, however, because she fails to acknowledge that this "strategy" works *at the expense of* women's historical specificity. Having described the "use" to which this "composite figure" is put in *The French Lieutenant's Woman* ("to trigger the discursive and documentary interruptions to the narrative flow, in which comparisons are drawn between nineteenth- and twentieth-century attitudes and practices, sexual, social, and literary"), Lovell suggests that Fowles's novel might provide evidence for the claim "which links narrative disruption with progressive politics and aesthetics" (116). The disruptive impact of the unknowable woman, the woman who exceeds history and representation, in this novel is less the effect of a "progressive politics and aesthetics" than of the mobilization of a powerful literary convention. Indeed, this notion of political and aesthetic progress sits uneasily with the rest of Lovell's analysis. Later in her essay, she notes the conservatism of the novel when she argues that "Fowles uses gender as *the* polarity which structures all aspects of human life. ... [Sarah] stands for 'woman'—timeless, unchanging, mysterious" (120).

Lovell draws on Tzvetan Todorov's interpretation of narrative as a progression through "order—disturbance—reordering" in order to analyze Sarah's narrative function. In Todorov's analysis, it is the appearance of something out of order on the fictional scene which initiates the narrative process. Lovell notes the extent to which women tend to perform this narrative function: "It may be the sexual desire she provokes which constitutes the 'problem' which the narrative must resolve, or the anomalous position she occupies. Women may also function within the novel as catalyst, stumbling block or test of some kind for the male protagonist" (115). Sarah is the problem of *The French Lieutenant's Woman*. While in general terms there is nothing unique about the place Sarah holds or the role she fulfills in this book, she is a fascinating character to the extent that she exposes the mundane but nevertheless complex processes through which the heterosexual subject is formed. Also, her characterization helps to illustrate that the subject does not emerge fully formed and coherent from a single formative process—there is no one event which makes a subject, so to speak—but rather these processes are repeatedly played out, rehearsed and reinforced throughout a subject's life. To the extent that it might be said to "stage" the various performative and interpellative mechanisms which make a heterosexual subject what he or she is (and is not), *The French Lieutenant's Woman* allegorizes the processes of subjectification as a series of "scenes."

I turn now to a consideration of the extent to which Sarah's characterization proceeds in the terms of a still pervasive or habitual way of thinking about the relationship between sex and power in the Victorian age. (Indeed the same can be said about other key players in this novel. I will get to them a little later.) This will lead into a close analysis of the opening chapters of the novel: Charles Smithson and Ernestina Freeman's meeting with Sarah on the Cobb.

Sarah and the Myth of Victorian Sexuality

Fowles writes of his vision: "The woman had no face, no particular degree of sexuality. But she was Victorian ...." There is a telling slippage between these two sentences: the woman has "no particular degree of sexuality," *but* she is Victorian, a description which cannot help but invoke the question of sexuality. The force of that "but" is qualificatory: it brings into play a discourse of "negative" sexuality; "Victorianness" in what Fowles's narrator calls its "derogatory sense" (234). Post-Foucault, we are in familiar territory here. Fowles's rhetorical maneuver is enabled by the "repressive hypothesis," first defined by Foucault in Part 1 of *The History of Sexuality, Volume 1*: "We 'Other Victorians.'" Fowles characterizes the woman on the quay as an "outcast," rebuked by but also rebuking Victorian society. The rhetoric of repression which produces and sustains this description of a cast-out Victorian woman is circumscribed by the sexual despite Fowles's statement to the contrary ("I didn't know her crime, but I wished to protect her"). To this extent, the nature of her crime is an open secret. This pretty scene, presented to us in "static long shot" by Fowles, is a snapshot of what Fowles would call the "hypocrisy" of Victorian sexuality.

The "Victorian age" in this novel describes, quite simply, the "age of repression" (Foucault 5); in a sense, the ontological link between sex and repression "belongs" to the Victorian age. Foucault prefaces his introduction of the term "repressive hypothesis" with a recitation of the discourse which his term describes. He begins: "For a long time, *the story goes*, we supported a Victorian regime and we continue to be dominated by it even today" (3, my emphasis). In simple terms *The French Lieutenant's Woman* can be read as one such story. Fowles's tale of Victorian sexuality, of the relationship between Victorian and contemporary sexuality, depends upon the repressive hypothesis in order to make sense.

Foucault suggests that we must "ask why we burden ourselves today with so much guilt for having once made sex a sin. What paths have brought us to the point where we are 'at fault' with respect to our own sex? And how have we come to be a civilization so peculiar as to tell itself that, through an abuse of power which has not ended, it has long 'sinned' against sex?" (9) In his early study of Fowles, Barry Olshen writes that "heterosexual love and the nature of freedom are the thematic centers of all his work" (14). Foucault helps bring the link between these two themes into focus:

> And the sexual cause—the demand for sexual freedom, but also for the knowledge to be gained from sex and the right to speak about it—becomes legitimately associated with the honor of a political cause: sex too is placed on the agenda for the future. (6)

To a certain extent, Sarah's sexuality is the catalyst for Charles's liberation from the bounds of Victorian propriety by the end of the novel. When they first kiss, the narrator remarks that "[w]hat lay behind them did not matter. The moment overcame the age" (217). The repressive hypothesis produces the very rhetoric which enables and sustains this narrative trajectory.[5] Related to this is the fact that Fowles returns again and again, both in the novel itself and in his comments about it, to the suggestion that Sarah and Charles are existentialists before their time. While I will make comparatively little reference to the novel's engagement with existentialism here, it is important to note the extent to which the novel's preoccupation with the question of individual freedom depends upon an assumption that sex and freedom are ontologically linked. (This is, of course, the flip-side to the sex/repression conjunction.)

By implication then, the sexuality of the woman in Fowles's vision is not so much of no particular consequence, as it is at once "illegitimate" and somehow "progressive." In "We 'Other Victorians'" Foucault writes:

> If it was truly necessary to make room for illegitimate sexualities, it was reasoned, let them take their infernal mischief elsewhere: to a place where they could be reintegrated, if not in the circuits of production, at least in those of profit. The brothel and the mental hospital would be those places of tolerance: the prostitute, the client, and the pimp, together with the psychiatrist and the hysteric—those "other Victorians," as Steven Marcus would say—seem to have surreptitiously transferred the pleasures that are unspoken into the order of things that are counted. Words and gestures, quietly authorized, could be exchanged there at the going rate. Only in those places would untrammeled sex have a right to (safely insularized) forms of reality, and only to clandestine, circumscribed, and coded types of discourse. Everywhere else, modern puritanism imposed its triple edict of taboo, nonexistence, and silence. (4–5)

In the novel, it is Sarah's improper "sexuality" which disturbs and challenges Victorian propriety. Further, the brothel and the asylum are the very sites which both organize and threaten to contain Sarah's scandalous behavior, her "shame." From the perspective of the "respectable" residents of Lyme Regis, Mrs Poulteney and

---

5   Bruce Woodcock's analysis of what he calls the "masculine ideology" of Fowles's fiction is also useful here. Woodcock presents a detailed and careful examination of the extent to which Fowles's novels depend upon an idealization of the "feminine" (what Fowles calls the "feminine principle") and a corresponding "hunt structure"; women function as catalysts for men's quests for personal freedom. He cites a number of statements from Fowles which reinforce this view, e.g. "I find it difficult to think fictionally except in terms of quest, solitude, sexuality, the mania for freedom" (18). Woodcock's study underscores the close link between heterosexuality and freedom that *The French Lieutenant's Woman* presumes.

Dr Grogan for example, her insistence on displaying rather than hiding her shame means that she must be either mad or a whore.

Sarah is characterized as an "other Victorian" in two senses. First, she is an "improper" Victorian. She frequents precisely those places where a "proper" woman would not be seen: most notably Ware Commons, that "running sore" (81) on the outskirts of Lyme Regis, of which it "is sufficient to say that among the more respectable townsfolk one only had to speak of a boy or girl as 'one of the Ware Commons kind' to tar them for life. The boy must henceforth be a satyr; and the girl, a hedge-prostitute" (81); and Exeter, "notoriously a place to hide, ... [a] safe sanctuar[y] from the stern moral tide that swept elsewhere through the life of the country" (238). In this sense, Sarah belongs to the Victorian age as a necessary foil to propriety. She is the improper figure without whom the notion of a proper Victorian wouldn't make sense. She occupies the constitutive outside of normative society; throughout the novel, her movements map the relationship between the inside and the outside, the center and the margins. Both literally and symbolically, Sarah frequents those places which lie outside the bounds of proper society: the very end of the quay; Ware Commons. She must, however, be seen to occupy these sites in order for the narrative to proceed in the way that it does. That Sarah quite deliberately displays her preference for the margins of society is central to my reading of this novel. In a second sense, however, Sarah does not "belong" to the Victorian age but rather exceeds it; she is beyond her time and hence an other Victorian in the sense that she is *not* Victorian. It is precisely the dispersal of the figure of woman across time that makes this second sense possible. In terms of the novel's own rhetoric, history cannot contain Sarah; she stands outside of her age as a critical observer. To be an "other Victorian" in this double sense is to be simultaneously an object of censure and an object of desire. It is also, it must be said, to be the agent of a censuring gaze. These gazes, censuring and desiring, criss-cross throughout the novel in mutually informing and contradictory ways.

Alice Ferrebe reads *The French Lieutenant's Woman* and Fowles's earlier novel *The Magus* (1966) as "a complex interplay between the deconstruction and reinscription of traditional gender roles" (207). She explains the difficulty Fowles's fiction poses for feminist critics in terms of what she calls its "scopic politics." The opening chapters of *The French Lieutenant's Woman*, in which Charles Smithson and his fiancé, Ernestina Freeman, first meet Sarah Woodruff, bring into play a powerful scopic or visual narrative economy according to which characters recognize (or misrecognize) each other within the terms of a discourse of repression. Like Ferrebe, I am fascinated by just how semantically and narratologically dense these opening scenes are. The relationships between Sarah, Charles, and Ernestina, as they play out in the novel's first two chapters, are my interpretive focus for the remainder of this chapter. As I will show, by the end of these chapters we already suspect a great deal about the parameters of these relationships; that is to say, they anticipate a quite particular kind of love story.

Sarah's appearance on the quay at the conclusion of Chapter 1 initiates the heterosexual romance narrative; she is the "figure from myth" who will call forth the romantic speech act:

But where the telescopist would have been at sea himself was with the other figure on that sombre, curving mole. It stood right at the seawardmost end, apparently leaning against an old cannon-barrel up-ended as a bollard. Its clothes were black. The wind moved them, but the figure stood motionless, staring, staring out to sea, more like a living memorial to the drowned, a figure from myth, than any proper fragment of the petty provincial day. (9)

What one cannot help but notice about this figure is the extent to which it doesn't quite belong in its historical setting; it is not a "proper" provincial Victorian. Unlike the other two figures on the Cobb, Charles and Ernestina, a pair about whom "a person of curiosity could have at once deduced strong probabilities" (7), this character is marked by its improbability, its strangeness. She is something out of order on the landscape. (Despite the lack of a gendered pronoun, I would argue that this figure is absolutely gendered.) The passage above follows detailed descriptions of a young lady and gentleman walking down the quay, or at least detailed descriptions of their clothing and its suitability according to the fashions of the age. In contrast, however, this other figure is uncostumed and apparently unable to be "read" according to the customs of the day. The "static long shot" (Fowles, "Notes" 136) of Sarah standing at the end of the quay which introduces this novel only has such semantic and narrative force because we know that this well-dressed couple are walking along the Cobb towards her.

Having anticipated the novel's opening scenes in "Notes," Fowles jumps immediately to the question of how to represent two Victorians in bed. The picture of a man who "walks down the quay and sees that mysterious back, feminine, silent ... turned to the horizon," leads to the question of "how they made love, what they said to each other in their most intimate moments, what they felt then" (141). Fowles confides that trying to write the sex scene between these two characters was like trying to write science fiction. In order for Fowles to eventually bring this scene off Sarah must, as I have already argued, be something other than Victorian (or an "other" Victorian) from the very outset. Ernestina, however, the properly dressed (and hence "proper") Victorian woman cannot phrase romance for Charles. Instead, these early chapters seal her fate. Rather than inspiring love in her fiancé, she will present an obstacle to his love for Sarah. Ernestina represents a threat to romance. She is the mundane and hence absolutely knowable woman (the truly repressed Victorian woman) who will stand as a foil for the mysterious and unknowable Sarah. Unlike Sarah, Ernestina has "exactly the right face for her age" (27). She is, in the terms of the novel, absolutely representable as a "Victorian." In his book *The Romances of John Fowles* Simon Loveday writes: "A male writer creating female characters is faced with a logical problem ..., since his characters will have depths he himself cannot plumb." He goes on to applaud Fowles's characterization of Sarah as inscrutable and thus unrepresentable as an "ingenious solution to this problem" (60). What Loveday simply fails to acknowledge is that other female characters, most particularly Ernestina, are absolutely knowable: they are mundane (Ernestina, Mrs Tranter) or contemptible (Mrs Poulteney) precisely in their opposition to Sarah.

The first thing we notice about Sarah is that she is out of place; she stands alone on the Cobb and looks away from the "harmonious" (8) prospect of Lyme Regis.

Charles, having "noticed, or at least realized the sex of, the figure at the end" (12) is immediately curious. It is significant that it is Ernestina who first gives the title character her name (or names):

> "It must be poor Tragedy."
> "Tragedy?"
> "A nickname. One of her nicknames."
> "And what are the others?"
> "The fishermen have a gross name for her."
> "My dear Tina you can surely——"
> "They call her the French Lieutenant's ... Woman."
> "Indeed. And she is so ostracized that she has to spend her days out here?"
> "She is ... a little mad. Let us turn. I don't like to go near her." (12)

Ernestina is too coy to utter the fishermen's "gross name" for Sarah and substitutes "Woman" for "Whore." The two sites, the brothel and the asylum, which the "other Victorian" inhabits come immediately into play in Ernestina's troubled naming of Sarah; Sarah is both prostitute and madwoman. The only vocabulary available to Ernestina with which to name this other woman is a vocabulary which she cannot quite use. The ellipses in Ernestina's direct speech ("French Lieutenant's ... Woman," "She is ... a little mad") both signal her embarrassment (or shame) in the face of sex, and introduce a syntactical and semantic register according to which she herself can only speak (or, as I will discuss in Chapter 6, think) about sex in elliptical terms.

The conversation cited above continues as follows (note that Ernestina's speech continues to be elliptical):

> They stopped. He stared at the black figure.
> "But I'm intrigued. Who is this French lieutenant?"
> "A man she is said to have ..."
> "Fallen in love with?"
> "Worse than that."
> "And he abandoned her? There is a child?"
> "No. I think no child. It is all gossip."
> "But what is she doing there?"
> "They say she waits for him to return."
> "But ... does no one care for her?" (12)

Charles's curiosity is further provoked by Ernestina's tale and he insists on walking to the end of the quay despite her protests. Rather than closing the subject, Ernestina's reticence only heightens his interest in the woman at the end of the quay. Precisely because Sarah cannot be easily named by or *as* a "Victorian," she, not Charles's betrothed, is the figure of romance. "He stared at the black figure"; the initial image of Sarah on the Cobb initiates the chain of events which will eventually lead to Charles saying "I love you." Charles scolds Ernestina for telling him the "sordid facts" about Sarah: "That's the trouble with provincial life. Everyone knows everyone and there is no mystery. No romance" (14). Charles's rebuke is fascinating because Ernestina's coy speech does not so much cancel out as augment Sarah's "mystery" for him. His introduction to "mystery" leads him, somewhat curiously, to lament its loss. Ernestina misinterprets the implications of Charles's castigation of her: "She teased him then: the scientist, the despiser of novels" (14). To the contrary, Charles is the character who comes to reject facts and desire a "novel" by the conclusion of Chapter 2; he is cast as Sarah's key witness, so to speak. (In effect, he will join "us" and the "novelist" in the garden outside Sarah's darkened bedroom window.)

Importantly, Ernestina is literally too "short-sighted" to see anything but a "dark shape" at the end of the quay, so can only guess who the figure might be from her knowledge of Lyme Regis gossip. Sarah's gaze, however, is "aimed like a rifle at the farthest horizon" (13). Whereas Ernestina is characterized by a failure to see things accurately, Sarah is credited with a special type and potency of vision. When she turns towards Charles, she looks "through" rather than at him. She is, by implication, not quite there. Sarah's preoccupation with the horizon in this scene brings about the spatial and temporal collapse according to which she belongs to both another place and another time, a collapse which is also enacted by a "true" Victorian's inability to see her as anything but an indistinct figure on the horizon. The heavily symbolic exchange between Charles and Sarah which begins with her distracted look is wordless; they stare at one another. A look which lasts "two or three seconds at the most" (13) establishes an intensely affective relationship between Charles and Sarah which excludes Ernestina. The description of Charles and Sarah's exchange of looks maps the affective and narratological relationships between the three central characters. Further, this episode highlights the extent to which these three characters have significantly different relationships from those expected by what the narrator refers to again and again as "their age."

Rather than hang her head or avert her eyes when they meet Charles's, Sarah holds his gaze. Her look is "not as [Charles] had expected; for theirs was an age when the favoured feminine look was the demure, the obedient, the shy" (13). The characteristics which she does not express are, of course, the very ones which Ernestina has just performed to the letter. As a "good" Victorian woman, Ernestina is characterized by such displays of modesty *or of shame* throughout the novel: "At first meetings she could cast down her eyes very prettily, as if she might faint should any gentleman dare to address her" (27; see also 131, 291). The characteristic response of the shamed subject is to avoid the gaze of the other; to perform shame is to look away (when you have already been seen). Sarah performs shame in these opening scenes, though in a somewhat different way to Ernestina. She is, as we have seen, immediately recognizable as an outcast, a shamed subject, who directs her gaze away from the society which would cast her out. However, from the outset, her relationship to her shame is not straightforward; she is not simply shamed, but herself shames another when she turns to look at Charles. She is also, we might add, "shameless," to the extent that she does not behave as a proper Victorian woman should and stares back at Charles. Once Charles and Ernestina are close enough to see it, Sarah's black coat is described as "more like a man's ... than any woman's coat that had been in fashion those past forty years" (13). In contrast, Ernestina is brightly dressed according to the fashions of the day. Sarah's behaviour, we can guess (if we haven't already), will not be as expected.[6] Her look figuratively penetrates Charles; it is described as a "lance" both here and on numerous other occasions throughout the novel (109, 143, 163, 224).

Despite the fact that Sarah represents a disturbance to the Victorian conventionality and propriety represented by this well-dressed and newly betrothed couple, Charles is the one who feels like an intruder in this scene:

> Charles felt immediately as if he had trespassed; as if the Cobb belonged to that face, and not to the Ancient Borough of Lyme. It was not a pretty face, like Ernestina's. It was certainly not a beautiful face, by any period's standard or taste. But it was an unforgettable face, and a tragic face. Its sorrow welled out of it as purely, naturally and unstoppably as water out of a woodland spring. There was no artifice there, no hypocrisy, no hysteria, no mask; and above all, no sign of madness. [...]
>
> Again and again, afterwards, Charles thought of that look as a lance; and to think so is of course not merely to describe an object but the effect it has. He felt himself in that brief instant an unjust enemy; both pierced and deservedly diminished. (13)

This passage echoes Nietzsche's description of the experience of shame in *Human, All-Too-Human*. The following passage from Friedrich Nietzsche's account almost reads like a philosophical paraphrase of the scene cited above:[7]

> Why do we feel shame when some virtue or merit is attributed to us which, as the saying goes, "we have not deserved"? Because we appear to have intruded upon a territory to which we do not belong, from which we should be excluded, as from a holy place or holy of holies, which ought not to be trodden by our foot ... In all shame there is a mystery, which seems desecrated or in danger of desecration through us. (Nietzsche qtd. in Schneider 9–10)

To read Nietzsche's account of shame alongside Fowles's characterization of the relationship between Charles and Sarah anticipates my argument that this novel demonstrates the mutual implication of love and shame in the representation (and construction) of the heterosexual romantic subject. Nietzsche returns again and again to the metaphor of truth as a woman before whom one exercises a sense of shame. "Woman," in his analysis, becomes the bearer of secrets, the place of mystery, whom "man" must desire if he is to achieve true humanity, if he is to become "noble," to use Nietzsche's term. In his 1977 study of shame, *Shame, Exposure, and Privacy*, Carl N. Schneider describes Nietzsche as the philosopher "who most tenaciously stalked the significance of shame for our understanding of the human" (6). He writes, "[a]ccording to Nietzsche, no structure will save us; only men who are 'self-overcoming' and who know that truth is hard yet crave it will avail" (9). There is a heteronormative logic to Nietzsche's account of the search for truth: truth is a

---

6   In an important sense, Sarah is distinguished from the proper Victorian woman by her failure to be "feminine," or her "masculinity." As I discussed in the previous chapter, the twentieth-century popular romance heroine is typically distinguishable by her ability to be "like" men, or to have a "spirit" which the mundanely feminine woman lacks. Sarah Woodruff is no exception. See also: "There *was* something male about her there" (157).

7   Charles repeatedly feels himself to be reproached by Sarah (78, 143, 157, 224).

woman desired by man (as generic human). Further, woman can only remain the bearer of truth if she is virginal: "In the end [truth] is a woman: she should not be violate" (11). This is precisely the narrative trajectory which Fowles mobilizes in *The French Lieutenant's Woman*. Sarah is the bearer of truth (and morality) before whom Charles feels shame. He experiences a sense of shame because he recognizes himself as a threat to her purity; to her integrity as the bearer of truth. In order to become "noble" (or, in Fowles's terms, one of the "few"), Charles must abandon Ernestina for Sarah; he must realize that the "structures" of Victorian propriety will not allow him to become free (or "noble" in the Nietzschean sense). He must desire truth, and then realize its unattainability (Sarah as impenetrable mystery) in order to reach his "happy ending."[8]

---

8   Again Woodcock's account of the "masculine ideology" of Fowles's fiction is relevant here.

Chapter 6

"Shame on You": Affective Speech Acts in *The French Lieutenant's Woman*

The French Lieutenant's Woman is organized and propelled by two affective speech acts: "I love you," and "Shame on you." This chapter continues my investigation of "I love you" as the ontological and narrative turning-point of heterosexual romance narratives. The introduction of "Shame on you" into my analysis is designed to complicate and hopefully to invigorate this investigation by suggesting the ways in which the romantic performative functions in mutually constitutive ways with other performatives. This chapter thus points to a broader or more general interest in the relationship between affect, the performative, and narrative. My focus continues to be on the ways in which what we might call the discursive field of the heterosexual romance narrative can be fruitfully interrogated from the perspective of performativity theory.

In the previous chapter, I considered the narrative function of Sarah Woodruff, the "shameful" woman in this novel. This chapter begins with a brief discussion of Sedgwick's theory of shame. I then go on to suggest how her claims for the foundational importance of "Shame on you" shed light on the linguistic and discursive mechanisms which produce and reproduce the heterosexual subject. I pursue this argument by examining the ways in which this particular novel might be said to "stage" the constitutive relationship between "shame" and "love." My analysis of *The French Lieutenant's Woman* aims to put pressure both on the ways in which this particular novel is read and on the ways in which we read historical romance novels in general. I continue to pay particular attention to the characterization of Sarah and to her function in the narrative. Taking its cue from Judith Butler's work on the "politics of the performative" and theories of subjection, my close discussion of the novel facilitates a rethinking of the relationship between performativity and interpellation. Bringing Louis Althusser's original formulation of the interpellative moment (and Butler's reformulation of it) to bear on Fowles's novel highlights the extent to which this is a novel "about" the policing of sexuality—a thematic preoccupation (and narrative mode) of particular significance in a novel which, as I have shown, so mobilizes the myth of Victorian sexuality.

The first two chapters of *The French Lieutenant's Woman* anticipate the possibility of a declaration of love between Charles and Sarah which, if it is to be felicitous, must be spoken over Charles's earlier promise to Ernestina. The happiness of such an utterance is threatened to the extent that Charles's own behavior would be shameful from the perspective of polite Victorian society; he would become guilty of a "breach of promise." This is, of course, exactly what happens later in the novel when he breaks off his engagement with Ernestina and is forced to sign a confession of guilt. Charles's breach of promise is brought about by his perception of a greater promise: a sincere "I love you" as opposed to a premature and thus insincere "I love you" which cannot stand for romance. In effect, in order to pursue Sarah, Charles must himself suffer the charge "Shame on you" from two fronts; he finds himself in David H. Walker's words, "caught, as it were, between two accusing stares" (64). There are, in effect, two registers of shame at work here. The first lays claim to universality and timelessness and is represented by Sarah; she stands for a truth and "nobility" which cuts across history. The second is more mundane and is in effect the scorned object of the first. It is historically anchored and represented by the figures of polite Victorian society who populate the novel: Ernestina and her father; Mrs Poulteney; Dr Grogan; and so on. The Freemans' breach of promise charge and the *confessio delicti* they hold against him can be read as a legal speech act which amounts to "Shame on you." Charles's dilemma arises from his confusion about how best to reconcile these two registers and indeed his ultimate failure to do so. We might name them according to that familiar Victorian dichotomy (a dichotomy with which this novel is obsessed): the opposition of duty and passion.

Fowles mobilizes certain powerful speech acts crucial to the formulation of heterosexual romance narratives, and to the formation or individuation of the heterosexual romantic subject: "I love you" and "Shame on you." One of my aims in Chapter 5 was to begin to be attentive to the workings of these speech acts and to present a kind of introductory proof of my key claim about this novel—my aim was, so to speak, to make these utterances heard. Of course, neither "I love you" nor "Shame on you" is actually uttered by any of the characters present on the Cobb in those crucial opening scenes; however, my assumption here and throughout this book is that what Austin calls "explicit performatives" also circulate *implicitly* to the extent that they can be said to initiate, propel, and organize stories. In order to think about speech acts in this way one needs to be aware of what might be termed the "conventions of usage" in the context of which a given speech act circulates; one needs, that is, to keep in view Austin's "Doctrine of the Infelicities," his list of rules which determine the "happiness" (or "unhappiness") of each instance of a speech act. My suggestion is that these rules, which in effect map the conventional procedure for a speech act, provide us with a framework to do more than simply assess the success or failure of a particular utterance. They also help us recognize the workings of an utterance even when it is not explicitly spoken. Indeed, the scopic narrative economy I described in my analysis of the scene on the Cobb is peculiarly suited to a novel about love and shame. The experiences of love and shame are typically described through what we might term a trope of sight ("I've loved you since the moment I saw you"; "I [the "shamefaced" person] can't bear to look him in the eyes."). In fact, the connection between shame and the gaze is so well-recognized that a number of psychoanalysts have floated the idea that the "ocular zone" be identified as the bodily place of shame (Schneider 33).

In this chapter I examine a number of key scenes from later in the novel which stage the relationship between the romantic performative and "Shame on you." This approach means that I pay little to no attention to some aspects of *The French Lieutenant's Woman* which have been heavily discussed by other commentators on the novel. My main interest continues to be in the way we can *use* texts to rethink the ways in which we see the world. So, while I want, of course, to present an insightful and persuasive reading of this particular book, I am also keen to ask what it can tell us about history, romance, and heterosexuality. I argue in this chapter that the narrative trajectory offered by this novel is enabled by a relationship between the affective utterances "I love you" and "Shame on you." I also contend that these two speech acts are always already implicated in any representation of the heterosexual romantic subject. I am certain, for instance, that the conventional scene of utterance for "Shame on you" is unimaginable without an understanding of the workings of the repressive hypothesis.

Shame, Love and the Heterosexual Romantic Subject

> Few words, after all, could be more performative in the Austinian sense than "shame": "Shame on you," "For shame," or just "Shame!," the locutions that give sense to the word, do not describe or refer to shame, but themselves confer it. (Sedgwick, "Socratic" 126)

My first step here is to bring into play a performative which, while not occupying center stage in this book, is nevertheless of crucial importance to my understanding of heterosexual romance fiction. A brief flash-forward to Chapter 46 of *The French Lieutenant's Woman* helps: Sarah and Charles lie in bed together after having sex: "A minute passed, his hand smoothing her hair as if she were a child. But his mind was elsewhere. As if she sensed it, she at last spoke. 'I know you cannot marry me'" (306). Their affective and now sexual relationship can anticipate only the possibility or the impossibility of that most classic of speech acts, "I do…"

In her essay "Queer Performativity: Henry James's *The Art of the Novel*" Eve Kosofsky Sedgwick considers the "weird centrality of the marriage example for performativity theory" (3). If, as Sedgwick suggests, Austinian performativity "lives in the examples," then it lives most fully—as any reader of Austin will recognize—in his favorite example "I do (take this woman to be my lawful wedded wife)." Having read *How to Do Things with Words*, one might say that "I do…" is the founding performative, the speech act which introduces and sustains Austin's category of the explicit performative, and in which he indulges most frequently. Sandy Petrey calls marriage the "prototypical performative rite" (40).[1] Butler writes:

> The centrality of the marriage example in J.L. Austin's examples of performativity suggests that heterosexualization of the social bond is the paradigmatic form for those speech acts which bring about what they name. "I pronounce you…" puts into effect the relation that it names. But from where and when does such a performative draw its force, and what happens to the performative when its purpose is precisely to undo the presumptive force of the heterosexual ceremonial? (*Bodies* 224–5)

Significantly, Butler cites "I pronounce you…" rather than Austin's "I do…," as the utterance which solemnizes a marriage. In an editor's note to *How to Do Things with Words*, J.O. Urmson writes: "Austin realized that the expression 'I do' is not

---

1   Petrey also calls marriage the "locus classicus for speech-act theory's assertion that social sense is always consubstantial with social conventions" (66).

used in the marriage ceremony too late to correct his mistake. We have let it remain in the text *as it is philosophically unimportant that it is a mistake*" (5). Butler's substitution of "I pronounce you..." for "I do..." implicitly shares this assumption. To the contrary, I suggest that the persistence of "I do..." in Austin's work and in the work of speech act theorists after him is *philosophically remarkable*.

In Austin's own terms, the operations of "I do..." are precisely "parasitic." Not only does "I do..." circulate outside the parameters of "ordinary speech," with which Austin claims he is wholly and solely concerned; it circulates as an immediately recognizable signifier of marriage *despite* its absence from the *traditional* wedding ceremony: it is a fiction. The status of "I do..." in performativity theory becomes, to invoke Sedgwick's telling descriptor, weirder still when we consider its decidedly odd relationship to the ceremony it purports to signify. Sedgwick suggests that an alternate title for *How to Do Things with Words* might have been *How to say (or write) "I do" about twenty million times without winding up any more married than you started out*, or in short, *I Do—Not!* She goes on to say that this new title rings true "both because most of the 'I do's ... in the book are offered as examples of the different things that can go *wrong* with performative utterances ...; but even more because it is *as* examples they are offered in the first place—hence as, performatively, voided in advance" (3). If the marriage example is the paradigmatic case for performativity, and, further, if that exemplary status follows in the first instance from the persistence of "I do..." in Austin's original formulation of the performative, then the question of the "presumptive force" of the "heterosexualization of the social bond" becomes a peculiarly troubled one. What happens once we realize that the special status of the marriage example in *How to Do Things with Words* is constituted by its failure from the very beginning?

Sedgwick invites us to imagine theories of performativity which might begin by offering other types of speech acts as "exemplary." She writes:

> Austin keeps going back to that formula "first person singular present indicative active,"
> ... and the marriage example makes me wonder about the apparently natural way the
> first-person speaking, acting, and pointing subject, like the (wedding) present itself, gets
> constituted in marriage through a confident appeal to state authority, through the calm
> interpellation of others present as "witnesses," and through the logic of the (heterosexual)
> supplement whereby individual subjective agency is guaranteed by the welding into a
> cross-gender dyad. Persons who self-identify as queer, by contrast, will be those whose
> subjectivity is lodged in refusals or deflections of (or by) the logic of the heterosexual
> supplement; in far less simple associations attaching to state authority; in far less
> complacent relation to the witness of others. The emergence of the first person, of the
> singular, of the present, of the active, and of the indicative are all questions, rather than
> presumptions, for queer performativity. (3–4)

The uneasy relation of the non-heterosexual subject to the marriage ceremony prompts Sedgwick to consider a theory of performativity which "might begin with the example, not 'I do...' but, let us say, 'Shame on you.'" In Chapter 2 I suggested a comparison between this affective speech act and "I love you." My aim in this chapter is to bring these two utterances into closer relation in an analysis of a novel in which I argue they play a mutually constitutive role for the heterosexual subject. The institutional performative which organizes their relation to each other is, we might say, that particularly weird, but nevertheless persistent, example of performativity, "I do…" Certainly the persistence of the marriage example makes me wonder about the "apparently" natural way in which the heterosexual subject is constituted; however, it also makes me wonder about the extent to which that process of acculturation is only "apparently" natural. My broader belief is that *no* subject exists in a comfortable— or "straight"—relation to the marriage example in particular, or in more general institutional terms, to heterosexual hegemony. That is to say, my object is not to reclaim Sedgwick's terms in order to "queer" the heterosexual romantic subject, but rather to unsettle the assumption that the confidence or the calm of that subject is something that we can take for granted in our analyses. To return to Diane Elam: "Thinking romance is a question of how it is that one may say 'I love you'" (26). It may also be a question of how it is that one may say (or hear) "Shame on you." This last point will become clearer as I proceed.

In her work on shame, Sedgwick is an enthusiastic reader of psychologist Silvan Tomkins, who she argues "offers by far the richest theory and phenomenology of this affect" (4–5; see also *Touching Feeling*).[2] She pays attention also to the work of other development psychologists such as Michael Franz Basch and Francis Broucek. This bringing together of socio-linguistics and developmental psychology is designed to facilitate a theory of shame which does away with the idea that prohibition (and, by association, repression) is the key to understanding shame. Her working hypothesis is that shame can be productively rethought for an anti-homophobic politics to the extent that the experience of shame has nothing to do with repression. Sedgwick cites psychological studies of the "proto-affect" shame in infants as evidence that shame is not the product or result of prohibition or disapproval, but is instead a "disruptive moment, in a circuit of identity-constituting identificatory identification" (5) The experience of shame, in Sedgwick's analysis, becomes an extraordinarily complicated and circuitous drama (which is not, in itself, a bad thing) in which the very terms of identity—and indeed theories of performativity—are under constant renegotiation.

My contention is that to attempt to excise the question of repression (or prohibition) from a study of shame is both to miss the point of Foucault's critique of the repressive hypothesis and to ignore the extent to which "performances" of shame cannot be understood without an acknowledgment of the continued currency of the repressive hypothesis. On one level, my analysis of *The French Lieutenant's Woman* is intended to demonstrate that the representation of characters as shamed and/or shaming subjects is enabled by a discourse of shame which assumes it is engendered by prohibition. A close reading of *The French Lieutenant's Woman* illustrates the extent to which shame and (heterosexual) love are mutually implicated. My working hypothesis is that "love" and "shame" are codependent terms in the heteronormative

---

2   See also Sedgwick's most recent book, *Touching Feeling: Affect, Pedagogy, Performativity*. This volume includes a number of essays published in earlier versions: "Queer Performativity: Henry James's *The Art of the Novel*," "Socratic Raptures, Socratic Ruptures: Notes Towards Queer Performativity," "Shame and Performativity: Henry James's New York Edition Prefaces," and "Shame in the Cybernetic Fold: Reading Silvan Tomkins" (written with Adam Frank). For the most part, my references are to these earlier texts.

narrative of romance. The entanglement of discourses of shame with discourses of love and desire persists because of the legacy of the repressive hypothesis, a legacy which dates, so the story goes, from the Victorian Age.

Sedgwick joins Tomkins and a long line of thinkers before him to insist that, "Shame … makes identity" (Sedgwick, "Queer" 5).[3] "Shame," she writes, "is a bad feeling attaching to what one is: one therefore *is something*, in experiencing shame. The place of identity, the structure 'identity,' marked by shame's threshold between sociability and introversion, may be established and naturalized in the first instance *through shame*" (12). Shame, then, is circuitously individual and sociable; the shamed subject is simultaneously isolated from and inextricably bound to others through shame. This is very close to the way I have characterized the experience of love throughout this book. Sedgwick, however, grants shame a primacy in the formation of identity which I have tried to avoid giving love. While it might be necessary for the purposes of analysis to consider speech acts in isolation from one another, the singling out of an utterance is always arbitrary. This kind of work must carry a cover note of sorts which states that speech acts are discursive units which circulate and have effects only because they are inextricably related to other speech acts. In addition, speech acts are intensely ideological; they are inextricably linked to the set of signs and practices which work to produce and reproduce hegemonic social structures. One of the most important things to notice about speech acts is, of course, that they can only be identified as such because they are reiterated. Like "I love you," "Shame on you" is *an instance* in the linguistic and grammatical suturing of formations and assumptions of "identity" through its insistent *reiteration*. In the final analysis, it is impossible to consider fully the operations of these two speech acts in isolation from one another. Shame, as Tomkins shows us, is constitutively related to "interest" (the heading under which we might consider love).

In their essay "Shame in the Cybernetic Fold: Reading Silvan Tomkins," Sedgwick and Adam Frank cite the following long passage from Tomkins's *Affect, Imagery, Consciousness*. Tomkins's theory is that shame exists at one end of the affect polarity "shame-interest"; we can only feel shame if we have first felt pleasure. It also alludes to the bodily gestures which typically accompany shame: lowered head and diverted eyes, and, we might add, the blush.

> Like disgust, [shame] operates only after interest or enjoyment has been activated, and inhibits one or the other or both. The innate activator of shame is the incomplete reduction of interest or joy. Hence any barrier to further exploration which partially reduces interest … will activate the lowering of the head and eyes in shame and reduce further exploration or self-exposure … Such a barrier might be because one is suddenly looked at by one who is strange, or because one wishes to look at or commune with another person but suddenly cannot because he is strange, or one expected him to be familiar but he suddenly appears unfamiliar, or one started to smile but found one was smiling at a stranger. (500)

---

3   This "long line of thinkers" includes people such as Thomas Burgess, Charles Darwin and Nietzsche. For a summary of philosophies of shame which identify shame as constitutive of the human, see Schneider.

Tomkins's theory of affect was inspired by his close observations of an infant in 1955; "he was able," Sedgwick and Frank write, "to locate early expressions of shame at a period (around seven months) before the infant could have any concept of prohibition" (501). While I find Sedgwick's (and Frank's) work on shame both useful and engaging, I am somewhat troubled by the extent to which she extrapolates a discursive theory of adult shame as performative (or constitutive of identity) from psychological accounts of infantile "proto-shame." Whether or not shame is produced—in the first instance—by prohibition or repression, *performances* of shame cannot help, I would argue, but invoke a discourse of prohibition (and repression). That Sedgwick's analysis of shame is so haunted by the presumption of prohibition signals, I think, that her efforts to *expel* it from consideration are excessive. Immediately following the passage above, Sedgwick and Frank write: "The emphasis in this account on the strange, rather than on the prohibited or disapproved, was congenial with our motivating intuition that the phenomenon of shame might offer new ways of short-circuiting the seemingly near-inescapable habits of thought that Foucault groups together under the term *repressive hypothesis*" (500). To the contrary, I would suggest this passage emphasizes what we might call "prohibition" no more and no less than it emphasizes the strange: shame *inhibits* interest; *any barrier* to interest will produce shame.

What Foucault demonstrates in "We 'Other Victorians'" is that the repressive hypothesis persistently circulates in our understanding of the relationship between power and sexuality despite its being, for Foucault, a theoretical problem. "Let there be no misunderstanding," he writes,

> I do not claim that sex has not been prohibited or barred or masked or misapprehended since the classical age ... I do not maintain that the prohibition of sex is a ruse; but it is a ruse to make prohibition into the basic and constitutive element from which one would be able to write the history of what has been said concerning sex starting from the modern epoch. (12)

Surely what Foucault's critique of the repressive hypothesis teaches us is *precisely* that it is a "habit of thought"; to attempt to deny the significance of a discourse of repression in representations *or* experiences of shame is thus to short-circuit our analyses from the very beginning. Any characterization of a shamed or shaming subject must make reference to a discourse of repression in order to be recognizable as such; even Tomkins—who Sedgwick argues dispels the idea of prohibition from his theory of affect—depends upon a vocabulary of repression to describe the experience of shame. This is not to suggest that "some version of prohibition is the most important [read 'only'] thing to understand" (501) about shame, but that prohibition is a modality of power which participates in the production of the shameful subject; it is not, as my reading of *The French Lieutenant's Woman* will insist, necessarily efficacious.

Carl D. Schneider describes shame as a "drama to be enacted" (xiii). Similarly, Sedgwick talks about shame as a "drama" which is "enacted" in the context of her discussion of Henry James's *The Art of the Novel* (7). The semantic force of "to be" in Schneider's phrase is to insist that the experience of shame is a *necessary* process for the individual in society. Sedgwick says something very close to this. She writes: "The forms taken by shame are not distinct 'toxic' parts of a group or individual identity that can be excised: they are instead integral to and residual in the processes by which identity itself is formed" (13). While their political motivations are certainly very different, both Sedgwick and Schneider oppose those commentators who talk about shame only in negative terms—who campaign against it, so to speak. They are keen to reclaim shame as a *positive* affect of foundational importance in the construction of identity.

The very "dramas" which preoccupy Sedgwick, both in her work on shame and elsewhere, are also those which Schneider says have a special relationship to shame. He writes: "Shame is intimately tied to the central human dramas of covering and uncovering, speech and silence, the literal and the inexpressible, concealment and disclosure, community and alienation. Under the spell of rationalism, science, and individualism, however, our society perceives not a *drama to be enacted*, but a problem to be solved" (xiii). Sedgwick insists that the experience of shame is always in some sense about "performance." She follows Tomkins's theory and phenomenology of shame to sketch a picture of the shamed subject: "shame effaces itself; shame points and projects; shame turns itself skin side outside; shame and pride, shame and self-display, shame and exhibitionism are different interlinings of the same glove: shame, it might finally be said, transformational shame, *is performance*. I mean theatrical performance" (5). The shamed subject attempts to hide that which has already been seen. Shame, that is, straddles the threshold between display and dissemblance, unmasking and masking, introversion and extroversion, confession and secrecy. The notion of shame as a role or a scene which is played or performed as on a stage—of an affect as "performance"—is crucial to my reading of *The French Lieutenant's Woman*.

I am struck by just how much of what Sedgwick says about shame chimes with my thinking about love. Love straddles the very same thresholds as shame. Love is always undecidably individual and sociable. My guess is that these two affects do not play the dynamic of interiority and exteriority in isolation from one another: love and shame are not mutually exclusive. Love, then, it might be said, *is performance*. If shame and love exist in a definitional relationship to *performance* (if performance defines shame and love so to speak), then these affects and their interrelationship can be seen to be especially available for deception.

Sedgwick's theorization of shame (and my theorization of the relationship between shame and love) is enabled by the close and somewhat complex relationship between the concepts of performance, the performative and performativity. "I love you" and "Shame on you" are explicit performatives in the Austinian sense; they are speech acts. Sedgwick explains the "performative force" of "Shame on you" by reference to its "transformational grammar." I discussed this material at some length in Chapter 2 when I first pointed out a similarity between "I love you" and "Shame on you" as relational speech acts. Sedgwick writes "'Shame on you' is performatively efficacious because its grammar ... *is* a transformational grammar: both at the level of pronoun positioning ... and at the level of the relational grammar of the affect shame itself" (4). That is, this utterance does what it says: it confers shame and thus produces a shamed subject. The utterance of the affective speech act or performative leads to the performance of shame in Sedgwick's analysis. Sedgwick skips somewhat lightly

I think from the question of an utterance which *confers* shame to the description of a shamed or shameful subject. Her emphasis on the efficacy of "Shame on you" elides a consideration of the possibility that a subject who is addressed by the speech act "Shame on you" (whether explicitly or implicitly) might ignore the address and thus *fail* to perform shame, might perform shame *insincerely*, or—perhaps more interestingly—might have deliberately stepped in the way of the utterance in order to be addressed by it.

The French Lieutenant's Woman enacts the constitutive relationship between shame and love in the construction of the heterosexual romantic subject. Pulling this argument off involves an examination of the ways in which various characters can be said to "perform" shame, specifically Sarah, Charles, and Ernestina. A number of critics have noted what might be termed the *theatricality* of this text: the way in which the narrative is tempered by a kind of metaphorics of the stage (Le Bouille; Walker). What I want to add to this observation is the thesis that this novel is in a sense about the foundational (and ever-perplexing) dynamic between performance and performativity. Throughout this book, I use the phrase "scene of utterance" to describe the context within which speech can be said to "act." Reading the fictional scenes of utterance this book can be said to "stage" (redoubled scenes to the extent that they are organized by at least two interrelated speech acts) allows us to gain a fresh perspective on the relationship between discourse and the subject, and to closely consider the workings of these affective speech acts in society generally. For the most part, the following section is a comparison of the characterization of Sarah and Ernestina (Charles gets more attention later in this chapter). I use this comparison to develop a response to theoretical questions about the place of "agency" in performative theories of subject formation. This will involve consideration of Butler's argument about agency in *Excitable Speech*. Additionally, Ann Pellegrini explains how reading fictional performances helps us to gain an understanding of performativity. Her explanation is pertinent here; throughout this book I assume that the value of scrutinizing literary texts lies in what they can tell us about the world within which they were produced, what they can help us to see about "us":

> If I try to get to what performativity means by citing specific performances … perhaps this is because "we" (the collective and collaborative "we" of writer and reader, performer and audience) can only catch ourselves in the act of becoming subject when we see ourselves as if through the other's "I." Theatrical, cinematic, and textual scenes of identification restage that other scene, but with a critical distance built in. … [T]here is—as Anne Deavere Smith says—the possibility of "stepping back, stepping back, stepping back, stepping back" and getting a different view of things, gaining a renewed sense of ourselves. (10–11)

Performativity and Performance: The Scene of Shame and Love in *The French Lieutenant's Woman*

Ernestina's successful interpellation into the marriage plot is intimately related to her internalization of the injunction "Shame on you." She is a "proper" Victorian woman to the extent that her behavior is determined by the regulatory force of shame. The novel's fifth chapter provides a detailed portrait of Ernestina in exactly these terms. It begins with Ernestina going up to her room to "catch a last glimpse of her betrothed through the lace curtains" (27). Having "duly admired" Charles from the window, she takes off her dress and stands "before her mirror in her chemise and petticoats":

> [S]he raised her arms and unloosed her hair, a thing she knew to be vaguely sinful, yet necessary, like a hot bath or a warm bed on a winter's night. She imagined herself for a truly sinful moment as someone wicked—a dancer, an actress. And then, if you had been watching, you would have seen something very curious. For she suddenly stopped turning and admiring herself in profile; gave an abrupt look up at the ceiling. Her lips moved. And she hastily opened one of her wardrobes and drew on a *peignoir*.
>
> For what had crossed her mind—a corner of her bed having chanced, as she pirouetted, to catch her eye in the mirror—was a sexual thought: an imagining, a kind of dimly glimpsed Laocoön embrace of naked limbs. [...]
>
> Thus she had evolved a kind of private commandment—those inaudible words were simply "I must not"—whenever the physical female implications of her body, sexual, menstrual, parturitional, tried to force an entry into her consciousness. But though one may try to keep the wolves from one's door, they still howl out there in the darkness. (29–30)

Ernestina's mantra of self control, "I must not," is in this context a first-person version of "Shame on you." Her silent address heavenwards pictures, of course, a scene of prayer or confession and thus invokes God as the imagined witness to her "sinful moment" or indeed as the one who confers shame. The drawing on of a *peignoir* is precisely to hide that which has *already been seen*. The link between performativity and performance is an "active question" (Parker and Sedgwick 8) in this apparently private scene of feminine self-regulation (as indeed it is throughout this book). Ernestina flirts with sin (and with shame) by imagining herself as a performer on a stage, an actress or a dancer.

Ernestina's bedroom becomes an intensely theatrical space both in terms of her narcissistic play in front of the mirror and in terms of the constitutive relationship between "acting" and "identity" which this scene negotiates. It's instructive to dwell for a moment on the "theatricality" of this episode. The image of Ernestina pirouetting on a stage immediately prompts the question of audience: "And then, *if you had been watching*, you would have seen something very curious." The reader is interpellated as a witness, as a "fly on the wall," so to speak, to an intensely private scene. To get a handle on the performative force of any utterance it is necessary, following Sedgwick and Parker's test-case analysis of "I dare you," to attempt a "disimpaction of the scene, as well as the act, of utterance." The first thing to notice is that while an explicit performance, "I dare you" or "Shame on you" for instance, seemingly involves only a speaker and an addressee (actors), it functions only by virtue of the presence (or virtual presence) of witnesses (an audience). Ernestina suddenly stops twirling before the mirror, mouths something towards the ceiling, and covers herself with a dressing gown—just as if she has been *caught in the act*. She is, it seems, playing the part of shame—but for whom?

Having "quelled the wolves" (at least for the moment), Ernestina unlocks a drawer in her dressing table, and takes out her locked diary, which she in turn unlocks using a key hidden in another drawer. On the back page of this book, she has listed the dates between her betrothal to Charles and their impending marriage: "Neat lines were drawn already through two months; some ninety numbers remained; and now Ernestina took the ivory-topped pencil from the top of the diary and struck through March 26^(th)" (31). She has pressed a sprig of jasmine in the diary as a memento of the day of her betrothal:

> She stared at it a moment, then bent to smell it. Her loosened hair fell over the page, and she closed her eyes to see if once again she could summon up the most delicious, the day she had thought she would die of joy, had cried endlessly, the ineffable …
> But she heard Aunt Tranter's feet on the stairs, hastily put the book away, and began to comb her lithe brown hair. (31)

Whereas Ernestina recites her "I must not" in order to suppress visions and feelings which the "physical female implications of her body" insist upon her, the too carefully concealed diary makes a secret of things which are, in a sense, publicly known. That is to say, whereas a "sexual thought" comes to her unbidden and unwelcome and thus invokes the fear of God, her girlish delight in her impending marriage is both permissible and expected. The sound of Aunt Tranter's feet on the stairs does not invoke fear of censure but a very particular delight in secrecy. The imagined "embrace of naked limbs" which so unsettles Ernestina signals a "truth," a bodily truth, which in these terms demands to surface and so must be immediately repressed. Ernestina's prudery and shame in the face of sex are figured throughout as symptomatic of her Victorianism. The model of power implicit in the narration of Ernestina's self-censorship is precisely the model which Foucault critiques in his discussion of confession in *The History of Sexuality*. That is to say, power only comes into play in this scene when a figure of authority, a repressive God, intervenes to prevent the truth from surfacing. In the terms of this narration, truth, and quite specifically here the truth of sex, "does not belong to the order of power" (Foucault 60): "But though one may keep the wolves from one's door, they still howl out there in the darkness."

Further, the hiding of her diary enacts the mechanism of the open secret as I defined it in Chapter 2: this scene describes a habit of behavior for Ernestina which is comforting and pleasurable to the extent that it reinforces her sense of herself as a private subject. We might consider also the possibility that this chapter is quite specifically about "feminine" rituals of self-definition. One implication of Ernestina's properly feminine displays of demureness—her proclivity to blush, avert her eyes, hang her head, speak elliptically and so on—is that women are *properly* secretive: it is a woman's rôle to cover over the "truth," to veil herself, to be shy in the face of sex, to be mysterious (for men). Secrecy and shame intersect in this scene; to perform shame is to go through a ritual of concealment, to secrete.

In Chapter 32, guilty about her reaction to the news that Charles is no longer to inherit his uncle's property at Winsyatt ("I am shameful, I have behaved like a draper's daughter"), Ernestina looks out of her bedroom window towards Charles's windows at the White Lion (the inn he stays at in Lyme Regis). She misreads the fact that his light remains burning until well into the night as a sign that he is displeased

with her. (Charles is, of course, battling with guilt over his feelings for Sarah, but I'll
get to *his* experiences of shame and love later.) Ernestina again pulls on her *peignoir*
and unlocks her diary in a scene which closely echoes the one I have described
above. Her performances can be described as "scenes of utterance" to the extent
that they are ordered by the overlapping force of the speech acts "I love you" ("I
confess..." "I promise..." etc) and "Shame on you!" ("I/you must not..."). She is
defined (and defines herself) as a good woman (or indeed as a "woman") through a
certain obedience to the demands and the implications of these two speech acts.

My interpretation of these two scenes is meant, in part, to draw attention back
to the scopic narrative economy which I identified earlier to invite consideration
of both the "hither and thither" side of the utterance. This novel makes it explicit
that the imagined spectators of Ernestina's performances in her bedroom are, in her
mind, God and Charles: "Perhaps Charles would see that *her* window was also still
penitentially bright in the heavy darkness that followed the thunderstorm" (219).
Her misinterpretation of Charles's late-burning light follows of course from the
assumption that just as he is her virtual witness (her confessor in this scene), so too
is she an imagined presence in his room. Except, and this is important, she does
not so much imagine herself as a spectator (although she does watch his window)
as understand herself to be the object of his spectatorship; she turns her light on
to signal that she is doing penance under his gaze. When she writes in her diary,
"just as she hoped he might see the late light in her room, so did she envisage a day
when he might coax her into sharing this intimate record of her prenuptial soul. She
wrote partly for his eyes—as, like every other Victorian woman, she wrote partly
for *His* eyes" (219–20). I have already referred to the novel's tendency to conflate
the perspectives of Charles, the narrator, and, indeed, Fowles himself. This scene
resonates with the novelist's claim in Chapter 13 that this manifold gaze is shared by
God, or, perhaps more accurately, that this multiplex system is, in its very operations,
"Godlike." This God, however, is an "omniscient and decreeing" or Victorian one.

It is beyond the scope of this study fully to analyze the extent to which the
discourse of repression it recites is, in large part, a religious discourse, except to
briefly address the idea that the novel's representation of the relationship between
sex and power turns on the recognition of the authority of God. What I want to
emphasize instead is that what Ernestina does in these scenes is, in a quite particular
sense, *perform*. She plays out a little drama of subjection which only makes sense
or succeeds to the degree that she imagines an audience for it. Indeed the idea of an
audience must, in some sense, already be in place before she can perform. It is for
this reason that the figure of God has such potent symbolic force: the success of her
performance depends upon the imagined presence of an omniscient spectator.

While it is Sarah, and clearly not Ernestina, who most explicitly plays the role
of the shameful (or "fallen") woman in this novel, I hope that I have made it clear
that Ernestina's behavior is also informed and conditioned by a discourse of shame.
Although to varying degrees and with quite different dramatic consequences, *both*
women act out the relationship between "shame" and "love." This observation is
crucial to my argument that even the most apparently mundane heterosexual subject
exists in a complex and uneasy relation to the heterosexual matrix. Further, the
constitution of such a subject does not take place through a singular act but must

be enacted over and over and over again if the dangers inherent in processes of subjectification are to be thwarted. To a certain extent, Sarah's performances shed light on Ernestina's; her relatively self-conscious manipulation of the conventional scene or space of utterance draws attention to the fact that she is not the only character "acting" in this novel. Again: the relationship between performance and performativity is an "active question" in this novel.

A number of difficult questions must be negotiated if I'm going to talk about the characters as "actors" in this way. I must consider, first of all, the semantic tangle between the terms performance, performative, and performativity. As I have been at pains to point out throughout this book, an ever-present trap for anyone using theories of performativity in their analyses is the apparent ease with which these three terms can be collapsed into one another. Conflating "performance" with the "performative" is what led to the fairly ubiquitous misreadings of Butler's *Gender Trouble*. However, to leave the question of "performance" out of our analyses entirely would be to make an error of no less consequence. To say that these terms do not mean the same thing is not to say that they don't mean something *in relation to each other*. In fact, the terms "performative" and "performativity" mean something (as does "speech act") because of their intimate etymological relationship with the notion of "performance." If one was to put together a kind of lexicon of some of the terms and "semantic clusters" most often used by speech-act and performativity theorists, it would have to include words like the following (and any number of variations on them): perform, act, actor, play, drama, stage, imitate, comedy, script, display, scene, costume, masquerade, dissemble, artifice, copy, mimic, (re)cite.[4] Despite the pitfalls, performativity theorists' use of the vocabulary and idiom of the "stage" has enabled an effective and subtle critical analysis of the relationship between the subject and society. This strategy only becomes all the more useful when one comes up against a text which itself uses these very same "semantic clusters" to tell a tale about the troubled relationship of individuals to their "age."

In order to read this novel most effectively, I would argue, it is important to keep the space between "performance" and "performativity" in view; indeed this is the very space I have focused on in my close reading. As will become clearer as I go on, it is in this space, in which notions of performance and performativity feed into and off one another, that the potential for resistance to hegemonic discourses might be said to reside. In the context of theories of performativity, questions of resistance and resignification almost always raise the particularly vexed question of "agency." When I say that Ernestina and Sarah (and indeed the other characters) are most usefully conceptualized as "actors," I am clearly risking precisely the voluntarist misinterpretation of "performativity" which I criticized in Chapter 4. Who is the subject of the verb "perform" in this context? If it is simply the character, or the shamed subject, then how is this approach useful for a constructivist theory of subjectivity? There are, in very simple terms, two senses of the verb "to perform"

---

4   This notion of generating a lexicon in order to demonstrate the prevalence of certain discursive structures, and—in my case—certain recurrent rhetorical and theoretical strategies in a given body of texts, comes from Sedgwick's "Shame and Performativity: Henry James's New York Edition Prefaces" (228).

in play here: one assumes an actor who is "conscious" that he or she is performing a "ritual, ceremonial, or scripted behaviour" (Parker and Sedgwick 2), whereas the other assumes an actor who is "unconscious" of their performance. It is the latter sense of performance which makes theories of performativity possible. However, and again this should become clearer as I go on, a politics of the performative has to allow for the possibility that these two senses of "perform" cannot, in the final analysis, be so simply opposed.

Lucien Le Bouille notes that "space is treated as an open theater" or a "symbolic stage" (209) in *The French Lieutenant's Woman*. Just as Ernestina's performances in her bedroom require the (virtual) presence of an audience in order to proceed, Sarah must play shame before the eyes of others if her performance is to be successful. Whereas Ernestina imagines herself an exhibitionist—"a dancer, an actress"—in the "privacy" of her own bedroom, Sarah's infamy in the town depends on a more public exhibitionism. Related to this is the extent to which Ernestina and Sarah tend to occupy quite distinct spaces in the novel: if Ernestina's "symbolic stage" is her room, or at least the interior of her aunt's house (we very rarely see her outdoors), then Sarah's is the outdoors, and most particularly the Undercliff, a lush coastal landscape to the West of Lyme Regis: "an English Garden of Eden" (62). The implications are fairly clear. Ernestina is defined by her domesticity. Her narrative confinement within the walls of upper-middle-class Victorian homes for much of the novel is symbolic of exactly the model of repressive power I discussed above. The proper Victorian woman is trapped, immobilized in a sense, by the structures which define and rule her. Ernestina is not, however, an unwilling prisoner; she has after all "a very proper respect for convention" (28). (Note, for example that one of her favourite pastimes is planning and daydreaming about the interior decorations of her future home.) Sarah, in contrast, refuses to be contained by the very same spaces. Remember her fixation on the "farthest horizon" in the opening scenes on the windswept quay; Ernestina, you will also remember, was keen to return to the relative safety of Lyme Regis. Further, Sarah insists on walking alone in the Undercliff despite her employer, Mrs Poulteney's, orders to the contrary. Importantly, she does not endeavor to keep these walks a secret, but *allows herself to be seen* by Poulteney's housekeeper, Mrs Fairley, thus ensuring that her disobedience will be found out. (A clear example of this is the scene when Sarah chooses to take the path by the dairy—and thus be seen by the dairyman from whom she knows Mrs Fairley buys her milk—rather than take the concealed path she has taken in the past.)

Mrs Poulteney, variously described as an "awesome Lady" (22), a "plump vulture" (22), and, sarcastically, "a pillar of the community" (130), employs Sarah as a companion early in the novel. Mrs Poulteney, whose house stands as an "elegantly clear simile of her social status, in a commanding position on one of the steep hills behind Lyme Regis" (21), is partly persuaded to employ Sarah because of her "*seeming* so castdown, so annihilated by circumstance" (36, my emphasis). In her eyes, employing Sarah is a Christian act of charity; she has welcomed a repentant sinner into her home and thus made some move towards ensuring the good favor of the Lord. At the conclusion of their initial interview, Poulteney "put her most difficult question":

"What if this … person returns; what then?"

But again Sarah did the best possible thing: she said nothing, and simply bowed her head and shook it. In her increasingly favourable mood Mrs Poulteney allowed this to be an indication of speechless repentance. (37)

Poulteney's characterization of Sarah as both ashamed of her past behavior and now repentant is not based on any actual disclosure or confession on Sarah's part ("I do not wish to speak of it ma'm" (37)). Instead, she reads her silence, her bowed head, as evidence enough. Sarah indeed does the "best possible thing" and Mrs Poulteney "allows" her behavior to signal a willingness to do penance. What this passage lets slip is the suggestion that there may be no necessary correspondence between Sarah's actual feelings or intentions and her body language. The following passage reinforces this idea: "It had not occurred to her, of course, to ask why Sarah, who had refused offers of work from less sternly Christian souls than Mrs Poulteney's, should wish to enter her house" (37). One of the reasons is simply that "Marlborough House commanded a magnificent prospect of Lyme Bay" (37). Next to the end of the quay, this house is the best place from which to watch for her lover, or, more accurately as it turns out, Marlborough House allows Sarah to keep staring towards the horizon: this passage gestures towards the same spatial and temporal collapse which I described earlier as fundamental to Sarah's characterization. (Again, that is to say, the novel contrasts the "view" of the "Victorian" with that of the "other Victorian.")

Just as Mrs Poulteney reads Sarah's behavior in her house as evidence of repentance (silence, averted eyes, bowed head, her obvious desire for privacy and so on), so too she reads "the pattern of her exterior movements" (57) as evidence that she "[s]till shows signs of attachment to her seducer" (56). (Notice that this opposition of proper and improper behavior can again be mapped in terms of an opposition of interiority to exteriority. The spatial metaphors in this novel are strikingly suited to the myth of Victorianism it promotes.) Not surprisingly, Poulteney rarely ventures outdoors and must rely on the eyes of her housekeeper, Mrs Fairley, to keep track of Sarah's movements; Mrs Fairley, in turn, has a "wide network of relations and acquaintances at her command." Sarah's "every movement and expression" (57) are thus efficiently reported back to her employer. In Chapter 9, Sarah is chastised for "exhibiting her shame" (59): "'I am told, Miss Woodruff, that you are always to be seen in the same places when you go out.' Sarah looked down before the accusing eyes. 'You look to sea'" (58). Sarah agrees to Poulteney's request to only walk by the sea on occasion ("and pray do not stand and stare so" (59)) and alters her walking habits accordingly. While Mrs Fairley continues to report to her mistress every occasion on which Sarah does stand and stare to her mistress, they are rare. In any case, "Sarah had by this time acquired a kind of ascendancy of suffering over Mrs Poulteney that saved her from any serious criticism. And after all, as the spy and the mistress often reminded each other, poor 'Tragedy' was mad" (59). Again, respectable society can only account for Sarah's difference by reference to the figures of the prostitute and the madwoman. This episode (and there are many like it in the book) is a telling one: again Sarah is the focus of a manifold gaze, censorious *and* fascinated. Mrs Poulteney and her spies can only view her from the historically determined and thus limited perspective available to them. That is, this episode highlights the possibility that Sarah may very well be

exploiting the narrow purview of those who would watch (and judge) her. We finally
have this suspicion confirmed for us at the conclusion of Chapter 9:

> You will no doubt have guessed the truth: that she was far less mad than she seemed ...
> or at least not mad in the way that was generally supposed. Her exhibition of her shame
> had a kind of purpose; and people with purposes know when they have been sufficiently
> attained and can be allowed to rest in abeyance for a while. (60)

This is, particularly with the aims of my analysis in mind, a fascinating passage. In
The French Lieutenant's Woman, Sarah manipulates conventional scenes of utterance
in order to bring about certain illocutionary and perlocutionary effects. Sarah accepts,
or more precisely invites, the injunction "Shame on you." She quite deliberately
plays the part of a "fallen woman" and thus puts herself beyond the pale of Victorian
propriety—in order to become an "other Victorian." Sarah's performance guarantees
her circulation as a character in Lyme Regis's social gossip network, and as an object
for censure. Unlike Poulteney and the milieu she represents, Sarah is attuned to
the performative dimensions of language and behavior. Further, her deception is
successful because she understands the relationship between the performative and
narrative: speech acts anticipate certain effects; they can be said to initiate, propel,
and organize narratives. Her capacity to deceive (and, in Charles's case, to seduce)
in this way is closely linked to her characterization as an "Other Victorian" in the
sense I have discussed above, and, in a broader sense, to the representation of her as
an archetypal mysterious woman, as a figure who cuts across or transcends history
and who can also, so the book implies, defy the distinction between the diegetic and
extra-diegetic world and thus exert her influence outside of the text and force the
"novelist" to reveal his presence in the text.[5]

---

5   Another way to analyze the force of Sarah's deception might be to characterize her
as a "liar" rather than a "performer." Gian Balsamo comments that *"The French Lieutenant's
Woman* is characterised by [a] never-ending, ceaseless flow of conflicting levels of un-truth,
quasi-truth, semi-truth" (147). To lie is to make an utterance for which there is no referent,
yet the lie cannot be adequately assessed or judged on the basis of its falsity. We lie because
we want something to happen, we want to achieve or to avoid certain effects. In fact to lie
is to rely upon the conventionality of illocutionary *and* perlocutionary effects. Sarah, quite
simply, tells lies. Her utterances are felicitous as lies for precisely the same reasons they are
infelicitous as confessions. They function as confessions in the social field despite the fact that
they might be said to be "unhappy"; as lies, however, her utterances are very "happy" indeed.
Of course, all utterances are vulnerable to insincerity. However, my guess is that the threat of
the false performance, or of the "lie," has peculiar resonance when it comes to the questions of
love and shame. The notion of the lie could well be used to organize an interpretation of *The
French Lieutenant's Woman* not dissimilar to my own. In these terms, this novel is about lying.
It is fascinating, that is, to consider the "lie" as a type of speech act. Perhaps what accounts for
the continued usefulness of Austin's *How to Do Things With Words*—and, by the way, what
produces its casual, jocular tone—is the sense that Austin is not telling us anything we didn't
already know. There's a confidence about his invention of the category of the performative
which obviates the need for a detailed, philosophical justification of the claim that when we
utter certain things, we are not so much saying as doing something. By correcting the error of
traditional philosophies of language—their focus on the statement, on testing utterances on

After their initial and portentous encounter on the Cobb, an intensely romantic relationship between Sarah and Charles develops over the course of a number of meetings, mostly in the Undercliff. Charles is initially drawn there by his interest in fossils; however, it soon becomes the setting for a more profound and difficult quest, one which will put into question his entire sense of self, and lead him to end his betrothal to Ernestina. Their first meeting anticipates the terms within which this "quest" will proceed. Charles stumbles across Sarah asleep on a grassy ledge and is reminded fleetingly of a girl he had once known in Paris. Sarah is immediately associated with a more liberal and "foreign" sexuality than that which his age permits; again her difference from properly feminine women is the focus.[6] Charles studies her face while she sleeps and cannot "imagine what, besides despair, could drive her, in an age where women were semi-static, timid, incapable of sustained physical effort, to this wild place" (65). He comes "to his sense of what was proper" when she wakes and is startled by his presence: "She said nothing, but fixed him with a look of shock and bewilderment, perhaps not untinged with shame" (65). He excuses himself and quickly walks away. The concluding passage of this episode is a telling one:

> Charles did not know it, but in those brief poised seconds above the waiting sea, in that luminous evening silence broken only by the waves' quiet wash, the whole Victorian Age was lost. And I do not mean he had taken the wrong path. (66)

It is on his return from this walk that he sees Sarah walk defiantly by the dairy and is told by the dairyman that "she been't no lady. She be the French Loot'n'nt's Hoer" (77). He is again bowled over by the sight of her face: "It was as if after each sight of it, he could not believe its effect, and had to see it again. It seemed both to envelop and reject him; as if she were a figure in a dream, both standing still and yet always receding" (78). He rushes to catch up with her, but she refuses his company: "she stared at the ground a moment. 'And please tell no one you have seen me in this place'" (78). Left with the "after-image of those eyes—... abnormally large as if able to *see* more and suffer more" (78, my emphasis), Charles again finds himself "rebuffed" and drawn into a strange complicity with Sarah, the "scarlet woman of Lyme" (107).

One opposition which is starkly in play in Charles and Sarah's romance is, of course, that between "Duty" and "Passion." Sarah's capacity to transfix and unsettle Charles is directly contrasted with the chasteness and inhibition which colors his relationship with Ernestina. The chapter which bridges the narration of "those brief, poised seconds" above the sea and their meeting by the dairy, has as its first

---

the basis of whether they are true or false—Austin drew our attention to an error that was so glaringly obvious, it's amazing no one had remarked on it (at least in so memorable a way) before. From the moment a subject enters into language, enters into culture, he or she knows that "speech" produces effects: we all know "how to do things with words." It's at this point that the idea of the lie as speech act becomes most pertinent.

6   An important marker of Sarah's difference from the proper Victorian woman throughout this novel is her apparent "likeness" to foreign, particularly French, women. See also 105–6.

epigraph a poem by A.H. Clough aptly titled "Duty."[7] This chapter tells the tale of Charles and Ernestina's betrothal, after which "[e]verything had become quite simple. He loved Ernestina" (74), and Charles can imagine the pleasure of waking with her "legitimately in the eyes of both God and man beside him" (74). That is, their relationship brings to his mind a bedroom image of a quite different kind to that which Sarah's sleeping form provokes. Charles is, at least in part, motivated to marry Ernestina for the sex. Since his first sexual encounter at university threw him into a period of deep inner torment and guilt, Charles has travelled overseas to satisfy his sexual desires (with exactly the kind of "foreign" woman Sarah reminds him of). Midway through the novel he begins to doubt the wisdom of his decision: "In this vital matter of the woman with whom he had elected to share his life, had he not been only too conventional? Instead of doing the most intelligent thing had he not done the most obvious? What then would have been the most intelligent thing? To have waited" (114). He begins to imagine himself hampered by his betrothal to Ernestina: "His future had always seemed to him of vast potential; and now suddenly it was a fixed voyage to a known place. [Sarah] had reminded him of that" (114).

Sarah beseeches Charles to meet her in the Undercliff to hear the tale of her seduction by Varguennes, the French Lieutenant. While she confesses that she embraced shame in order to claim an identity for herself, we later learn that the story she tells Charles is itself a fabrication:

> I did it so that I should never be the same again. I did it so that people *should* point at me, *should* say, there walks the French Lieutenant's Whore—oh yes, let the word be said. So that they should know I have suffered, and suffer, as others suffer in every town and village in this land. I could not marry that man. So I married shame. I do not mean that I knew what I did, that it was in cold blood that I let Varguennes have his will of me. It seemed to me then as if I threw myself off a precipice or plunged a knife into my heart. It was a kind of suicide. An act of despair, Mr Smithson. I know it was wicked … blasphemous, but I know no other way to break out of what I was. If I had left that room, and returned to Mrs Talbot's, and resumed my former existence, I know that by now I should truly be dead … and by my own hand. What has kept me alive is my shame, my knowing that I am truly not like other women. I shall never have children, a husband, and those innocent happinesses they have. And they will never understand the reason for my crime. […] Sometimes I almost pity them. I think I have a freedom they cannot understand. No insult, no blame, can touch me. Because I have set myself beyond the pale. I am nothing, I am hardly human any more. I am the French Lieutenant's Whore. (152–3)

Sarah steps in the way of an authoritative utterance. She makes herself available for censure by playing a part before the eyes of a community of witnesses. By declaring herself an outcast (by inviting the stares and the injunctions of those who would cast her out), she steps outside of the bounds of proper society and thus makes herself

---

7   With the form conforming duly,
     Senseless what it meaneth truly,
     Go to church—the world require you,
     To balls—the world require you too,
     And marry—papa and mama desire you,
     And your sisters and schoolfellows do (67).

"other." Importantly though, in the terms of the novel her exclusion does not follow from but rather necessitates her performance, and indeed makes her capable of it. Educated beyond her class and gifted with an exceptional intelligence, Sarah can "never see the world except as the generality to which I must be the exception" (149). Her tale of illicit sex in a cheap tavern has, as you may well guess, an extraordinary impact on Charles. He imagines himself both as Varguennes and as the man who would strike him down and, correspondingly, sees Sarah both as an "innocent victim" (153) and a "wild, abandoned woman" (154). The narrator tells us that "[s]uch a shift of sexual key is impossible today." Whereas in Charles's age "private minds did not admit the desires banned by the public mind," in our own time "[a] man and a woman are no sooner in any but the most casual contact than they consider the possibility of a physical relationship" (154). Men and women only make sense to each other in this novel through a heterosexual rubric; the distinction is between a time when the imagined sexual encounter between every man and every woman is a secret, a repressed truth, and a time when it is not. Hence a sexual relationship between a man and a woman who force a dialogue between these two times can come to stand for "truth" or the struggle for "truth" in a greater sense. Sarah's story offers Charles a "glimpse of an ideal world" (154) and thus she, and no other woman, is the proper object of his love.

What impresses me the most about Sarah's characterization in this novel is the way in which her *relatively* self-conscious performances of affect—even if enabled by a less than progressive discourse of gender and sexuality—help us to see the ways in which all experiences of affect are always already in some sense "performances." I hope that I have avoided granting Sarah any kind of autonomous interiority which places her outside the constraints and strictures of language and discourse. Such a move would be complicit with what I have critiqued as the generative conceit of this novel: the lie that Sarah is in some primary way, *self-authoring*. Despite appearances, she is no less discursively or culturally constituted than the other characters who populate the novel. Nevertheless, Sarah's characterization does force us to reconsider the status of the subject in theories of performativity. She functions, in a very important sense, as the agent of the novel's action. This does not mean, however, that in the final analysis Sarah represents a subject, an "I," who is coterminous with Power, a subject who is, in some final sense, in control. Instead, this novel, perhaps inadvertently, reveals at almost every turn that "we" can only act within the parameters of an already defined social and linguistic field. What it also reveals, through Sarah I think, is that this field is never fully defined and thus always vulnerable to redefinition.

The tension between these two ideas, between the notion of a discursive field which is already defined and one which can be redefined, might name the main problem in any attempt to develop a "politics of the performative." In the introduction to *Excitable Speech: The Politics of the Performative*, Butler distinguishes between "sovereignty" and "agency" in her explanation of what it means to "act" in the context of a social and discursive field. For Butler, "agency begins where sovereignty wanes" (16). She writes: "The one who acts (who is not the same as the sovereign subject) acts precisely to the extent that he or she is constituted as an actor and, hence, operating within a linguistic field of enabling constraints from the outset" (16). This almost-oxymoronic notion of "enabling constraints" is a difficult one. (It's also, I think, quintessential Butler, in the sense that the figure it invokes is of something "turning back on itself.") She explains what she means through a discussion of the "responsibility" of the subject who speaks ("acts"): responsibility, she argues, does not follow from any originary relationship with "speech," but rather from the "citational character of speech" (39). The underlying metaphorics at work here is, of course and again, a metaphorics of the stage: the subject is understood as an "actor" who speaks (who reads a script).

Butler returns in earnest to the question of "agency" in the chapter "Implicit Censorship and Discursive Agency." Butler's notion of "discursive agency" pictures a subject who is not, as it were, hamstrung from the outset, or, to use Butler's term, a subject who is not "redundant." Certainly, the subject makes linguistic decisions "only in the context of an already circumscribed field of linguistic possibilities. One decides on the condition of an already decided field of language, but this repetition does not constitute the decision of the speaking subject as a redundancy. The gap between redundancy and repetition is the space of agency" (129). The agency of the subject, that is, "is constrained but not determined in advance" (139). Butler clarifies this point in the introduction to *Undoing Gender* where she explains agency in terms of enabling constraints: "If I have any agency, it is opened up by the fact that I am constituted by a social world I never chose" (3). This is not unrelated to my claim that the space between performance and performativity is the very space within which the relationship of the speaking subject to the social field is under constant renegotiation.

Sarah's performance in *The French Lieutenant's Woman* enables fruitful consideration of this space of renegotiation. Further, the drama she plays out highlights the performative or, to use another term, the *interpellative* force of such formulaic or idiomatically prescribed utterances as "I love you" and Shame on you." This novel has things to teach us, although inadvertently, both about the usefulness of theories of performativity and about the theories themselves. Butler writes that the performative needs to be rethought as "social ritual"; it is precisely this kind of rethinking which this novel can inspire.

Butler elaborates on the "tacit performativity of power." Her (re)definition of the performative intersects in fascinating ways with the kind of claims I've been making about the force of (implicit) speech acts, both as represented in this novel and beyond it:

> The "constructive" power of the tacit performative is precisely its ability to establish a practical sense for the body, not only a sense of what the body is, but how it can or cannot negotiate space, its "location" in terms of prevailing cultural coordinates. The performative is not a singular act used by an already established subject, but one of the powerful and insidious ways in which subjects are called into social being from diffuse social quarters, inaugurated into sociality by a variety of diffuse and powerful interpellations. In this sense the social performative is a crucial part not only of subject *formation*, but of the ongoing political contestation and reformulation of the subject as well. The performative is not only a ritual practice: it is one of the influential rituals by which subjects are formed and reformulated. (*Excitable Speech* 159–60)

It is exactly such a mapping of the space, the "'location' in terms of powerful cultural coordinates," of the subject in society which I intended to emerge from my reading of what I have termed the "scopic narrative economy" of *The French Lieutenant's Woman*. While I tend to talk about performatives in terms of temporality (in terms of moments, instances, illocutionary and perlocutionary effects, narrative trajectories), this discussion gestures towards a consideration of the space of performatives, as indeed do my frequent references to the "scene of utterance." Each citation of a particular speech act instantiates what Sedgwick calls "a neighborhood of language around or touching the performative." Close scrutiny of the ideological parameters of this novel's characterizations and principle narrative trajectory proceeds must fruitfully when we acknowledge and examine the ways in which it represents or "stages" various "social rituals" crucial to the formation of the heterosexual romantic subject. From my perspective, contemporary theories of performativity are ideally suited to such an approach.

Performativity and Interpellation: Charles Smithson, the Law, and Love

In a broad sense, my key theoretical interest is to interrogate the relation of "*act* to *identity*."[8] In their introduction to *Performativity and Performance*, Parker and Sedgwick argue for the continued currency of Austin's formulation of the speech act to such an endeavor. They write: "Viewed through the lenses of a postmodern deconstruction of agency, Austin can be seen to have tacitly performed two radical condensations: of the complex producing and underwriting relations of the 'hither' side of the utterance, and of the no-less-constitutive negotiations that comprise its uptake" (7). They thus suggest the importance of shifting the critical focus to the "thither" side of the utterance, arguing that if Austin's formulation of the speech act makes "a deconstruction of the *performer* both necessary and possible," it has even more to offer to a consideration of the "complex process (or, with a more postmodernist inflection, the complex space) of uptake" (7). The implication of much of this chapter has been that a subject who occupies what might be called the "thither" side of a formulaic utterance may be no less a "*performer*" than the subject who speaks. Further, I have been concerned to open up the space of utterance by examining the ways in which speech acts can be said to circulate implicitly, to be taken up, so to speak, without needing to be spoken or heard as direct speech. This involves imagining a cast much larger than the "I" and "you" who are usually the star players in analyses of the scene of utterance.

Sedgwick and Parker note that "Austin's rather bland invocation of 'the proper context' (in which a person's saying something is to count as doing something) has opened, under pressure of recent theory, onto a populous and contested scene in which the role of silent or implied witnesses, for example, or the quality and structuration of the bonds that unite auditors or link them to speakers, bears as much weight as do

---

8   This phrase comes from Parker and Sedgwick's introduction to *Performativity and Performance*, where they remark that "highly detailed interrogations of the relations of *speech* to *act* are occurring in the space of a relatively recent interrogation of the relation of *act* to *identity*" (6).

the particular speech acts of supposed individual speech agents" (7). My own work is clearly informed by such recent theory as I aim to be sensitive to the workings of speech acts in a social context, when that context is less easy to locate or to map than early proponents of speech act theory suggested. I use the interpretation of a number of key scenes in *The French Lieutenant's Woman*—a novel which I maintain is *about* the relation between *act* and *identity*—to explore the fraught and fascinating space of uptake, to attempt to chart the ways in which formulaic utterances can be said to be constitutive not just of subjects, but of subjects in their sociality, of social relations.

Sedgwick and Parker go on to suggest that theories of "interpellation" may be one of the best places to begin analysis of this newly complicated space, but remark that current theories of interpellation are not up to the task (7). Butler takes up this challenge in *Excitable Speech* and *The Psychic Life of Power*. She reformulates Althusser's original account of the scene of interpellation in order both to bring it up to speed with her more complex and metatheoretical account of the processes of subjection and, in turn, to use this reformulation to clarify and qualify, once more, her understanding of the performative character of these processes. The kind of analysis of *The French Lieutenant's Woman* that I am attempting here both helps us to make sense of the relationship between performativity and interpellation as Butler articulates it, and suggests ways in which some of her conclusions might be usefully extended.

How might speech acts be said to "interpellate" subjects? In Althusser's original formulation of the scene of interpellation it is precisely through an act of speech that individuals are "hailed" as subjects; the individual comes to recognize itself as a subject (and as the object of authoritative discourse) through that hailing. Indeed, as Butler's critique makes clear, the potential for a correspondence between Althusser and Austin is apparent in the vocabulary and metaphorics of Althusser's account of the interpellative moment as the "hailing" of an individual by authoritative speech; to be interpellated is to be addressed or spoken to. Further, Althusser characterizes his quasi-fictional narration of the way ideology "acts" as a "little theoretical theatre" (174), populated by "'*actors*' [who] in this *mise en scène* of interpellation, and their respective roles, are reflected in the structure of all ideology" (177, my emphasis). An individual walking along a street is called by a policeman, "Hey, you there!" Recognizing him or herself to be the object of that address, the individual turns around, and, through that turning, becomes a subject. As Althusser insists, however, "*individuals are always-already subjects*" (176). The individual who turns is best conceived of as a "place-holder," acting out a moment in every subject's history which can never be witnessed or remembered, indeed never happened in any literal sense, but which must be *imagined* if we are to make sense of the way in which the subject is produced. Nor does Althusser offer his account of the interpellative scene as a description of some primary and unambiguous process by which we come to be and are thus complete. His qualifying remarks make it clear that the process he names "interpellation" is precisely reiterative and thus, in the final analysis, unable to be fully and accurately narrated as a single scene: "I only wish to point out that you and I are *always already* subjects, and as such constantly practice the rituals of ideological recognition, which guarantee for us that we are indeed concrete, individual, distinguishable and (naturally) irreplaceable subjects" (172–3). His description of interpellation as a scene is useful to the extent that it allows him to clarify certain things about the relationship of ideology to subjects, including, paradoxically enough, things about that relationship which his scene cannot show: "The existence of ideology and the hailing or interpellation of individuals as subjects are one and the same thing" (175). Althusser's recourse to a model of speech and response as the best way to illustrate the process of subjection, and, of course, the grammatical strictures of narration, imposes a linear and progressive temporality where none exists: "in reality these things happen without any succession" (175).

Nevertheless, as Butler explains, this scene is "exemplary and allegorical and as such never needs to happen for its effectivity to be presumed" (*Psychic* 106). Her definition of interpellation in these terms is a particularly useful one:

> Indeed, if it is allegorical in Benjamin's sense, then the process literalized by the allegory is precisely what resists narration, what exceeds the narrativizability of events. Interpellation, on this account, is not an event, but a certain way of *staging the call*, where the call, as staged, becomes deliteralized in the course of its exposition or *darstellung*. The call itself is figured as a demand to align oneself with the law, a turning around (to face the law, to find a face for the law?) and an entrance into the language of self-ascription—"Here I am"—through the appropriation of guilt. (106–107)

The individual who turns around in response to the policeman's call recognizes himself as a subject, by recognizing himself as a subject before the law. Before becoming a subject then, the individual must already be constituted by some prior awareness of and obedience to the law, to authority. Why does the hailed individual almost always turn around in Althusser's formulation of interpellation ("nine times out of ten")? He writes, "it is a strange phenomenon, and one which cannot be explained solely by 'guilt feelings,' despite the large numbers who 'have something on their consciences'" (174). The tenor of his discussion suggests the question, as Butler puts it, "Might the theory of interpellation require a theory of conscience?" (5) She goes to great lengths to elaborate such a theory in *The Psychic Life of Power*.

It's impossible to do full justice to Butler's dense and detailed interrogation of the process of subjection here; however, her key argument, as I understand it, is particularly useful and suggestive. This argument is best explained through reference to the "figure of turning" which she invokes over and over again to explain her assumptions and conclusions about the relationship between the subject and power, between the subject and discourse. For Butler, this "figure of turning"—of a subject who turns towards the law as it turns back on itself—encapsulates the paradox of subjection as she defines it: "'Subjection' signifies the process of becoming subordinated by power as well as the process of becoming a subject" (2); thus the synchronicity of self-recognition with recognition of and obedience to the law in Althusser's formulation of the moment of interpellation. The man on the street can recognize himself as a subject only by recognizing himself as always already subjected. The subject does not exist prior to discourse, just as discourse does not exist prior to the subject.

I want now to consider one scene from *The French Lieutenant's Woman* alongside Althusser's scene of interpellation: the sex scene between Charles and Sarah in Endicott's Family Hotel. By considering this scene alongside that allegorical scene involving a pedestrian and a policeman, I hope to be able to draw certain conclusions about the ways in which this novel represents the relationship between the (heterosexual) subject and power. From the outset, I want to suggest that what this scene does, like so many others in this novel, is stage a call, stage a scene of utterance. Such a suggestion only makes sense if we accept that *as performatives* "Shame on you!" and "I love you" are *interpellative* to the extent that they function to call subjects to order. When he sees Sarah again, Charles is "overcome with a violent sexual desire" (302).

> He strained that body into his, straining his mouth upon hers, with all the hunger of a long frustration—not merely sexual, for a whole ungovernable torrent of things banned, romance, adventure, sin, madness, animality, all these coursed wildly through him. (304)

Immediately thereafter, Charles is seized by "an immediate and universal horror" (305). He imagines Ernestina and her father as the imagined witnesses to his infidelity and hears a noise outside:

> And he held her a little closer. Her hand reached timidly and embraced his. The rain stopped. Heavy footsteps, slow, measured, passed somewhere beneath the window. A police officer, perhaps. The Law.
> Charles said, "I am worse than Varguennes." (305)

As in the scene depicting Ernestina's self-regulation ("I must not") which I discussed earlier, a figure of the "law" comes into the bedroom to suppress an "ungovernable torrent." Still a "Victorian," Charles is defined by a constitutive vulnerability to a repressive regulatory norm. His obedience is guaranteed by his always anticipating the charge "Shame on you"; the performative need not be heard in order for an individual to be constituted by it. Charles recognizes himself as a "bad subject" before the law; it is, of course, Sarah who has led him to this point. His love for her will come to represent a greater law; the demand Sarah represents will exceed and thus cancel out the demands of his betrothal to Ernestina. Breaking his promise to Ernestina and his willingness to sign the *confessio delicti* follows from his perception of a greater responsibility—to the "law" Sarah represents. The lie, however, is that whereas his vulnerability to the regulatory norms of his age, represented by the figure of the police officer, is conventional and historical, the "law" Sarah represents is not figured as a "law" but rather as a "truth."

When he sees blood on his shirt tails, Charles immediately realizes that he has been the object of an extraordinary and perplexing deception; Sarah never slept with Varguennes. He sees also that, if he was so easily deceived, then he is not quite in possession of himself in the way that Sarah is. Her only explanation for her behavior is to turn back on the utterance which has been the key to their entire relationship, "I love you": "'Do not ask me to explain what I have done. I cannot explain it. It is not to be explained'" (308–309). Her behavior doesn't have to make sense because it was motivated by love and hence is inexplicable. Yet, as I have insisted throughout this chapter, the success of her manipulation, and indeed the novel's entire narrative trajectory, depends on a certain conventionality of romance; on the conventionality of scenes of utterance and the vulnerability to manipulation which follows from this.

Butler invites us to reimagine Althusser's scene of interpellation. While Althusser emphasizes the success of interpellation, Butler is ever keen to highlight its potential for failure. What if, she asks, the one who is hailed doesn't turn around, or turns around only to "protest the name"?

> And then imagine that the name continues to force itself upon you, to delineate the space you occupy, to construct a social positionality. Indifferent to your protests, the force of interpellation continues to work. One is still constituted by discourse, but at a distance from oneself. Interpellation is an address that regularly misses its mark, it requires a recognition of an authority at the same time that it confers identity through successfully compelling that recognition. Identity is a function of that circuit, but does not preexist it. The mark interpellation makes is not descriptive, but inaugurative. It seeks to introduce a reality rather than report on an existing one; it accomplishes this introduction through a citation of existing convention. Interpellation is an act of speech whose "content" is neither true nor false: it does not have description as its primary task. Its purpose is to indicate and establish a subject in subjection, to produce its social contours in space and time. Its reiterative operation has the effect of sedimenting its "positionality" over time. (*Excitable* 33–4)

Sarah makes me think about yet another way to reimagine this scene: What if the one who is hailed has deliberately stepped in the way of a social performative and accepts the name at a distance from it? Her manipulation of the conventionality of interpellation helps us to see that the relationship of the subject to discourse is best understood through a model of social iterability. That is, her performance reveals that there is no natural or necessary correspondence between the name and the subject it purports to describe; the social performative only masquerades as descriptive. Sarah accepts, even invites, her name "The French Lieutenant's Whore," aware that its potency does not follow from its truth, but rather from the capacity of names to produce effects. Sarah helps us to realize, to take some words of Butler's a little out of context, that "a critical perspective on the kinds of language that govern the regulation and constitution of subjects becomes all the more imperative once we realize how inevitable is our dependency on the ways we are addressed in order to exercise any agency at all" (27). Throughout the novel, her performance untethers agency from mastery by wresting from the sole ownership of the figure of law the capacity to make speech *act*.

Frederick Holmes describes Sarah as the "narrating novelist's surrogate within the fictional world" ("The Novel" 195). He argues that while all of the central characters "fictionalize," Sarah alone understands that the fictions she creates are *fictions*; she is not self-delusional in the way that Charles, Ernestina, Grogan, or Poulteney are. Further, I would add that Sarah uses other characters' trust in the proper course of fictions to her own advantage. From my perspective, she manipulates the relationship between performatives and narratives; she relies on the perlocutionary force of speech acts. As Holmes points out, the characters in this novel have different levels of hermeneutic competency; Sarah is clearly the best reader (and writer) amongst them. In the next chapter, I analyze a novel in which the relationship between reading and heterosexual romance is a central theme: A.S. Byatt's Victorian historical romance *Possession*. My interpretation of this novel illustrates the foundational relationship between performativity and narrativity.

Chapter 7

Performatives and Narratives: A.S. Byatt's *Possession: A Romance*

What's love got to do with it? Everything it seems. (Buxton 200)

A.S. Byatt's "People in Paper Houses: Attitudes to 'Realism' and 'Experiment' in English Post-War Fiction," first published in 1979, includes a critique of *The French Lieutenant's Woman*. Byatt dismisses John Fowles's treatment of Victorianism as "crude" (174).[1] She is fascinated, however, by the way in which his "Victorian novel within a novel" brings "realism" and "experiment" "curiously close together" (173). What she likes about his novel is that it offers a "realist" reading experience at the same time as it invites us to reflect on the fictionality of that experience. But this dual pleasure is spoiled for Byatt by the inclusion of two possible endings for the novel. She argues that they do not suggest "a plurality of possible stories," but "are a programmatic denial of the reality of any" (174). For Byatt, Fowles's alternative endings "painfully destroy the narrative 'reality' of the central events, which have happily withstood authorial shifts in style, interjections, and essays on Victorian reality" (174). Further, she argues that Fowles's experiment doesn't work because *The French Lieutenant's Woman* is set in the past. Without any recourse to the "future tense," readers cannot imagine the two endings as "real" alternatives; "They therefore cancel each other out, and cancel their participants" (174). Byatt's argument is that the two endings upset verisimilitude to such an extent that the reading experience becomes a less enjoyable one; readers' faith in the "reality," or "truth," of the characters and their story is destroyed. In her terms, the alternative endings to Fowles's historical romance privilege "experiment" over "realism," and, as a consequence, deny its readers the pleasures of narrative coherence and closure.

Byatt's disappointment with *The French Lieutenant's Woman* can be understood within the context of her preference for reading and writing what she calls "self-conscious moral realism." She defends this position in a number of the essays published in *Passions of the Mind* (4, 22–3, 181). The key to understanding how Byatt means this term is the idea of balance. She gives her most useful definition of it in "People in Paper Houses," when she praises three novels (Iris Murdoch's *The Black Prince* (1973), Angus Wilson's *As If by Magic* (1973) and Doris Lessing's *The Golden Notebook* (1962)) for fulfilling the dual aims she hopes to promote through her use of this term:

---

1 Byatt restates her opposition to Fowles's novel in her collection of essays, *On Histories and Stories* 56, 79, 85–6, 102.

an awareness of the difficulty of "realism" combined with a strong moral attachment to its values, a formal need to comment on their fictiveness combined with a strong sense of the value of a habitable imagined world, a sense that models, literature and "the tradition" are ambiguous and problematic goods combined with a profound nostalgia for, rather than rejection of, the great works of the past. (181)

In contrast, she sees *The French Lieutenant's Woman* as a poor example of self-conscious moral realism to the extent that it fails to sustain a happy balance between these seemingly contradictory impulses. In praise of Fowles's novel, she writes, "the reader is allowed, invited, both to experience imaginatively the sexual urgency and tension it evokes, and to place such imagining as a function of that kind of story, that kind of style, and, Fowles suggests, that period of history" (173). Her problem with it is that intellectual and literary self-consciousness ultimately undermine the novel's realist aspects; they do not work well together. Her emphasis is emphatically not on the contradictions between self-consciousness and the realist mode, but on their potential to act as counterweights to one another and to thus produce a more roundly satisfying novel.

It is no surprise that the usual approach to Byatt's Victorian romance *Possession* is to point out that its apparent postmodernism is belied by Byatt's commitment to a coherent narrative structure. Commentators variously oppose the novel's postmodernist gestures and strategies to its "modernism" or its "Victorianism" (Bronfen, Buxton, Holmes, Hulbert, Kaiser, Kelly, Shiller, Shinn, Yelin). This has been a fruitful approach and has produced a number of engaging analyses, most particularly those by Jackie Buxton, Elisabeth Bronfen, and Frederick Holmes. Indeed, *Possession* seems to present somewhat of a challenge for reviewers and scholars keen to classify it. Danny Karlin remarks that "[t]he book's genre is hard to pin down" (17) and a number of critics have identified it as an example of a new type or genre of novel. In her essay about *Possession* Thelma Shinn coins the term "meronymic novel" to "describe novels which seek to balance and encompass seeming contradictions in style and in content" (164). Dana Shiller makes similar claims with her term, "neo-Victorian novel," which she defines as a subset of the historical novel "at once characteristic of postmodernism and imbued with a historicity reminiscent of the nineteenth-century novel" (1). Del Ivan Janik's classification of *Possession* shifts the emphasis somewhat and is certainly more interesting for it. He singles out *Possession* as the clearest example of a new type of English historical novel which he argues emerged in the 1980s and 1990s. Janik cites *The French Lieutenant's Woman* as a key precursor of the new historical novel and discusses novels by Graham Swift, Julian Barnes, Kazuo Ishiguro, and Peter Ackroyd as examples of the trend. Like Shinn and Shiller, Janik notes that *Possession* and other books like it are only inadequately described by monikers like "modernist" and "postmodernist" because of the extent to which they employ devices and strategies proper to both literary approaches. He remarks further that *Possession* has "all the earmarks of a Victorian 'good read'" (162). Rather than dwell on the questions of contradiction and balance which such an observation usually raises, Janik expressly dismisses the usefulness of classifying these novels according to their predominant literary devices and strategies. More importantly for Janik, what they share is "an affirmation of the importance of history to the understanding of contemporary existence" (162). He writes that this new type of historical novel is "characterized by a foregrounding of the historical consciousness, most often through a dual or even multiple focus on the fictional present and one or more crucial 'pasts'" (161). Like Shinn and Shiller, Janik is keen to distinguish *Possession*, to make claims about the ways in which this book does something different or new in its treatment of the past and, indeed, of the present. In contrast, my focus is on the ways in which *Possession* is anything but remarkable in this regard. That is to say I am more interested in thinking through the idea that both Byatt's use of certain literary strategies and devices to propel a fairly straightforward heterosexual romance plot and her treatment of history are entirely conventional. From the outset then, my aim is to point out the similarities, rather than the differences, between *Possession* and other historical romances, both popular and literary.

In a sense, *Possession* is a study and a defence of the modes of writing by which Byatt is most excited. Buxton writes that *Possession* "unashamedly celebrates romance in both its 'high' and 'vulgar' forms" (212). Byatt's historical romance has easily as much in common with the popular examples of the form I discuss in Chapters 3 and 4 as it does with Fowles's literary romance and others like it. Byatt is, as it turns out, a self-confessed Georgette Heyer fan. One of the few literary scholars who have taken Heyer's historical romances seriously, Byatt has published two essays in her defence. In "The Ferocious Reticence of Georgette Heyer" she gives a detailed description of Heyer's extensive reference library and of her carefully indexed and historically rigorous notebooks on Regency life and language. In contrast to her frustration with Fowles's historical inaccuracy, she is impressed by Heyer's devoted attention to historical detail, and concludes that "the very act of research was for Georgette Heyer, the act of recreating a past to inhabit" (37). Importantly, the focus of both Byatt's criticism of Fowles and her commendation of Heyer is on the value of what she calls a "habitable imagined world," the object of which is to enable readers to imaginatively project themselves into the fiction. What Heyer's novels, including *These Old Shades* and *The Masqueraders*, satisfy for Byatt is "the perennial need for a happy ending and ... a curiosity about historical *facts* of daily life and thought" ("An Honourable Escape" 259); they give her exactly the kind of reading pleasure which *The French Lieutenant's Woman* does not.

As evidence of Heyer's rigorous historical method, Byatt points out that, despite having been written in a grass hut in Africa, "*The Masqueraders* turned out to have only one anachronism ... —White's Club had been made to open a year before it did" ("The Ferocious Reticence" 83). Even if we accept Byatt's neat distinction between history and romance, the claim that this novel contains only one minor historical inaccuracy simply doesn't make sense. As I suggested in my discussion of *The Masqueraders* and throughout this book, the "historical" or factual aspects of historical romance fictions cannot be assessed in isolation from their "fantastic plots." As Linda Hutcheon points out, both novels and historical narratives "derive force more from verisimilitude than from any objective truth" (*Poetics* 105). Indeed, Byatt's own description of Heyer's fictional world as a "myth and an idealization" belies her insistence that this world is true to the historical reality it represents. Byatt writes that Heyer's carefully drawn picture of a particular historical period provides a perfect backdrop for adventure and romance:

> An impossibly desirable world of prettiness, silliness and ultimate good sense where men and women really *talk* to each other, know what is going on between them, and plan to spend the rest of their lives together developing the relationship. In her romantic novels, as in Jane Austen's, it is love the people are looking for, and love they give each other, guaranteed by the cushions, bonnets and dances at Almack's, and by the absence of sex-in-the-head. It is a myth and an idealization, but it is one we were brought up to believe whether or not we really had Jane Austen in our schoolroom. And because of Georgette Heyer's innocence and lack of prurience we can still retreat into this Paradise of ideal solutions, knowing it for what it is, comforted by the temporary actuality, nostalgically refreshed for coping with the quite different tangle of preconceptions, conventions and social emphases we have to live with. ("An Honourable Escape" 265)

The contradictions in Byatt's appraisal of Heyer reveal the conceptual problems inherent to her notion of balance. Her claims for the historical accuracy of Heyer's fictional setting do not equate with her description of it as an "impossibly desirable world." In line with this emphasis on a "Paradise of ideal solutions," Byatt describes Heyer as a "superlatively good writer of honourable escape" ("An Honourable Escape" 258). She rejects the charge that Heyer wrote simple naïve escapism. Instead, she praises her for achieving a "clever balance between genuine romance and a saving comic mockery of romance within romance" (261). For Byatt, Heyer's novels are saved from mediocrity by precisely the kind of self-parody described (although with a different emphasis) in my analysis of *These Old Shades* and *The Masqueraders*. They achieve, in her terms, an equilibrium between cleverness and sincerity not unlike that which Byatt expected of *The French Lieutenant's Woman*. She locates the clue to Heyer's success "in the *precise* balance she achieves between romance and reality, fantastic plot and real detail" (265). I interrogate the relationship between history and romance by closely considering the way representations of the past are used in historical romances to set the stage for heterosexual love. In simple terms, Heyer's historical setting anticipates romance; love is "guaranteed by the cushions, bonnets and dances at Almack's." To complicate matters, I showed in my analysis of *These Old Shades* and *The Masqueraders* that such a guarantee or promise of heterosexual love proceeds on the basis of a series of interrelated silences and exclusions and, further, that such omissions are only ever provisionally successful. I make similar claims about *Possession*. By telling a late twentieth-century love story alongside and through a late nineteenth-century one, Byatt contrives an intimate and fascinating relationship between the past and the present, and, more pertinently for my purposes, between a certain approach to history and the course of heterosexual romance.

Definitions of romance almost always emphasize the importance of another time and place to its narrative structure. In Gillian Beer's concise history of the romance genre, she notes that "romance depends considerably upon a certain set *distance* in the relationship between its audience and its subject-matter" (5). She makes the point that "romance can be distinguished from other forms of fiction by the relationship it imposes between reader and romance-world" (8). Romance, in her analysis, is essentially "authoritarian"; it demands that we inhabit the ideal fictional world it offers. To refuse to do so is to read romance improperly and thus to expose ourselves to the "absurdities" (8) of the romance which, Beer makes clear, are inherent to its representation of ideal worlds. Further, Beer argues that the "imaginative functions" (8) of the romance are twofold: "Because romance shows us the ideal it is implicitly instructive as well as escapist" (9). Beer's general points about the romance are strikingly similar to Byatt's specific claims about Heyer's Regency romances. Beer writes that "[p]art of the delight of the romance is that we know we are not required to live full-time in its ideal worlds. It amplifies our experience; it does not press home upon us our immediate everyday concerns" (9). Clearly, neither Byatt nor Beer are using the term "ideal" in quite the politically and theoretically loaded way I use it: to denote the authoritative cultural fiction of a happy heterosexual couple and, by implication, that fiction's dependence on normative assumptions about sex and gender. Nevertheless, it is instructive to follow the link which does exist between our usages and thus to think through the possibility that historical romance novels in general and *Possession: A Romance* in particular are, almost by definition, internally troubled by the essential impossibility of the ideals they represent.

Romance's structural dependence on "distance," to use Beer's term, not only exposes the fissure between the ideal and the actual which lies at the heart of heterosexual romance narratives, but hints that the "actual" is itself defined by cultural fictions and imagined ideals. This idea, and it is certainly not without precedent, is only made more pertinent by an examination of what is perhaps romance's weightiest subgenre, historical romance fiction. The literal opposition which persists between its two key terms, "history" and "romance," is no small matter in this regard. As I have already argued, anachronism is inherent to historical romance fictions. I do not simply mean that errors of historical fact are unavoidable when fictional stories are set in the past. Rather, what my reading of *Possession* illustrates, like my interpretations of the cross-dressing romances and *The French Lieutenant's Woman*, is that the heterosexual romance plot is always anachronistic; it is constitutionally out of time. It is only ever a fiction. One thing that Byatt's novel does make clear is that to believe in love is a question of accepting anachronism; it involves inhabiting an imagined past.

As Byatt has said in interview, she hasn't "used the plot naïvely" (Buxton 214). To the contrary, she has written a sophisticated and remarkably self-aware novel which invites its readers both to immerse themselves in an engrossing tale of history and romance and to reflect on the discursive mechanisms which propel that tale, to think about the particular elements which give this novel's love stories force despite its relentless self-analysis. "But," she goes on to say:

> it has given me intense pleasure. I love those Victorian novels in which, when you come to the end, you're told the whole history of every character from the end of the story until their dying day. I love that kind of thing, it makes me very happy. I don't see why we shouldn't have it: it's not wicked, as we were told in the sixties, it's just pleasant. Everybody knows it's fiction, but then everybody knows the whole thing is fiction. (Buxton 214–15)

Byatt says: "Everybody knows it's fiction, but then everybody knows the whole thing is fiction." This sentence strikes me as a fascinating statement about the relationship between narrative and performativity. It suggests that our acceptance of the illusion of continuity and coherence in a novel is a benign activity because it is, after all, in sync with our "happy" collusion in a whole series of carefully maintained fictions (or elaborate lies) in our daily lives; "everybody knows the whole thing is fiction." Claims for the force of speech acts and of performative acts more generally only make sense because of an implicit acceptance that these acts always take place in the context of a conventional narrative or story (or more accurately in the context of a whole series of overlapping stories). I have touched on this question a number of times—most directly in my discussion of the "implicit performative"—however, I have left close consideration of it until now.

There is a complex thematics at work in *Possession* which makes it an ideal focus for the concluding chapter of this book. Byatt's novel is about the plotting of heterosexual romance and thus inspires me to pursue the idea that there is a constitutive relationship between stories and speech acts, narratives and performatives. Like *The French Lieutenant's Woman*, *Possession* is self-conscious about the pivotal relationship between "I love you" and the heterosexual romance plot, between the romantic speech act and the formation of the heterosexual romantic subject. Further, not only does *Possession* take for granted the importance of open secrecy to heterosexual romance, but demonstrates a kind of faith in the value of its pleasures. My earlier discussion of the workings of the open secret informs my reading later in this chapter of Byatt's use of costume in the representation of her characters' dealings with the past and with each other. This novel is painfully aware that the heterosexual ideal is a fiction, but insists that not only does this make it no less compelling, but, in a very important sense, it makes it no less "true." This capacity to "know" one thing, but to "believe" in quite another is precisely what enables the present-day love story to persist and to make sense despite the book's relentless self-consciousness. This is, I think, a process which *Possession* celebrates and invites us to take pleasure in: "it's not wicked … it's just pleasant." Indeed, Byatt draws our attention to exactly these kinds of considerations with Maud and Roland's own self-consciousness about the progress of their romance. In a sense *Possession* takes issue with one of the key points of this book, namely my emphasis on the inherent instability of the romantic speech act and its correlate, heterosexual romance. The test is to see how my argument that the romantic speech act is always already unstable stands up against this book, which is—in an important sense—about the triumph of love over that instability.

The first section of this chapter, "Writing a Victorian Romance: Byatt versus Fowles," is a comparative discussion of *The French Lieutenant's Woman* and *Possession* in which I pay particular attention to the characterization of Christabel LaMotte. *Possession* is clearly informed by the ideas which motivated Byatt's criticism of *The French Lieutenant's Woman*, her defence of Georgette Heyer, and her promotion of "self-conscious moral realism." While the correspondence between her critical work and this novel informs my analysis of it, my priority is not close speculation about Byatt's personal agenda (an almost irresistible urge when reading her fiction). Instead, my objective is to read this novel in the context of its subscription to and strategic use of an established form: the historical romance. In the following section, "Love's 'Happy Ending': The Story of Maud Bailey and

Roland Michell" my interpretive focus is on the relationship between the novel's twentieth-century protagonists. This discussion continues my use of speech act and performativity theories to unravel the discursive links between the terms history, romance, and heterosexuality.

Writing a Victorian Romance: Byatt versus Fowles

Byatt has said that she was "partly provoked" by Fowles's Victorian romance to write her own (qtd. in Kellaway 45).[2] It is no surprise then that *The French Lieutenant's Woman* is frequently cited by reviewers of A.S. Byatt's novel *Possession: A Romance* as one of its most important antecedents.[3] Nevertheless, for Richard Todd, arguably the most prolific commentator on Byatt's work, this is merely a "commonplace comparison" between these two novels, "bred of a superficial similarity in iconoclastic treatments of Victorian sexuality" (*Consuming* 31). The comparisons follow, he implies, from not reading either novel closely enough and from a consequent failure to appreciate their very different representations of the Victorian past. The connections, however, that many writers have drawn between these two novels cannot be quite so easily dismissed. Not only is Todd's broad-sweeping criticism unfair because he fails to acknowledge that most writers do note the important differences between the two books, but there is clearly a relationship between *The French Lieutenant's Woman* and *Possession* which it falls to reviewers and literary scholars to discuss. Anita Brookner begins her review of *Possession* by noting that Byatt's publishers compare it with *The French Lieutenant's Woman* "on the not unreasonable grounds that both are Victorian dramas secured to the present day": "[t]he comparison" she says, "is inevitable."

Despite Todd's frustration with comparisons between these two novels, he has remarked that the 1981 film adaptation of *The French Lieutenant's Woman* "achieves a similar effect visually" to *Possession*. Like Karel Reisz's film, Byatt's novel tells a twentieth-century love story alongside (and through) a Victorian one. In short, *Possession* tells the story of two contemporary literary scholars, Roland Michell and Maud Bailey, who discover that their respective objects of study, Victorian poets Randolph Henry Ash and Christabel LaMotte, had a brief but passionate love affair. In their efforts to learn what happened between the Victorian poets, Roland and Maud—and we along with them—become engrossed in a paper trail of letters, short stories, poems, essays and diaries. The cumulative effect of these carefully crafted "Victorian" manuscripts is to build exactly the kind of engrossing fictional history or narrative reality that Byatt enjoyed and then lamented when reading *The French Lieutenant's Woman*. While we are invited to reflect on the relationship between

---

2   Byatt's opposition to *The French Lieutenant's Woman* also influenced her approach to *Angels and Insects*: "My own intentions [behind *Possession* and *Angels and Insects*], as I recollect them, were more to do with rescuing the complicated Victorian thinkers from modern diminishing parodies like those of Fowles and Lytton Strachey" (*On Histories* 79).

3   See Brookner; Buxton 208; Giobbi 47–8; Holmes 319–20; Hulbert 56; Janik 181, 187; Kelly xii; Lehmann-Haupt; Shiller; Stout 13; Thurman 151; Todd "Retrieval" 104. Kathryn Hughes cites *The French Lieutenant's Woman* in her review of *Angels and Insects* 49.

narrative and history, Byatt's "ventriloquism" is not just a postmodern device designed to draw our attention to the fictiveness of her historical tale, or, indeed, of history more generally.[4] If the effect of Fowles's alternative endings on the narrative reality is, for Byatt, to "reduce it to paperiness again" ("People in Paper Houses" 174), the sheer volume of material (or evidence) she presents us with in *Possession* contributes to the sense that the past her Victorian lovers inhabit is much more than a papery postmodern conceit. One of the aims of the novel is to strike a more satisfying balance between "realism" and "experiment" than she felt Fowles did in *The French Lieutenant's Woman*; to answer the challenge, as she sees it, of writing a novel in which literary self-consciousness, crucially important for Byatt, doesn't spoil the pleasures of a "good read."

Jackie Buxton goes considerably further than most critics in her comparison of Byatt's historical romance with Fowles's when she cites a number of scenes in *Possession* as direct evidence of "postmodernist hat-tipping" to Fowles. She identifies "a young man with a hammer and sack … busy chipping away at the rock-face" (269), when Roland and Maud visit the Yorkshire coast, as an "intertextual transposition of Charles Smithson" (218). Most interestingly, however, she points out a parallel between the narrator's intrusion into Charles's train compartment towards the end of *The French Lieutenant's Woman* and Byatt's chapter in which an omniscient narrator tells the story of Randolph Henry Ash and Christabel LaMotte's journey to Yorkshire. As Buxton notes, this episode represents an important break from the twentieth-century perspective which has been maintained to this point. She describes it as an "omniscient time capsule," then asks, "Or is it omniscient?" She writes:

> The poets are introduced through the speculations of a "hypothetical observer" who studiously documents their appearance and demeanour in an attempt to discern their relationship. Implicitly the reader (and the writer) is that observer, projected into the novel as a fellow traveller. Although certainly not as emphatically authorial as John Fowles's intrusion, the situation, description and tone of this episode echoes Fowles's embodied entrance into his own fiction. (208)

While I am persuaded that there is a correspondence of sorts between these two episodes, I am not convinced by the key claim of Buxton's comparative analysis. Byatt does not so much repeat what Fowles does in *The French Lieutenant's Woman* as *take issue with it*. The appearance of Fowles's narrator near the end of the novel is clearly designed to unsettle readers' expectations of narrative closure. Byatt's switch to omniscient "Victorian" storytelling promises the very coherence Fowles rejects.

There are fundamental differences between Ash and LaMotte's "hypothetical observer" and Charles's "inquisitive" and "magistral" "travelling companion." The former is precisely hypothetical; there is no observer but if there were, as the three brief references to the possibility make clear, they would have been able to discern little about

---

4   In her essay "Robert Browning: Fact, Fiction, Lies, Incarnation and Art" Byatt remarks that while "[I]t is often seen as a modern discovery that history is necessarily fictive; it was in fact a pervasive nineteenth-century perception" (35). Related to this is her "[d]efiance [in the story 'Sugar'] of the aesthetic imperative that all good fiction is now overtly fictive and about fictiveness. 'Sugar' is that, but it does try to be truthful" ("Sugar" 25).

LaMotte and Ash or about their relationship (273, 274). There is no suggestion that the observer shares the writer/narrator's omniscient perspective; after careful observation he or she can decide little about the circumstances or the character of the two travellers and certainly has no knowledge of their past (let alone their future). "The hypothetical observer might have been unable to decide whether his subject pursued an active or a contemplative life" (274): moments like this do not undercut the illusion of reality, of a real history, so much as they augment it. In the terms of this carefully crafted historical fiction, the illusion that two Victorian lovers travelled to Yorkshire on a train in 1859 is important to sustain; hence the suggestion that somebody else travelling on the same train might have seen or even paid close attention to them. I don't so much want to refute Buxton's claim that "the reader (and the writer) is that observer, projected into the novel as a fellow traveller" (208), as to shift its emphasis. The "bearded man who stares at Charles" is likened to an "omnipotent god" visiting the world he has created in order to try and work out what to do with it. His intrusion on the scene expressly reminds readers that the narrative reality is an artfully contrived fiction. The aim of this episode is to distance readers from the text. In contrast, Byatt works to bring us closer. The observer operates as a vehicle for the readers to institute themselves in the romance, to experience imaginatively the drama of the fictional past.

In *On Histories and Stories* Byatt makes explicit the opposition between her version of a nineteenth-century narrator and Fowles's:

> Fowles has said that the nineteenth-century narrator was assuming the omniscience of a god. I think rather the opposite is the case—this kind of fictive narrator can creep closer to the feelings and inner life of characters—as well as providing a Greek chorus—than any first-person mimicry. In *Possession* I used this kind of narrator deliberately three times in the historical narrative—always to tell what the historians and biographers of my fiction never discovered, always to heighten the reader's imaginative entry into the world of the text. (55–6)

The story of Ash and LaMotte's trip to Yorkshire is strewn with references to their pasts and their futures; it issues a promise to readers that there will be an ending to their romance. At the same time, however, in this chapter as in their letters, Byatt uses Ash and LaMotte's imaginings or perceptions of themselves as characters in a story to deftly remind us that we are reading carefully crafted and multilayered fiction. To the same end, they explain their situation to themselves and to each other by reference to literature and folklore. Their contemporary counterparts are similarly self-reflective. Whereas it is the narrator in *The French Lieutenant's Woman* who interrupts the narrative flow to deliver literary self-commentaries and analyses, Byatt gives much of this kind of work to her characters. This is a small but telling distinction. Almost all of *Possession*'s principal characters are readers and writers who continually assess the world and their relationship to it through literature. Much of this novel's explicit "self-referentiality" makes sense in the context of the story; it is not extra-diegetic to the same extent that Fowles's narratorial intrusions are. This is of course one aspect of Byatt's aim to produce a novel which is both thought-provoking and moving, or, in her words which "leaves space for thinking minds as well as feeling bodies" (4).

Byatt uses the term "ventriloquism" to describe the type of historical writing she offers in *Possession*. She does this "to avoid the loaded moral implications of 'parody' or 'pastiche'" (*On Histories* 43); it is part of an attempt to dissociate her work from the category of "postmodern writing." Byatt's ventriloquism seeks to enact a more intimate relationship between the past and the present—and especially between past and present literatures—than she feels is encouraged in the contemporary literary and academic climate. It is no accident that the central characters in this novel are poets and literary scholars, readers and writers. Byatt writes of a current "renaissance of the historical novel" (9). She cites novels by Penelope Fitzgerald, Ishiguro, Ackroyd, Graham Swift, and Jeanette Winterson as examples of this renewed interest in setting fiction in the past. From Byatt's perspective, this trend towards historical fiction is the result of a shared desire amongst writers and readers to rediscover the pleasure of narrative and, related to this, to work against the "vanishing of the past from the curriculum of much modern education" (93). Byatt compares her practice of ventriloquism in *Possession* and *Angels and Insects* to Ackroyd's use of the genre of the ghost story in *Chatterton*, *The Last Testament of Oscar Wilde*, and *Hawksmoor*. For Byatt, Ackroyd uses the ghost story "as an enactment of the relationship between readers and writers, between the living words of dead men and the modern conjurers of their spirits" (43). In these terms, the intertextuality which pervades novels like *Possession* is not so much a function of postmodernism as it is endemic to the processes of reading and writing which produce literary texts:

> As an innocent reader I learned to listen, again and again, to texts until they had revealed their whole shape, their articulation, the rhythms of their ideas and feelings. … As a writer I know very well that a text is all the words that are in it, and not only those words, but the other words that precede it, haunt it, and are echoed in it. (46)

The intertextuality which Byatt describes—and is excited by—is expressly not the kind of "parodic intertextuality" which Hutcheon discusses in *A Poetic of Postmodernism* (126). Rather than seek to critique nineteenth-century ideas of the author and the text through "parody," Byatt aims to renew them through "ventriloquism." The Victorian poems she wrote for *Possession* are a case in point: "For the Victorians were not simply Victorian. They read their past, and resuscitated it" (47).

While certain storytelling aims and priorities evident in *Possession* are clearly opposed to those of *The French Lieutenant's Woman*, there are key structural similarities between them. My analysis of the characterization and narrative function of Christabel LaMotte both draws attention to their common paradigmatic structure and reveals a deeper shared allegiance to the tenets and motives of heterosexual hegemony. The first epigraph to *Possession* is a passage from Nathaniel Hawthorne's Preface to *The House of the Seven Gables*. It concludes: "The point of view within which this tale comes under the Romantic definition lies in the attempt to connect a bygone time with the very present that is flitting away from us." It goes without saying that *Possession* is also a romance because it tells a love story. One of my aims is to tease out the connections between these two senses of the book's subtitle: "A Romance." My hypothesis is that there exists a mutual dependency between these two aspects of the book which is crucial to Byatt's project. Examination of the characterization of Christabel helps to draw this out.

In her review of *Possession*, Anita Brookner writes "Christabel is an altogether grittier Victorian subject [than Randolph Henry Ash], and here the comparison with *The French Lieutenant's Woman* is valid, for Christabel is passionate, secretive, virtuous, pure and slightly mad." Like Sarah Woodruff, Christabel is less properly "Victorian" than her lover, though the similarities between them run a little deeper than shared personality traits. In Chapter 5, I showed how analysis of the representation of Sarah as an eccentric and mysterious woman reveals the normative assumptions about sex, gender, and sexuality which inform and structure Fowles's historical romance. Following Diane Elam, I argued that characters like Sarah—and, I want to add, Christabel—enable the kind of negotiation of the past and the present which Fowles and Byatt offer. Through their representation as both historical and outside of history these characters provide the conduit, so to speak, for the elaborate to-ing and fro-ing between the Victorian age and the latter half of the twentieth century which is central to both novels. The double aspect of these characters depends on allegorical stereotyping of women as both "mystery" and "truth." They enable, in Elam's words, "a re-engendering of the historical past as romance" (16).[5]

An extract from fictional poet Randolph Henry Ash's poem, "The Garden of Proserpina," provides the epigraph for *Possession's* first chapter. It begins:

These things are there. The garden and the tree
The serpent at its root, the fruit of gold
The woman in the shadow of the boughs
The running water and the grassy space.
They are and were there. ...

Like *The French Lieutenant's Woman*, *Possession* begins with a poetic image of an ever-present and "shadowy" woman. The invocation of the continuous present in this context begins the very process of "en-gendering" which Elam describes. Just as the Thomas Hardy verse which introduces *The French Lieutenant's Woman* tells

---

5 Elam's argument about the function of female characters in "postmodern romance" also rings true in relation to the spate of recent historical novels based on the life of Johannes Vermeer: Tracy Chevalier's *Girl with a Pearl Earring*; Deborah Moggach's *Tulip Fever*; Susan Vreeland's *Girl in Hyacinth Blue*; and Gregory Maguire's *Confessions of an Ugly Stepsister*. As pointed out by Gary Schwartz, the heroines of these novels are all remarkably similar. They are all romantic figures linked to Vermeer by a "secret love". For example, like Sarah Woodruff and—as I argue in Chapter 6—Byatt's Christabel LaMotte, Chevalier's heroine Griet is distinguished by her uneasy relationship to the time in which she lives. In fact, this is a characteristic common to the heroines in all three of Chevalier's historical romance novels: *The Virgin Blue*; *Girl with a Pearl Earring*; *Falling Angels;* and her latest bestseller, *The Lady and the Unicorn*. The heroines of Susan Sontag's two historical romance novels, Catherine in *The Volcano Lover* and Maryna in *In America*, are also available for this type of analysis. I would argue that both narratives pivot on the characterization of these two women as unknowable "historical" figures. Our apparent preference for remembering the past by turning it into a heterosexual love story is demonstrated in numerous texts. A recent example which merits further attention is Peter Carey's Booker Prize-winning novel, *True History of the Kelly Gang*, in which Carey's invention of a fictional lover for Kelly functions to hold the narrative together.

us something about the role of Sarah, so too this poem is suggestive of Christabel's place and function in the novel. She is, in a very important sense, "[t]he woman in the shadow" who stands at the centre of Byatt's tale.

Reviewer Elaine Feinstein is certainly right when she claims that "it is the characterization of Christabel Lamotte that is central" [sic]. She elaborates on this point:

> Lamotte's passion for the making of poems gives her the ability to live a withdrawn life which rewards her with a freedom women in the 20th century hardly recognise. She and her companion would inevitably these days have been mistaken for Lesbian. Indeed we never do discover the full nature of her relationship with poor Blanche Glover, who is driven to suicide when Lamotte departs with Ash.

In his review, Richard Jenkyns describes Byatt's portrayal of Christabel as a "triumph":

> We feel her both as a child of her time and as an individual: in her letters we meet a keen intelligence wrestling with some awkwardness and angularity, in her verse a passionate reticence, a quirky lyricism, nervous but refined. But Byatt is wise enough not to tell us everything; Christabel keeps some of her secret, including the nature of her feelings for Blanche Glover, and that is as it should be.

Feinstein and Jenkyns highlight two of the most important aspects of Christabel's character: she is and is not of her time, just as she is and is not a lesbian. Both reviewers read with the text in their appraisal of Christabel's impressive literary sensibility and in their awkward dismissal of lesbianism. In Chapter 5 I dealt closely with the idea that the role of a central female character such as Sarah or Christabel is to facilitate the temporal and spatial bridgework which supports the historical novel's engagement with the past. Feinstein and Jenkyns's indication that Christabel (like Sarah) stands out in her time is easily supported with evidence from the text. Rather than rehearse arguments I have already posed and defended in my interpretation of *The French Lieutenant's Woman*, I want to focus here on the second aspect of Christabel's character which Feinstein and Jenkyns highlight and, in so doing, to suggest a link between her purported lesbianism and her capacity to hold time. Feinstein's certainty that, if they were alive today, Christabel and Blanche would be "mistaken" for lesbians is based on prevailing myths about Victorian sexuality which I discussed in my reading of *The French Lieutenant's Woman*. We would misrecognize them as lovers, Feinstein assumes, because we belong to an age which is distinguished from theirs precisely by our attitudes to sex and sexuality; twentieth-century prurience is contrasted to nineteenth-century innocence. Fowles's narrator warns us against making a similar mistake about Sarah when she is described sleeping with her arms around Mrs Poulteney's maid, Millie: "A thought has swept into your mind; but you forget we are in the year 1867 ... some vices were then so unnatural that they did not exist" (137). Nevertheless, when Charles finds Sarah living in Christina Rossetti's house at the end of the novel, he imagines the very possibility which the narrator has so emphatically denied: "What new enormity was threatened now! Another woman, who knew and understood her better than ... this house inhabited by ... he dared not say to himself" (389). The narrator's earlier insistence that his nineteenth-century characters are incapable of such thoughts is belied by Charles's fears. There is a similar contradiction or slippage in Feinstein's commentary on *Possession* and indeed in the novel itself: we would be wrong to think of Blanche and Christabel as lesbians, and yet she says that we can't be certain otherwise. Just as readers of *The French Lieutenant's Woman* are chastised for inappropriate and anachronistic suspicions about Sarah only to be reminded of them later on, so too Byatt allows but refuses to dwell on the possibility that Christabel and Blanche's relationship is sexual. Jenkyns's judgment, "that is as it should be," is true to *Possession*'s prevailing temper and tone. As Buxton points out, "*Possession* is hardly a subversive text; indeed its ideology is a heterosexual, humanist one" (216). It is important not to underestimate or downplay the significance of a politics of heteronormativity to the storytelling and proselytizing priorities of this novel, and to its underlying and related narrative structure.

Buxton writes that Byatt is "(coyly?) silent on the exact details of the purportedly lesbian nature of Blanche Glover's relationship with Christabel LaMotte" (216). In answer to her implied question, I don't believe that there is anything coy in Byatt's treatment of lesbianism in this book, neither in the representation of Blanche Glover nor, amongst the contemporary characters, in the portrayal of Leonora Stern (I discuss Leonora's characterization in the next section). In the ideological terms of this novel, lesbianism is an aberrance; it is an interruption or an obstacle to the proper course of narrative and of history which must be removed. Buxton points out that whereas the message of this book seems to be that "[w]e *can* know everything" (216), the only Victorian character about whom we are not told all is Blanche Glover. She is, I think, written in simply to be written out; lesbianism is not simply left out of this text, but is raised as a possibility to be explicitly rejected. To this extent, there is an ideological continuity between *Possession* and the banishment of the specter and threat of male homosexuality in popular cross-dressing historical romances.

The morning after Ash and LaMotte first have sex, Ash washes the blood from his thighs. Like Charles Smithson, although for different reasons and less violently, Ash is unsettled by the physical evidence of his lover's virginity:

> He had thought, the ultimate things, she did *not* know, and here was ancient proof. He stood, sponge in hand, and puzzled over her. Such delicate skills, such informed desire, and yet a virgin. There were possibilities, of which the most obvious to him was slightly repugnant, and then, when he thought about it with determination, interesting, too. He could never ask. To show speculation, or even curiosity, would be to lose her. Then and there. He knew that, without thinking. It was like Melusina's prohibition, and no narrative bound him, unlike the unfortunate Raimondin, to exhibit indiscreet curiosity. He liked to know everything he could—even this—but he knew better than to be curious, he told himself, about things he could not hope to know. (284–5)

Ash's "love for this woman, known intimately and not at all, was voracious for information" (277), but he must not seek an explanation for the incongruity of Christabel's virginity and her apparent sexual experience. He knows without thinking that to do so would be to end their romance. He compares himself to Raimondin, the ill-fated hero of the legend of Melusina about which Christabel writes an epic poem. The most important point of this intra-textual allusion is not that Ash is different to

Raimondin, but that he is like him. Like Raimondin, Ash is forbidden from pursuing his lover's secrets: the difference is his obedience to the perceived authority. Ash also refers to this aspect of the legend in a letter to Christabel in which he confesses that he has broken an "unspoken spell of prohibition" by riding near her cottage in Richmond Park: *"Now on the level of* tales, *you know, all prohibitions are made only to be broken, must be broken—as is indeed instanced in your own* Melusina *with striking ill-luck to the disobedient knight"* (181). Why can't he use the same logic to justify breaking the prohibition against homosexuality, or rather against knowing about it? Why does the suggestion of lesbianism particularly compel him to forget rather than follow his desire to know everything about Christabel? These are important questions which cannot be answered simply by echoing Fowles's insistence on the impossibility of Victorian lesbianism. Ash cannot pursue the truth about Christabel's relationship with Blanche Glover because to do so would be to risk disrupting, if not destroying, the proper narrative progression of heterosexual romance by looking too deeply into what is, by definition, improper to it. My explanation is, on the surface, a structural one, but its deeper aim is to highlight *Possession*'s conservative positions on both sexuality and literature and to expose the extent to which they reinforce one another.

Just before the Victorian lovers spend their first night together, Ash remembers the moment which had been his "touchstone" (282). As a young boy he read *Roderick Random*, an English book in which "[t]here had been a happy ending. At the end, the hero had been left at the bedroom door by the writer, and then let in, as a kind of *post scriptum*. And She—he forgot her name, some Celia or Sophia, some characterless embodiment of physical and spiritual perfection, or more accurately of the male imagination—She had appeared in a silk sack with her limbs glimmering through it, and had then lifted this over her head and had turned to hero and reader, and had left the rest, the promise, to them" (282). Buxton notes that the "erotics of reading" which *Possession* presents is a "heterosexually-inflected one" (217). She doesn't elaborate on this point, but it is certainly worth dwelling on. This passage takes for granted the formative impact of fictions. It represents a neat model of the kind of deeply involved reading experience which Byatt cherishes by a straightforward identification of the male reader with the hero and his desire for the heroine. The object of reading (romance) is thus aligned with the object of love; *Roderick Random*'s ideal heroine, Christabel LaMotte and the abstract promise of romance are mapped one over the other. *Roderick Random* helps to give Ash's life meaning and purpose. He uses his memory of it to reflect on and explain his desire for Christabel, by an imaginative pairing of the two of them with the hero and heroine of *Roderick Random*. (A similar pairing is crucial to the effect reading Ash and LaMotte's letters has on Roland and Maud.) Further, we read this passage in the context of a richly intertextual and self-reflective novel and as just one of its copious references to the patterns and repetitions of mythical, popular, and literary romances. It points, therefore, not just to the citationality of love and desire, but to the performative force of romance fictions and of texts more generally. *Possession* illustrates Byatt's claim that "the stories we tell about ourselves take form from the larger paradigmatic narratives we inhabit" (*On Histories* 65).

Aware that the woman waiting for him upstairs is also a "reader" (282), and must, he assumes, interpret the world—as he does—through a complicated mesh of literary references, Ash wonders how she sees him. She rebuts his assertion that her decision to live as his wife when in Yorkshire is generous with the statement, "This is necessity" (276). The meaning of this claim is not explained simply by the intensity of her passion for him—although that is of course important—but by the idea that they are caught up in a *narrative*, "gripped by necessity" (279). In one sense, she is talking about fate, but I want to suggest that something more complicated and altogether more interesting is also going on here. Christabel says, "This is where I have always been coming to. Since my time began. And when I go away from here, this will be the midpoint, to which everything ran, before, and *from* which everything will run" (284). Ash sees her, or the experience of her, in equivalent terms. Focusing on Christabel's waist, he imagines her as the embodiment of time: "She held his time, she contained his past and his future, both now cramped together, with such ferocity and such gentleness, into this small circumference" (287). Both characters have the sense that their romance makes sense of their life, by giving it a shape and a coherence which it might otherwise have lacked; they make linear narratives of each other's lives. (Notably, Christabel's self-analysis discounts the centrality of her life with Blanche in her personal history; Blanche is, in her own words, "a superfluous person" (216).) Their new sense of themselves follows, of course, from having fallen in love. More importantly, by figuring Christabel's body as a kind of hour-glass, alluding to her pregnancy and forecasting her ancestral relationship to Maud, this episode mobilizes a metaphorics of reproduction which is crucial to the novel's underlying fantasy of heterosexual continuity, coherence, and *truth*.

In a letter to Christabel, Ash writes of the "*the plot which holds us, the conventions which bind us*," but then declares that he must act against such limitations on his course of action because compliance to them "*goes against nature*" (193). Throughout *Possession*, its central characters battle with the sense that their behavior is somehow scripted or preordained to an extent which they cannot adequately explain by belief in a notion of fate. Such an idea directly contradicts their desire to believe in "love," a concept which refuses such philosophical pragmatism and demands instead faith in its inherent and "human" truth, in its denotative integrity. The contemporary hero and heroine, Maud Bailey and Roland Michell, express this dilemma with particular lucidity. I am most interested in how they resolve it enough to say "I love you" with sincerity and force. This novel reveals both a fascination with and a refusal of the idea that love and romance are inherently citational. That is, it entertains, but is finally uncomfortable with, a *performative* understanding of the patterns of romance, the formation and reformation of the heterosexual romantic subject, and the difficult relationship between history and romance.

Love's "Happy Ending": The Story of Maud Bailey and Roland Michell

Byatt says that the germ of her novel was in fact the word which became its title: "possession." Her interest in the meanings of this word was first sparked in the early 1970s when she saw a scholar in the British Museum library who had spent her professional life studying Coleridge: "I thought, it's almost like a case of demonic possession, and I wondered—has she eaten up his life or has he eaten up hers?" She later thought about pursuing this idea in a novel about Robert Browning, but rejected this idea because of the limits such an endeavor would place on her imagination. Instead, she followed the advice of D.H. Lawrence to frame her novel: "I thought, I have to have two couples, which he says is the beginning of any novel" (Cassidy). In her review of *Possession*, Mary Kaiser remarks: "Predictably enough, the romance between Roland and Maud develops in tandem with their investigations of the romance between Ash and LaMotte." Yet the relationship between the present and the past is much more complicated than simple parallelism. While there is an obvious contiguity between the novel's central couples which is the basis for its plot, what is less obvious is Roland and Maud's dependence on the story of their Victorian counterparts; their romance is made possible by the secret Victorian romance they discover and pursue. There is, as Kaiser suggests, an element of inevitability to all of this. To some extent, this follows from our familiarity with established storytelling devices and rituals. More complexly, however, the mood of anticipation and promise which surrounds the central characters is germane to my argument that *Possession* assumes and dramatizes the importance of paradigmatic narrative structures to rituals of subject formation. Specifically, and in the terms of this book, it invites consideration of the performative dimensions of romance, not least by telling a self-reflexive tale about two lovers who fear that they have been possessed by a plot that is not their own. This sense of the unoriginality of their love follows not just from their imaginative proximity to Randolph Henry Ash and Christabel LaMotte, but from the uncomfortable suspicion that their behavior complies to prevailing generic and cultural imperatives to which these well-trained literary theorists exhibit a heightened sensitivity: "Roland had learned to see himself, theoretically, as a crossing-place for a number of systems, all loosely connected" (424).

Both Maud and Roland are troubled by the idea that they are entrapped by a plot that they do not and cannot own. This fear is enhanced when Maud discovers, near the end of the novel, that Ash and LaMotte are her great-grandparents. Roland traces her face with his hands and points out her physical likeness to them. He is surprised that he hasn't noticed it before. Maud is not comforted by this newly revealed explanation for her deep interest in the Victorian poets and their lives: "I don't quite like it. There's something unnaturally *determined* about it all. Daemonic. I feel they have taken me over" (505). On one level, this is a metafictional moment in the text. The development of Roland and Maud's late twentieth-century romance in parallel with their investigation of a hitherto secret Victorian love story is, as this deeply self-reflexive novel reminds us over and over, a literary contrivance which works to quite particular ends. In this regard, Maud's fear that the direction of her life might be "unnaturally determined" is well-founded. There is plenty of evidence in *Possession* to support an argument that this novel is, in a very important sense, about itself. Here and throughout the novel, we are expressly invited to pay attention to and to think about the novel's underlying narrative structure. I will discuss a number of the literary strategies and devices used in the novel which encourage such considerations shortly. For now I want to consider the implications of Maud and Roland's habitual self-analysis.

Like Maud, Roland is discomforted by the sense that they have become so caught up in their pursuit of Ash and LaMotte's story that the demand for narrative "coherence and closure" which increasingly drives their study is somehow dictating the terms of their own reality.

> Somewhere in the locked-away letters, Ash had referred to the plot or fate which seemed to hold or drive the dead lovers. Roland thought, partly with precise postmodernist pleasure, and partly with a real element of superstitious dread, that he and Maud were being driven by a plot or fate that seemed, at least possibly, to be not their plot or fate but that of those others. And it is possible that there is an element of superstitious dread in any self-referring, self-reflexive, inturned postmodernist mirror-game or plot-coil that recognises that it has got out of hand, that connections proliferate apparently at random, that is to say, with equal verisimilitude, apparently in response to some ferocious ordering principle, not controlled by conscious intention, which would of course, being a good postmodernist intention, *require* the aleatory or the multivalent or the "free," but structuring, but controlling, but driving, to some—to what?—end. Coherence and closure are deep human desires that are presently unfashionable. But they are always both frightening and enchantingly desirable. "Falling in love," characteristically, combs the appearance of the world, and of the particular lover's history, out of a random tangle and into a coherent plot. Roland was troubled by the idea that the opposite might be true. Finding themselves in a plot, they might suppose it appropriate to behave as though it was that sort of plot. And that would be to compromise some kind of integrity they had set out with. (421–2)

Roland fears for the "integrity" both of their academic research and of their personal relationship, aspects of their lives which are inextricably intertwined. His fear, however, extends beyond a "superstitious dread" that his and Maud's developing love may simply be a weak echo of what they seek and discover in the history of the Victorian poets. What this passage makes clear is that Ash and LaMotte are exemplary rather than originary in relation to the controlling plot which seems to be imposing order on the events of the novel's present, its "reality." Roland names the plot (and genre) which binds Maud and himself to the Victorian poets: "He was in a Romance, a vulgar and a high Romance simultaneously, a Romance was one of the systems that controlled him, as the expectations of Romance control almost everyone in the Western world, for better or worse, at some point or another" (425). Questions of metafiction aside, how it happens that a "plot," a structure proper to narrative fiction, organizes Maud and Roland's "real" lives is less easy to understand. The long passage cited above is a difficult one. It is unclear how much of its substance we can attribute to Roland and how much we can read as the narrator's commentary on or explanation of the progress of Roland's thoughts. Not only is the point-of-view thus muddied, but what is said (despite its perspective) is itself obscure. How does verisimilitude follow from randomness, and further, while it is clear that "connections proliferate," how can they seem to do so both randomly, without order and, at the same time, "in response to some ferocious ordering principle"? One answer might be (and it is one the novel's rhetoric supports) that the appearance of truth, and by extension the belief in truth, requires the denial of externally imposed method or structure, thus the parallels between Roland and Maud and Ash and LaMotte and the proliferating allusions and cross-references which circle around them must seem serendipitous rather than controlled. Of course, Roland and Maud are simply too well educated not to notice that their increasing obsession with both the story of Ash and LaMotte and with each other (although less openly) is motivated by a demand and a desire for ending, for a "happy ending," for a romance. Roland notes that the romantic form which defines their pursuit of Ash and LaMotte's story changes from "Quest" to "Chase and Race" as the novel progresses and as competing academics Mortimer Cropper, Leonora Stern, and James Blackadder become involved (425). While there is clearly textual evidence for a number of such changes of form in the novel, dwelling on them would obfuscate the overarching importance of a definition of the novel's generic structure which both encapsulates these subforms and describes the book as a whole. *Possession* is a romance because it is organized and structured by the demand for and structural necessity of a defining speech act, "I love you."

Roland recognizes that he is subject to the demands and imperatives of "Romance" *"for better or worse"* (425). The reference to traditional marriage vows in this context is a telling one, not just in its allusion to *the* paradigmatic happy ending but also because by citing precisely this ritual, this ceremony, it assumes and implies that Romance, in all its manifestations, is driven by, defined by and reserved for *heterosexual* love. At the heart of *Possession* is a naturalization of the relationship between heterosexuality and love, and by extension between heterosexuality and romance, even, I suggest, between heterosexuality and the pleasures and values of reading narrative fiction. While the novel is self-conscious about the structural inevitability of Roland and Maud's romance, their rôle as characters in a drama of predictable proportions, this is undercut by a more profound insistence on the absolute naturalness of their love; they cannot help falling in love because, to reiterate a cliché which the novel mobilizes with more sincerity than cynicism, they are meant for each other.

At the heart of this novel, which Ann Hulbert describes as a "lesson" to its readers, is a celebration of heterosexual love. Love, finally, is what holds it all together. The "happy" marriage of opposing wants—self-consciousness and realism—which Byatt's historical novel reaches for hinges on belief in "love," a term which, as I have demonstrated, manages to bear its contradictions with only apparent ease. *Possession* takes for granted the pivotal relationship between the romantic speech act—"I love you"—and the heterosexual romance plot. The story of Roland and Maud's romance narrates their journey to the point where they can say "I love you" to one another with sincerity and force. The resolution of their romance is, not surprisingly, a "happy" speech act. That they are "children of a time and culture which mistrusted love, 'in love', romantic love, romance *in toto*" (423), delays but does not prevent their acceptance of the terms of romance. Their cognizance of the conventionality of what they are saying and feeling, of its assumption of an essentially humanist ontology and its insistence on the existence of an internally coherent self, does not make them believe it any less: "'I love you,' said Roland. '… In the worst way. All the things we—we grew up not believing in. Total obsession, night and day. When I see you, you look *alive* and everything else—fades. All that" (506). Roland, of course, bears a close resemblance to Umberto Eco's hypothetical "man who loves a very cultivated woman": "As Barbara Cartland would say, I love you madly." His declaration of love is, self-consciously, both a confession and a cliché; the broader implication of Roland's speech is that the inherent contradictoriness of "I love you," its lie, doesn't really matter—he means what he says anyway. Roland and Maud are only able to say "I love you" in this way when they have completed the learning process which reading the Victorian romance provokes.

In the terms of this novel, heterosexual romance both is and is not a "plot" and "a system." It is at once historicized and evacuated of history. We are repeatedly reminded that whereas Ash and LaMotte belong to a time which believes in romance, which takes it seriously, Maud and Roland live in an era in which ideas of love and romance are dismissed as remainders of an earlier and superseded way of thinking which persists in the present but belongs more properly to the past. When the late twentieth-century scholars begin reading Ash and LaMotte's letters, Maud considers this distinction:

> I've been trying to imagine him. Them. They must have been—in an extreme state. I was thinking last night—about what you said about our generation and sex. We see it everywhere. As you say. We are very knowing. We know all sorts of other things, too—about how there isn't a unitary ego—how we're made up of conflicting, interacting systems of things—and I suppose we *believe* that? We know we are driven by desire, but we can't see it as they did, can we? We never say the word Love, do we—we know it's a suspect ideological construct—especially Romantic Love—so we have to make a real effort of imagination to know what it felt like to be them, here, believing in these things—Love—themselves—that what they did mattered—. (266–7)

As the novel progresses, this distinction between what Ash and LaMotte believed and what Maud and Roland believe, between Victorian and late twentieth-century ideas about love, becomes an opposition between sincerity and lies, between true and false knowledge. While neither couple marries at the book's conclusion, heterosexual love and its key systems and institutions are upheld. They are rendered universal and timeless by the relative ease with which Maud and Roland forget what they know in order to fall happily and truly in love. Essential to their achievement of this turnaround is the mechanism of open secrecy. We are not surprised by Maud and Roland's purported change of heart because their love is forecast and anticipated from the outset. We never really believe their stated mistrust of "love" because stronger evidence exists to contradict this. The clearest example of this is Maud and Roland's intense and unconscious physical response to each other's touch.

Both *Possession* and Byatt's critical work are based on the assumption that there is an essential division between "mind" and "body" which bifurcates our lives in crucial and indeed valuable ways. This dichotomy is central to her efforts to achieve an equilibrium in this novel between the intellectual and the emotional and, most interestingly for my purposes, between history and romance. It is also a key to mapping and making sense of the conceptual and ideological parameters of the novel's portrayal of a contemporary love story. In this regard, Catherine Belsey's argument about the function of "true love" in popular romances is as pertinent to *Possession* as it is to the Mills and Boon and Harlequin novels she cites. She writes, "True love as the romances portray it promises to bring mind and body back into perfect unity, to heal the rift in experience which divides individuals from themselves" (23). Belsey shows how popular romances typically highlight the gap between mind and body, with a view to closing it off by the novel's happy conclusion. The representation of Maud and Roland's intense physical response to one another and their gradual acceptance of its significance works to the same end. Maud feels it first. She arrives at Seal Court, the Bailey ancestral home where she and Roland discover and read through Ash and LaMotte's letters, but delays going inside to spend some time in the winter garden which Christabel adored. She remembers the poem Christabel wrote about fish suspended, frozen, in the garden's pond. "Maud bowed her head with the self-consciousness of such a gesture, and thought of Christabel, standing here, looking at this frozen surface" (141). Roland interrupts her reverie with a touch which announces, despite her initial failure to see it, the inevitability of their falling in love:

> She moved her hand in little circles, polishing, and saw, ghostly and pale in the metal-dark surface a woman's face, her own, bared like the moon under mackerel clouds, wavering up at her. Were there fish? She leaned forward. A figure loomed black on the white, a hand touched her hand with a huge banging, an unexpected electric shock. It was meek Roland. Maud screamed. (142)

Roland is similarly affected soon after, but is more circumspect about the significance of such physical signals. That evening he peers through the keyhole of the bathroom door to see if Maud has finished bathing. She opens the door and almost stumbles over him;

> [S]he put out a hand to steady herself on his shoulder and he threw up a hand and clasped a narrow haunch under the silk of the kimono.
>   And there it was, what Randolph Henry Ash had called the *kick galvanic*, the stunning blow like that emitted from the Moray eel from under its boulders to unsuspecting marine explorers. Roland got somehow on his feet, briefly clutching the silk and letting it go as though it stung ... Did she simply *emit* the electric shock, he wondered, or did she also feel it? His body knew perfectly well that she felt it. He did not trust his body. (147)

"Of course," as Belsey says of such scenes in popular romances, "in these specific instances the reader already has grounds for suspecting that the sexual encounters between the central figures are the prelude to true love, and we know in consequence that the apparent conflict between mind and body, sense and sensuality, will ultimately be revealed in these cases as largely illusory" (26).

Both of these scenes make explicit an opposition of mind and body, intellect and desire, which Maud and Roland must overcome for their story to end happily. Maud ignores the force of the "electric shock" she feels when she sees that it is only "meek Roland" who has touched her and whom she has already cast as a "gentle and unthreatening being" (140). Roland is more sensitive to the threat Maud poses to his sense of self. Her touch unsettles his habitual privileging of thought over feeling. These two moments in the text credit Roland and Maud's bodies with their own powers of knowledge and understanding. Their bodies know things that they don't know, or rather don't know yet: "His body knew perfectly well that she felt it. He did not trust his body." Roland's body's "perfect" knowledge is contrasted with his rational doubt just as the "huge banging" which Maud feels cannot be easily silenced by her considered dismissal of him as "meek." The tumult of feeling and sensation which both Roland and Maud experience when they accidentally touch insists that to ignore such signals is, in a fundamental way, to be insincere, to be false to themselves. These parallel episodes at Seal Court initiate the learning process which underscores their romance: Roland and Maud must learn to trust their bodies, to bring thought and feeling into alignment, before they can finally admit their mutual attraction to one another. The question they need to answer is, it almost goes without saying, one of balance. Their first mistake, these scenes imply, is to value one way of knowing at the expense of another; *love* will only be possible when they learn how to better handle the apparent conflict between mind and body without privileging one or the other. They do this by learning to be better readers.

It is partly because of their increasing imaginative engagement with and absorption in the story of Ash and LaMotte that Maud and Roland "find themselves in a romance." A metaphorics of reading organizes and defines the relationship between the two scholars and their subjects, the present and the past. This is, of course, related to Byatt's notion of "ventriloquism." More importantly, however, this metaphorics is part of the tangle Byatt's novel creates between heterosexual love, the desire for narrative, and the insistence of the past in the present. For Byatt, "we are narrative beings because we live in biological time. Whether we like it or not, our lives have beginnings, middles and ends. We narrate ourselves to each other in bars and beds" (*On Histories* 132). The scholarly interest which initially prompts Maud and Roland's research is quickly overtaken by a desire to know what happens in the story; they become romance readers. Their deepening immersion in the Victorian love story describes a process of escape. It parallels also the development of their own love. Maud and Roland's journeys to Yorkshire and France following in the footsteps of Ash and LaMotte literalize this process. However, the novel does not simply suggest that Maud and Roland's love is caused by their mutual attraction to Ash and LaMotte's story.

Possession attempts to sustain the apparent opposition between structure and nature through its efforts to naturalize the very terms of its own narrative: "Coherence and closure are deep human desires that are presently unfashionable." That *Possession* can be read as an elaborate defence of this point is best illustrated by examination of the novel's careful use of the term "necessity." The novel's ninth chapter is a fairytale by Christabel LaMotte called "The Glass Coffin." It tells of a "Childe" on a quest for a magical herb for his father. He reaches a threshold where, if he is to cross, he must choose one of three sisters as his guide: the "gold lady," the "silver lady," or the "half-invisible third." He chooses the third sister: "And you know, and I know, do we not, dear children, that he must always choose this last … for wisdom in all tales tells us this, and the last sister is always the true choice, is she not?" The story entertains but does not permit the possibility that it may have happened, or been written differently: "And one day we will write it otherwise, that he would not come, that he stayed, or chose the sparkling ones, or went out again onto the moors to live free of fate, if such can be. But you must know now, that it turned out as it must turn out, must you not? Such is the power of necessity in tales" (155). The fairytale can acknowledge the possibility that it might have ended differently but, if it is to be proper and true, if it is to be felicitous, it must conclude the quest it narrates; it must end as anticipated or promised. The idea of the "power of necessity in tales" is a fascinating one which has implications for the novel's principal narrative. The power it names follows from the predominance and familiarity of established narrative patterns and paradigms; a kind of logic of iterability drives and motivates each repetition of such a pattern. Alongside this acknowledgement of the force of citationality is an insistence on the importance of ending. The use of the term "necessity" in this context renders the anticipated and happy conclusion a "need" which will insist itself upon a tale regardless of what other possibilities may have been entertained. An assumption of and insistence on this need underpins the story of Roland and Maud's life-changing immersion in the story of Ash and LaMotte.

Self-reflexive commentary such as that offered in "The Threshold" invites us to think about questions such as the force of citationality and the performativity of narrative, but in the final analysis, such moments in the text are merely concessions to a way of thinking which it doesn't meet; they are not followed through. On the train to Yorkshire, Christabel insists that her decision to accompany Ash and to act as his wife is not "generosity," as he suggests, but "necessity" (276). Her choice of words gives him "an idea for a poem about necessity" (279). This poem appears as an epigraph to *Possession*'s closing chapters and provides a neat focal point for the conclusion of my analysis of the relationship between the novel's two couples:

In certain moods we eat our lives away
In fast successive greed; we must have more
Although that *more* depletes our little stock
Of time and peace remaining. We are driven
By endings as by hunger. We *must know*
How it comes out, the shape o' the whole, the thread
Whose links are weak or solid, intricate
Or boldly welded in great clumsy loops
Of primitive workmanship. We feel our way
Along the links and we cannot let go
Of this bright chain of curiosity
Which is become our fetter. So it drags
Us through our time—"And *then*, and *then*, and *then*,"
Towards our figured consummation.
And we must have the knife, the dart, the noose,
The last embrace, the golden wedding ring
The trump of battle or the deathbed rasp
Although we know and must know, they're all one,
Finis, The End, the one consummate shock
That ends all shocks and us. Do we desire
We prancing, cogitating, nervous lives
Movement's cessation or a maw crammed full
Of sweetest certainty, though with that bliss
We cease as in his thrilling bridal dance
The male wasp finds the bliss and swift surcease
Of his small time i' the air. (476)

Ash's poem figuratively conflates life and fiction, living and reading. Most pointedly, this "nineteenth-century" poem rings as true for the lives of the novel's contemporary characters as it does for its historical ones. The poem's relevance to the events of the fictional present is highlighted by the poem's placement in the book—to introduce its conclusion. To this extent, Ash's poem is representative of the novel's insistence on the currency and vitality of habits of reading which it describes as "unfashionable." When Roland and Maud first begin to read through Ash and LaMotte's letters, she dismisses his suggestion that they read them together and in order. Instead, she insists that she reads LaMotte's letters and he Ash's and that they compare notes at the end. She is not persuaded by his suggestion that they would "lose any sense of the development of the narrative" and "retorted robustly that they lived in a time which valued narrative uncertainty" (129). By the novel's end, however, when Christabel's final letter to Ash has been exhumed from his grave and she reads it aloud to a gathering of the novel's central characters, she is emphatic and unwavering in her decision to do so: "We need the end of the story" (498); it is a necessity. Despite belonging to a time which values "narrative uncertainty" and, more disturbingly for the characters themselves, despite their schooling in an academy which habitually reads against rather than with texts, Roland and Maud find themselves profoundly subject to the compulsions and demands this poem describes. The demands for narrative certainty and closure are experienced by the central characters, both past and present, precisely as "deep human needs," universal and unhistorical. At the same time, however, Roland and Maud must learn how to read as their Victorian counterparts did; they must become "Victorian" readers if they are to be happy. To this extent, *Possession* both historicizes reading and seeks to banish history from its analysis of reading. At the same time, it describes love as something which must be resuscitated from the past; heterosexual love, like good reading, persists in the present despite threats to it. Heterosexual love is defiant in this novel; like "[c]oherence and closure" it is represented as a "deep human [desire] that [is] presently unfashionable."

As I have already argued, *Possession* takes a very particular pleasure in the processes of open secrecy. This point relates to my claim that the erotics of reading which this novel represents is resolutely heterosexual. In *On Histories and Stories* Byatt takes issue with her sister, Margaret Drabble, who opposes what she sees as a "nostalgia/heritage/fancy dress/costume drama industry" in contemporary literature. Drabble asks, "Where are the serious depictions of contemporary life?" Unlike her sister, Byatt believes passionately in the value of historical fictions: "I want to ask, why has history become imaginable and important again? Why are these books *not* costume drama or nostalgia?" (9) She uses this latest collection of essays to showcase "a large body of serious and ambitious fiction set in the past, not for the pleasures of escapism or bodice-ripping, but for complex aesthetic and intellectual reasons" (93). My claim throughout this book is that the pleasures of reading popular romance fiction and those of Byatt's novel and others like it are closer in kind than her dismissal of "costume drama" and "bodice-ripping" suggests. Certainly Byatt quite deliberately parodies popular romance forms in *Possession*. (She treats popular fiction quite differently than the literatures she claims to ventriloquize.) However, the close proximity between Byatt's romance and the novels I discuss in Chapters 3 and

4 is not simply a function of parody. Concealment of the heroine's femininity is used to fuel heterosexual desire in fairly straightforward ways in this novel. Historical costume undoubtedly plays a part in the novel's drama. However, *Possession* does not offer a clear message about the relationships between history and costume, or, to extrapolate, between performance and heterosexuality.

Early in the novel, Roland uses his memory of a portrait of Ellen Ash to arouse himself enough to have sex with his girlfriend, Val:

> At first Roland thought it was not going to work after all. There are certain things that cannot be done only on will power. ... He lit on an image, a woman in a library, a woman not naked but voluminously clothed, concealed in rustling silk and petticoats, fingers folded over the place where the tight black silk bodice met the springing skirts, a woman whose face was sweet and sad, a stiff bonnet framing loops of thick hair. (126)

Like Fowles's novel, *Possession* communicates an impatience with our post- (or anti-) Victorian openness about sexuality. Roland arouses himself by inhabiting an imagined past. There is a clear relationship here between historicity and dressing up. There is also a link between Roland's autoerotic vision of a woman "concealed" by her clothing and his drive to uncover the secrets of fictional and historical narratives. Reading stories is a question of (heterosexual) passion in this novel. Roland's heterosexuality is inextricably tied up with his desire to *read*. This is also true of Maud. Conversely, instead of dressing up, her story is one of undressing. Like the cross-dressed heroines of popular novels, Maud must reveal her true femininity before her romance can reach its happy ending. She must learn to look like a woman in order to be happy in love. Maud dresses to conceal her beauty. The focus of this symbolic narrative about concealment and truth is Maud's long blond hair which she wears tied "tightly into a turban" (38). When Roland asks Maud why she hides her hair, her reply reveals her "shame" in the face of heterosexual romance: "I once got hissed at a conference, for dyeing it to please men" (271). This novel shifts the experience of shame from its homosexual characters and onto its heterosexual ones. When Leonora Stern tries to kiss her, Maud's "shame" (317) is not the result of witnessing or experiencing homosexual desire, but because she cannot respond to the embrace. Letting her hair down comes to signify Maud's release from false ways of thinking, both as a reader and as a lover. Importantly, Leonora has no patience with concealment or secrecy. In a letter to Maud, she writes: "*I accept that [LaMotte's] inhibitions made her characteristically devious and secretive—but you do not give her sufficient credit for the strength with which she does nevertheless obliquely* speak out" (139). When Roland reads her essay about LaMotte's use of landscape, he has "a vision of the land they were to explore, covered with sucking human orifices and knotted human body hair" (246). This novel both values secrecy and yet also makes claims for the value of revelation; the point is that they work together. It's crucial to the course of Roland and Maud's love that Maud goes through a process of unveiling *for him*. When she looses her hair, Roland feels "as if something had been loosed in himself, that had been gripping him" (272). Leonora's clothing, by contrast, is used to represent her failure to appreciate the subtlety and beauty of secrets. She is described as a "majestically large woman, in all directions" (310). Whereas Maud's clothing signifies the repression of her femininity and her heterosexuality, Leonora "dressed up to her size" (310). In the terms of this novel, she is precisely unromantic. She is both a lesbian and a bad reader.

Conclusion

One of the things I like about *Possession* is that it helped me to see that the theory of speech acts and performatives which I have used and espoused in this book only makes sense because of an implicit theory of story. The easiest illustration is, of course, the explicit performative in the Austinian sense: the first person present indicative active speech act. Every utterance of a speech act ("I dare…," "I promise…") touches on, gestures towards, or drags behind it associated stories. The relationships I am pointing towards are ones of convention. This is not to say that the force of an utterance such as "I love you" is such that it can and will only be said in the context of a straight romance. Clearly such a claim would be absurd. The stories which might be said to be associated with any given speech act (as I explained in Chapter 2 the relationship can be defined as "perlocutionary") are multiple and variable. The ties between speech acts and their associated stories are elastic but ever present. They carry their history with them. I have made such claims about the operations of the phrase "I love you" and its relationship to romance throughout this book. My hope is that the ideas I have presented might invite speculation not just about the relationship of individual speech acts to literary genres, but of the way speech acts and performatives in broader terms work and circulate in Western culture generally.

Byatt uses a heterosexual romance plot to frame her "novel of ideas," as the basis for an elaborate defence of the values and pleasures of reading texts of the past; of a purportedly unconquerable "human" demand for narrative order, coherence and closure; and of the validity of a theory of language which emphasizes its capacity to tell the truth. Historical romance seems to have been the genre most suited to the literary, pedagogic, and political aims of such a project—aims which Byatt has repeatedly articulated and defended. Michael Westlake's argument about the best way to read Byatt's earlier novel, *Still Life*, rings as true for *Possession*: "The novel's hesitations, contradictions and formal equivocations, its failure to secure the stability it seeks can be read productively as an index of our larger cultural crisis." Westlake doesn't clearly state the dimensions of this crisis. However, his focus on Byatt's resistance to poststructuralist challenges to "prevailing notions of language, truth, reality and personal identity" (33) places her novel and its intellectual project in the context of a seemingly endless intellectual debate.[6] From my perspective, the crisis which *Still Life* and *Possession* might be said to tabulate runs deeper than Westlake's

---

6   Westlake argues that, "[w]ith the publication of *Still Life* … A.S. Byatt has emerged as a defender of a certain kind of literary and philosophic faith. In print and in person, she has taken up the challenge laid down by post-structuralist thought to prevailing notions of language, truth, reality and personal identity. While conceding that naïve ideas of correspondence of language to some pre-given reality are untenable, she fears that recent post-structuralist ideas, emphasising only the 'untrustworthiness' of language, undermine the social and logical possibility of truth" (33).

focus on contemporary academic debates implies. His idea of a text's "failure to secure the stability it seeks" resonates not only with my analysis of *Possession*, but of the form and function of heterosexual romance fictions in general. Throughout this book I have endeavored to read historical romance in the context of the crisis of definition which I argue is at the heart of ideas about gender and sexuality which predominate in Western culture. I have used speech act and performativity theories to demonstrate that the epistemological confusion which undermines heterosexual hegemony is secured to the deeper and finally irresolvable problem of the distinction between the descriptive and performative capacities of language (in its broadest definition). As I have argued, this distinction persists in Western culture, and quite particularly in its romancing of heterosexuality.

Works Cited

Primary Sources

Ackroyd, Peter. *Chatterton*. 1987. London: Penguin, 1993.
—. *Hawksmoor*. London: Abacus, 1986.
—. *The Last Testament of Oscar Wilde*. London: Hamish Hamilton, 1983.
Andrew, Sylvia. *Lord Trenchard's Choice*. Richmond: Mills & Boon, 2002.
Berger, John. 1972. *G. A Novel*. New York: Vintage, 1991.
Beverley, Jo. *My Lady Notorious*. New York: Avon-Hearst, 1993.
Brown, Rita Mae. *High Hearts*. Toronto: Bantam, 1986.
Byatt, A.S. *Angels and Insects*. London: Chatto & Windus, 1992.
—. *Possession: A Romance*. London: Vintage, 1991.
—. *Still Life*. London: Chatto & Windus, 1985.
Carey, Peter. *True History of the Kelly Gang*. St Lucia: U of Queensland P, 2001.
Cartland, Barbara. *The Enchanted Moment*. London: Rich and Cowan, 1949.
—. *The Fire of Love*. London: Hutchinson, 1964.
—. *The Irresistible Force*. London: Arrow, 1978.
—. *Love is the Enemy*. London: Rich and Cowan, 1952.
—. *The River of Love*. London: Pan, 1981.
Chevalier, Tracy. *Girl with a Pearl Earring*. London: HarperCollins, 2000.
—. *Falling Angels*. London: HarperCollins, 2001.
—. *The Lady and the Unicorn*. London: HarperCollins, 2004.
—. *The Virgin Blue*. London: Penguin, 1997.
Coulter, Catherine. *Lord Harry's Folly*. 1980. New York: Severn, 1993.
—. *Night Storm*. New York: Avon-Hearst, 1990.
Deveraux, Jude. *The Conquest*. New York: Pocket, 1991.
—. *Velvet Song*. 1984. London: Arrow, 1990.
Doctorow, E.L. *Ragtime*. 1975. Toronto: Bantam, 1981.
Eco, Umberto. *The Name of the Rose*. 1980. Trans. William Weaver. London: Picador, 1984.
Fowles, John. *The Aristos*. 1964. Boston: Little, Brown, 1970.
—. *The French Lieutenant's Woman*. 1969. London: Pan, 1987.
—. *A Maggot*. New York: Signet, 1986.
—. *The Magus*. 1966. Rev. ed. London: Triad/Panther-Granada, 1977.
Gedney, Mona. *Lady Diana's Daring Deed*. New York: Zebra-Kensington, 2000.
Henley, Virginia. *Seduced*. New York: Island-Bantam Doubleday Dell, 1994.
Hess, Norah. *Devil in Spurs*. New York: Leisure-Dorchester, 1990.
Heyer, Georgette. *Beauvallet*. 1930. Arrow-Random, 2006.
—. *The Corinthian*. 1941. London: Arrow-Random, 2004.
—. *Devil's Cub*. 1932. London: Heinemann, 1970.
—. *The Grand Sophy*. 1950. London; Mandarin-Random, 1997.

—. *The Masqueraders*. 1928. London: Arrow-Random, 2005.

—. *These Old Shades*. 1926. London: Arrow-Random, 2004.

—. *Venetia*. 1958. London: Arrow-Random, 2004.

Kinsale, Laura. *The Dream Hunter*. New York: Berkley, 1994.

—. *Prince of Midnight*. New York: Severn, 1990.

Lessing, Doris. 1962. *The Golden Notebook*. London: Grafton, 1989.

Lindsey, Johanna. *Fires of Winter*. Surrey: Severn, 1980.

—. *Gentle Rogue*. New York: Avon, 1990.

McBain, Laurie. *Moonstruck Madness*. 1977. London: Futura, 1994.

McPhee, Margaret. *The Captain's Lady*. 2004. *Regency Scandals*. Quills. Chatswood, NSW: Harlequin Mills & Boon, 2006. 282–524.

Maguire, Gregory. *Confessions of an Ugly Stepsister*. New York: ReganBooks-Harper Collins, 1999.

Moggach, Deborah. *Tulip Fever*. London: Heinemann, 1999.

Murdoch, Iris. *The Black Prince*. London: Chatto & Windus, 1973.

Orczy, Baroness. *The Scarlet Pimpernel*. 1913. London: Hodder and Stoughton, 1960.

Potter, Patricia. *Swampfire*. 1988. Chatswood, N.S.W: Harlequin, 1989.

Rosenthal, Pam. *Almost a Gentleman*. New York: Brava, 2003.

Rushdie, Salman. *Midnight's Children*. London: Picador, 1982.

Sabatini, Rafael. *Scaramouche*. London: Hutchinson, 1927.

Sontag, Susan. *In America*. London: Vintage, 2001.

—. *The Volcano Lover: A Romance*. London: Vintage, 1993.

Vreeland, Susan. *Girl in Hyacinth Blue*. New York: Penguin, 2000.

Weber, Katherine. *The Music Lesson*. New York: Crown, 1998.

Wilson, Angus. *As if By Magic*. London: Secker and Warburg, 1973.

Winterson, Jeanette. *Written on the Body*. 1992. London: Vintage, 1993.

Woodiwiss, Kathleen A. *Ashes in the Wind*. 1980. London: Futura-Macdonald, 1994.

Woolf, Virginia. *Orlando*. 1928. London: Grafton-Collins, 1990.

Secondary Sources

Abelove, Henry. "Some Speculations on the History of 'Sexual Intercourse' During the Long Eighteenth Century." *Nationalisms and Sexualities*. Ed. Andrew Parker, et al. London and New York: Routledge, 1992. 335–42.

Aiken-Hodge, Jane. *The Private World of Georgette Heyer*. London: Bodley Head, 1984.

Althusser, Louis. "Ideology and Ideological State Apparatuses (Notes Towards an Investigation)." *'Lenin and Philosophy' and Other Essays*. London: NLB, 1971.

Armstrong, Nancy. "A Brief Genealogy of 'Theme'." *The Return of Thematic Criticism*. Ed. Werner Sollors. Cambridge, Mass: Harvard UP, 1993. 38–45.

Assiter, Alison. "Romance Fiction: Porn for Women?" *Perspectives on Pornography: Sexuality in Film and Literature*. Ed. Gary Day and Clive Bloom. Basingstoke: Macmillan, 1988. 107–09.

Austin, J.L. *How to Do Things with Words*. 1962. 2nd ed. Cambridge, Massachusetts: Harvard UP, 1975.

—. *Philosophical Papers*. 3rd ed. Oxford: Clarendon, 1961.

Balsamo, Gian. "The Narrative Text as Historical Artifact: The Case of John Fowles." *Image and Ideology in Modern/Postmodern Discourse*. Ed. David B. Downing and Susan Bazargan. Albany: State U of New York P, 1991. 127–52.

Barnum, Carol M. *The Fiction of John Fowles: A Myth for Our Time*. Greenwood, Florida: Penkevill, 1988.

Barthes, Roland. *A Lover's Discourse: Fragments*. Trans. Richard Howard. New York: Hill and Wang, 1978.

—. *Mythologies*. London: Paladin, 1988.

Beer, Gillian. *The Romance*. London: Methuen, 1986.

Bell, Kathleen. "Cross-Dressing in Wartime: Georgette Heyer's *The Corinthians* in its 1940s Context." 1995. Fahnestock-Thomas 461–72.

Belsey, Catherine. *Desire: Love Stories in Western Culture*. Oxford: Blackwell, 1994.

Beverley, Jo. "Re: heroines disguised as boys," 1 Dec. 1995, online posting, newsgroup Romance Writers (RW-L@sjuvm.stjohns.edu).

Binns, Ronald. "John Fowles: Radical Romancer." *Critical Quarterly* 15.4 (1973): 317–34.

Black, Max. "Austin on Performatives." *Symposium on J.L. Austin*. Ed. K.T. Fann. London: Routledge, 1969. 401–11.

Boone, Joseph Allen. *Tradition Counter Tradition: Love and the Form of Fiction*. Chicago: Chicago UP, 1987.

Bratton, J.S. "Irrational Dress." *The New Woman and Her Sisters*. Ed. V. Gardner and S. Rutherford. London: Harvester Wheatsheaf, 1992. 83–94.

Bronfen, Elisabeth. "Romancing Difference, Courting Coherence: A.S. Byatt's *Possession* as Postmodern Moral Fiction." *Why Literature Matters: Theories and Functions of Literature*. Ed. Rudiger Ahrens and Laurenz Volkmann. Heidelberg: Winter, 1996. 117–34.

Brookner, Anita. "Eminent Victorians and Others." Rev. of *Possession: A Romance*, by A.S. Byatt. *The Spectator* 3 Mar. 1990: 35.

Brown, Ruth Christiani. "*The French Lieutenant's Woman* and *Pierre*: Echo and Answer." *Modern Fiction Studies* 31 (1985): 115–32.

Brunt, Rosalind. "A Career in Love: The Romantic World of Barbara Cartland." *Popular Fiction and Social Change*. Ed. Christopher Pawling. London: Macmillan, 1984. 127–56.

Bruzzi, Stella. *Undressing Cinema: Clothing and Identity in the Movies*. London: Routledge, 1997.

Burley, Stephanie. "What's a Nice Girl Like You Doing in a Book Like This? Homoerotic Reading and Popular Romance." *Doubled Plots: Romance and History*. Eds. Susan Strehle and Mary Paniccia Carden. Jackson, MI: UP of Mississippi, 2003. 127–46.

Butler, Judith. *Bodies That Matter: On the Discursive Limits of 'Sex'*. London and New York: Routledge, 1993.

—. "Contingent Foundations: Feminism and the Question of 'Postmodernism.'" *Feminists Theorize the Political*. Ed. Judith Butler and Joan W. Scott. New York: Routledge, 1992. 3–21.

—. *Excitable Speech: A Politics of the Performative*. London and New York: Routledge, 1997.

—. "Gender as Performance." *A Critical Sense: Interviews with Intellectuals*. Ed. Peter Osborne. London and New York: Routledge, 1996. 109–26.

—. *Gender Trouble: Feminism and the Subversion of Identity*. London and New York: Routledge, 1990.

—. "Imitation and Gender Insubordination." *Inside/Out: Lesbian Theories, Gay Theories*. Ed. Diana Fuss. London and New York: Routledge, 1991. 13–31.

—. *The Psychic Life of Power: Theories in Subjection*. Stanford: Stanford UP, 1997.

—. "There is a Person Here." Interview compiled by Warren J. Blumenfeld and Margaret Sönser Breen, with Susanne Baer, Robert Alan Brookey, Lynda Hall, Vicki Kirby, Robert Shail, and Natalie Wilson. *Butler Matters: Judith Butler's Impact on Feminist and Queer Studies*. Eds. Margaret Sönser Breen and Warren J. Blumenfeld. Hampshire: Ashgate, 2005. 9–25.

—. *Undoing Gender*. London and New York: Routledge, 2004.

Buxton, Jackie. "What's Love Got to Do With It? Postmodernism and *Possession*." *English Studies in Canada* 22.2 (1996): 199–219.

Byatt, A.S. "The Ferocious Reticence of Georgette Heyer." *The Sunday Times Magazine* 5 Oct. 1975: 28–38.

—. "An Honourable Escape: Georgette Heyer." Byatt, *Passions* 258–65.

—. *On Histories and Stories: Selected Essays*. London: Vintage, 2001.

—. *Passions of the Mind: Selected Writings*. London: Chatto & Windus, 1991.

—. "People in Paper Houses: Attitudes to 'Realism' and 'Experiment' in English Post-War Fiction." 1979. Byatt, *Passions* 165–88.

—. "Robert Browning: Fact, Fiction, Lies, Incarnation and Art." Byatt, *Passions* 29–71.

—. "'Sugar' / 'Le Sucre'" Byatt, *Passions* 21–5.

Bywaters, Barbara. "Decentering the Romance: Jane Austen, Georgette Heyer, and Popular Romance Fiction." 1999. Fahnestock-Thomas 493–508.

Callil, Carmen. "Subversive Sybils: Women's Popular Fiction this Century." 1996. Fahnestock-Thomas 476–79.

Cheah, Pheng, and Elizabeth Grosz. "The Future of Sexual Difference: An Interview with Judith Butler and Drucilla Cornell." *diacritics* 28.1 (1998): 19–42.

Cohn, Jan. *Romance and the Erotics of Property*. Durham: Duke UP, 1988.

Conradi, Peter. *John Fowles*. London: Methuen, 1982.

Crane, Lynda L. "Romance Novel Readers: In Search of Feminist Change?" *Women's Studies* 23.3 (1994): 257–69.

Cranny-Francis, Anne. *Feminist Fiction: Feminist Uses of Generic Fiction*. Cambridge: Polity, 1990.

Derrida, Jacques. *Limited Inc*. Ed. Gerald Graff. Trans. Samuel Weber and Jeffrey Mehlmann. Evanston, I.L: Northwestern UP, 1988.

Dubino, Jeanne. "The Cinderella Complex: Romance Fiction, Patriarchy and Capitalism." *Journal of Popular Culture* 27.3 (1993): 103–18.

Ebert, Teresa. "The Romance of Patriarchy: Ideology, Subjectivity and Postmodern Feminist Cultural Theory." *Cultural Critique* 10 (1988): 19–57.

Eco, Umberto. *Reflections on* The Name of the Rose. Trans. William Weaver. London: Secker & Warburg, 1985.

Eddins, Dwight. "John Fowles: Existence as Authorship." *Critical Essays on John Fowles*. Ed. Ellen Pifer. Boston: G. K. Hall & Co, 1986. 38–53.

Elam, Diane. *Romancing the Postmodern*. London and New York: Routledge, 1992.

Fahnestock-Thomas, Mary, ed. *Georgette Heyer: A Critical Retrospective*. Saraland, AL: PrinnyWorld, 2001.

Feinstein, Elaine. "Eloquent Victorians. Rev. of *Possession: A Romance*, by A.S. Byatt." *New Statesman and Society* 16 Mar. 1990: 38.

Felman, Shoshana. *The Scandal of the Speaking Body: Don Juan with J.L. Austin, or Seduction in Two Languages*. 1983. Trans. Catherine Porter. Stanford: Stanford UP, 2002.

Fenton, Kate. "I've Read Her Books to Ragged Shreds." *The Telegraph* 29 July 2002. 8 Feb 2006 <http://www.telegraph.co.uk/arts/main.jhtml?xml=/arts/2002/07/29/boheyer29.xml>.

Ferrebe, Alice. "The Gaze of the Magus: Sexual/Scopic Politics in the Novels of John Fowles." *Journal of Narrative Theory* 34.2 (2004): 207–26. *Project Muse*. 4 Apr. 2006. <http://muse.uq.edu.au/journals/journal_of_narrative_theory>.

Foucault, Michel. *The History of Sexuality, Volume 1, An Introduction*. Trans. Robert Hurley. Harmondsworth: Penguin, 1990.

Fowles, John. "Notes on an Unfinished Novel." *The Novel Today: Contemporary Writers on Modern Fiction*. Ed. Malcolm Bradbury. Manchester: Manchester UP, 1977. 136–50.

Frenier, Mariam Darce. *Goodbye Heathcliff: Changing Heroes, Heroines, Roles and Values in Women's Category Romances*. New York: Greenwood, 1988.

Gammel, Irene, ed. *Confessional Politics: Women's Sexual Self-Representations in Life Writing and Popular Media*. Carbondale and Edwardsville: Southern Illinois UP, 1999.

Garber, Marjorie. *Vested Interests: Cross-Dressing and Cultural Anxiety*. London and New York: Routledge, 1991.

Gelder, Kenneth. *Popular Fiction: The Logics and Practices of a Literary Field*. London and New York: Routledge, 2004.

Gilbert, Sandra M. "Costumes of the Mind: Transvestism as Metaphor in Modern Literature." *Critical Inquiry* 7.2 (1980): 391–417.

Giobbi, Giuliana. "Know the Past: Know Thyself. Literary Pursuits and Quest for Identity in A.S. Byatt's *Possession* and in F. Duranti's *Effetti Personali*." *Journal of European Studies* 24.1 (1994): 41–54.

Glass, E.R., and A. Mineo. "Georgette Heyer and the Uses of Regency." 1986. Fahnestock-Thomas 421–34.

Heyer, Georgette. Letter to Louisa Callender. 5 Mar. 1952. Correspondence between Heyer and William Heinemann. Baillieu Library, University of Melbourne, Parkville, Australia.

Holmes, Frederick. "The Historical Imagination and the Victorian Past: A.S. Byatt's *Possession.*" *English Studies in Canada* 20.3 (1994): 319–34.

—. "The Novel, Illusion and Reality: The Paradox of Omniscience in *The French Lieutenant's Woman.*" *Journal of Narrative Technique* 11.3 (1981): 184–98.

Hughes, Helen. *The Historical Romance.* London and New York: Routledge, 1993.

Hughes, Kathryn. "Repossession." Rev. of *Angels and Insects*, by A.S. Byatt. *New Statesman and Society* Nov. 6 1992: 49–50.

Hulbert, Ann. "The Great Ventriloquist: A.S. Byatt's *Possession: A Romance.*" *Contemporary British Women Writers: Narrative Strategies.* Ed. Robert E. Hosmer, Jr. New York: St. Martin's, 1993. 55–65.

Hutcheon, Linda. *Narcissistic Narrative: The Metafictional Paradox.* New York: Methuen, 1984.

—. *The Poetics of Postmodernism: History, Theory, Fiction.* London and New York: Routledge, 1988.

—. *The Politics of Postmodernism.* London and New York: Routledge, 1989.

—. "The 'Real World(s)' of Fiction: *The French Lieutenant's Woman.*" *Critical Essays on John Fowles.* Ed. Ellen Pifer. Boston: G.K. Hall, 1978. 118–32.

Jagose, Annamarie. *Queer Theory.* Melbourne: Melbourne UP, 1996.

Jameson, Fredric. "Magical Narratives: Romance as Genre." *New Literary History* 7 (1975): 135–63.

Janik, Del Ivan. "No End of History: Evidence from the Contemporary English Novel." *Twentieth Century Literature* 41.2 (1995): 160–90.

Jenkyns, Richard. "Disinterring Buried Lives. Rev. of *Possession: A Romance*, by A.S. Byatt." *Times Literary Supplement* 2 Mar 1990: 213.

Johnson, A.J.B. "Realism in *The French Lieutenant's Woman.*" *Journal of Modern Literature* 8 (1980–1981): 287–302.

Kaiser, Mary. "Rev. of *Possession: A Romance*, by A.S. Byatt." *World Literature Today* 65.4 (1991): 707.

Karlin, Danny. "Prolonging Her Absence." Rev. of *Possession: A Romance*, by A.S. Byatt. *London Review of Books* 8 Mar. 1990: 17–18.

Katz, Jonathan Ned. *The Invention of Heterosexuality.* New York: Penguin, 1996.

Kean, Danuta. "Georgette Heyer: Rejuvenating a Regency Romantic." *Bookseller.* 1 Apr. 2005: 22.

Kellaway, Kate. "Self-Portrait of a Victorian Polymath." *London Observer* 16 Sept. 1990: 45.

Kelly, Kathleen Coyne. *A.S. Byatt.* Ed. Kinley E. Roby. London: Twayne, 1996.

Kitt, Sandra. "Romance ... A Fundamental Lesson in Love." *Romantic Times Magazine* 147 (1996): 10–11.

Kloester, Jennifer. *Georgette Heyer's Regency World.* London: Heinemann, 2005.

Krentz, Jayne Ann, ed. *Dangerous Men and Adventurous Women: Romance Writers on the Appeal of Romance.* Philadelphia: U of Pennsylvania P, 1992.

Laski, Marghanita. "The Appeal of Georgette Heyer." 1970. Fahnestock-Thomas. 283–6.

Le Bouille, Lucien. "John Fowles: Looking for Guidelines." *Journal of Modern Literature* 8.2 (1980–1981): 203–10.

Lehmann-Haupt, Christopher. "When There Was Such a Thing as Romantic Love." Rev. of *Possession: A Romance*, by A.S. Byatt. *New York Times* 25 Oct. 1990: C 24.

Light, Alison. *Forever England : Femininity, Literature, and Conservatism between the Wars*. London and New York: Routledge, 1991.

—. "'Returning to Manderley': Romantic Fiction, Female Sexuality and Class." *Feminist Review* 16 (1984): 7–25.

Loveday, Simon. *The Romances of John Fowles*. London: Macmillan, 1985.

Lovell, Terry. "Feminism and Form in the Literary Adaptation: *The French Lieutenant's Woman.*" *Criticism and Critical Theory*. Ed. Jeremy Hawthorn. London: Edward Arnold, 1984. 112–26.

Lukács, Georg. *The Historical Novel*. Trans. Hannah and Stanley Mitchell. 3rd ed. London: Merlin, 1974.

McCafferty, Kate. "Palimpsest of Desire: The Re-Emergence of the American Captivity Narrative as Pulp Romance." *Journal of Popular Culture*. 27.4 (1994): 43–56.

Mansfield, Elizabeth. "A Sequence of Endings: The Manuscripts of *The French Lieutenant's Woman.*" *Journal of Modern Literature* 8.2 (1980–1981): 275–86.

Mann, Peter H. "The Romantic Novel and its Readers." *Journal of Popular Culture* 15.1 (1981): 9–19.

Rev. of *The Masqueraders*, by Georgette Heyer. *Outlook* 21 Aug. 1929.

Miller, D.A. "Secret Subjects, Open Secrets." *The Novel and the Police*. Berkeley: U of California P, 1988. 192–220.

Modleski, Tania. *Loving with a Vengeance: Mass Produced Fantasies for Women*. Hamden, Connecticut: Archon, 1982.

—. "My Life as a Romance Reader." *Old Wives' Tales and Other Women's Stories*. New York: New York UP, 1998. 47–65.

—. "My Life as a Romance Writer." *Old Wives' Tales*. 66–79.

Morrison, Jago. *Contemporary Fiction*. London: Routledge, 2003.

Mussell, Kay. *Fantasy and Reconciliation: Contemporary Formulas of Women's Romance Fiction*. Westport, Connecticut: Greenwood, 1984.

Olshen, Barry N. *John Fowles*. New York: Ungar, 1978.

Onega, Susana. *Form and Meaning in the Novels of John Fowles*. Ann Arbor: UMI Research, 1989.

Parker, Andrew, and Eve Kosofsky Sedgwick, eds. *Performativity and Performance*. London and New York: Routledge, 1995.

Pellegrini, Ann. *Performance Anxieties: Staging Psychoanalysis, Staging Race*. London and New York: Routledge, 1997.

Petrey, Sandy. *Speech Acts and Literary Theory*. London and New York: Routledge, 1990.

Pohler, Eva Mokry. "Genetic and Cultural Selection in *"The French Lieutenant's Woman."* *Mosaic: A Journal for the Interdisciplinary Study of Literature* 35.2 (2002): 57–72.

Radford, Jean, ed. *The Progress of Romance: The Politics of Popular Fiction.* London: Routledge and Kegan Paul, 1986.

Radway, Janice. *Reading the Romance: Women, Patriarchy and Popular Literature.* 1984. London: Verso, 1987.

Ramsdell, Kristin. *Romance Fiction: A Guide to the Genre.* Genreflecting Advisory Series. Ed. Diana Tixier Herald. Englewood, CO: Libraries Unlimited, 1999.

Rich, Adrienne. "Compulsory Heterosexuality and Lesbian Existence." *The Lesbian and Gay Studies Reader.* Ed. Henry Abelove, Michèle Aina Barale, and David M. Halperin. New York: Routledge, 1993. 227–54.

Ryan, Kate. "Theme Spotlight: Disguised as a Male." *Romantic Times Magazine* 148 (1996): 28–9.

Salami, Mahmoud. *John Fowles's Fiction and the Poetics of Postmodernism.* Rutherford: Fairleigh Dickinson UP, 1992.

Schneider, Carl D. *Shame, Exposure and Privacy.* New York: W.W. Norton and Company, 1992.

Schwartz, Gary. Rev. of *Confessions of an Ugly Stepsister* by Gregory Maguire; *Girl in Hyacinth Blue,* by Susan Vreeland; *Girl with a Pearl Earring,* by Tracy Chevalier; *The Music Lesson,* by Katherine Weber; and *Tulip Fever* by Deborah Moggach. *Art in America* 89.3 (2001): 104.

Sedgwick, Eve Kosofsky. *Epistemology of the Closet.* London: Penguin, 1994.

—. "Queer Performativity: Henry James's *The Art of the Novel.*" *GLQ* 1.1 (1993): 1–16.

—. "Socratic Raptures, Socratic Ruptures: Notes Towards Queer Performativity." *English Inside and Out: The Places of Literary Criticism.* Ed. Susan Gubar and Jonathan Kamholtz. London and New York: Routledge, 1993. 122–36.

—. "Shame and Performativity: Henry James's New York Edition Prefaces." *Henry James's New York Edition: The Construction of Authorship.* Ed. David McWhirter. Stanford, California: Stanford UP, 1995. 206–39.

—. *Touching Feeling: Affect, Pedagogy, Performativity.* Series Q. Eds. Michele Aina Barale, et al. Durham & London: Duke UP, 2003. Personal Copy.

Sedgwick, Eve Kosofsky, and Adam Frank. "Shame in the Cybernetic Fold: Reading Silvan Tomkins." *Critical Inquiry* 21 (1995): 496–522.

Shiller, Dana. "The Redemptive Past in the Neo-Victorian Novel." *Studies in the Novel* 29.4 (1997): 539–62.

Shinn, Thelma J. "'What's in a Word?' Possessing A.S. Byatt's Meronymic Novel." *Papers on Language and Literature* 31.2 (1995): 164–83.

Smith, Frederick N. "Revision and the Style of Revision in *The French Lieutenant's Woman.*" *Modern Fiction Studies* 31 (1985): 85–94.

Stout, Mira. "What Possessed A.S. Byatt?" *The New York Times Magazine* 26 May 1991: 12–15; 24.

Strehle, Susan and Mary Paniccia Carden. Introduction. *Doubled Plots: Romance and History.* Eds. Strehle, Susan and Mary Paniccia Carden. Jackson, MS: UP of Mississippi, 2003. xi–xxxiii.

Tarbox, Katherine. *The Art of John Fowles.* Athens: U of Georgia P, 1988.

Taylor, Helen. "Romantic Readers." *From My Guy to Sci-Fi: Genre and Women's Writing in the Postmodern World.* Ed. Helen Carr. London: Pandora, 1989. 58–77.

Thurman, Judith. Rev. of *Possession: A Romance*, by A.S. Byatt. *The New Yorker* 19 Nov. 1990: 151–5.

Thurston, Carol. "Popular Historical Romances: Agent for Social Change? An Exploration of Methodologies." *Journal of Popular Culture* 19.1 (1985): 35–49.

—. *The Romance Revolution: Erotic Novels for Women and the Quest for a New Sexual Identity*. Urbana: U of Illinois P, 1987.

Todd, Richard. *Consuming Fictions: The Booker Prize and Fiction in Britain*. London: Bloomsbury, 1996.

—. "The Retrieval of Unheard Voices in British Postmodernist Fiction: A.S. Byatt and Marina Warner." *Liminal Postmodernisms: The Postmodern, the (Post-) Colonial, and the (Post-)Feminist*. Ed. Theo D'haen and Hans Bertens. Amsterdam: Rodopi, 1994. 99–114.

Traub, Valerie. *Desire and Anxiety: Circulations of Sexuality in Shakespearean Drama*. London: New York, 1992.

Vasudevan, Aruna, ed. *Twentieth Century Romance and Historical Writers*. 3rd ed. Detroit: St James, 1994.

Walker, David H. "Remorse, Responsibility and Moral Dilemmas in Fowles's Fiction." *Critical Essays on John Fowles*. Ed. Ellen Pifer. Boston: G.K. Hall, 1978. 54–76.

Wallace, Diana. *The Woman's Historical Novel: British Women Writers, 1900–2000*. Houndsmills, Basingstoke, Hampshire, and New York: Palgrave Macmillan, 2005.

Weed, Elizabeth. "The More Things Change." *Differences* 6.2+3 (1994): 249–73.

Westlake, Michael. "The Hard Idea of Truth." *PN Review* 15.4 (1989): 33–7.

Westman, Karin E. "A Story of Her Weaving: The Self-Authoring Heroines of Georgette Heyer's Regency Romance." *Doubled Plots: Romance and History*. Eds. Susan Strehle and Mary Paniccia Carden. Jackson, MS: UP of Mississippi, 2003. 165–84.

Woodcock, Bruce. *Male Mythologies: John Fowles and Masculinity*. Brighton, Sussex: Harvester, 1984.

Woodruff, Juliette. "A Spate of Words, Full of Sound and Fury, Signifying Nothing: Or, How to Read in Harlequin." *Journal of Popular Culture* 19.2 (1985): 25–33.

Yelin, Louise. "Cultural Cartography: A.S. Byatt's *Possession* and the Politics of Victorian Studies." *Victorian Newsletter* 81 (1992): 38–41.

Index